D0889039

GOYA IN THE
DEMOCRATIC TRADITION

Frontispiece of the *Caprichos*

GOYA

IN THE
DEMOCRATIC TRADITION

F. D. KLINGENDER

INTRODUCTION BY HERBERT READ

SCHOCKEN BOOKS • NEW YORK

CONTENTS

INTRODUCTION
TO THE 1968 EDITION

WRITTEN during the early years of the Second World War, *Goya in the Democratic Tradition* remained unpublished until 1948. Another twenty years have passed before a publisher has ventured to issue a second edition of a book that is undoubtedly a classic of art criticism, or, to be more exact, of a particular kind of art criticism which the author himself defines in his Preface. Klingender (1907–55) was by training and experience primarily a sociologist, but as a sociologist he was aware of 'the intimate interaction between life and art'. He was therefore drawn to the study of the art of a society as a key to the interpretation of its history. A sensitive artist, an artist of genius, offers to the sociologist evidence far more reliable than mountains of historical documents. But you must choose your artist, and that element of choice, from another point of view—that of the philosopher of art—is apt to introduce bias or distortion.

Before discussing whether Klingender, as a sociologist, presents a true interpretation of Goya's art, it is desirable to give the reader some details of the life of the author. Francis Donald Klingender was born on February 18, 1907, of British parents who were at the time living in Germany. His father, Louis Henry Weston Klingender, was born in Liverpool in 1861, but settled in Germany in his youth and studied art in Düsseldorf under Carl Friedrich Deiker, a famous painter of animals. Louis Klingender also became an animal painter, specializing in realistic studies of animals in conflict. In 1902 he moved to Goslar with an English wife and, in addition to his painting, became Keeper of the Goslar Museum. Francis Klingender received a classical education at the Goslar Gymnasium, matriculating in 1925. Soon afterwards his parents (who had been treated as aliens during the First World War) decided to return to England. Francis then enrolled as an evening student in the London School of Economics and two years later obtained a ˙first-class honours degree. After taking this degree he undertook sociological field work in connection with a *New Survey of London Life and Labour* and in 1930 was given a research grant by the London School of Economics which enabled him to write a thesis on *The Black-Coated Worker in London* (1934), for which he was awarded a Ph.D. This thesis was later extended and published as a monograph on *The Condition of Clerical Labour in Britain* (1935). At the London School of Economics he had as teachers L. T. Hobhouse, Bronislaw Malinowski and Morris Ginsberg, all of whom he found inspiring. But none of them (unless possibly Malinowski) would have given him a particular interest in the sociology of art. That came from his father, and from the family background.

During his student years he was employed first in an advertising agency on market research, and later on similar work with Arcos Ltd., the export agency in London of the Soviet Union. In 1936 he undertook for John Grierson, at that time famous for his documentary films, an investigation into the financial structure of the British film industry (published in 1937 jointly with Stuart Legg as *Money Behind the Screen*). Klingender continued his association with Grierson and the documentary film movement, but meanwhile had been engaged by the Agricultural Research Council to conduct a nation-wide series of interviews with agricultural experts to discover why there was a time-lag between the discovery of new knowledge and its practical application on British farms. His report was published by an organization known as PEP (Politics, Economics and Planning), and this led to his appointment as research secretary to a joint committee of PEP and the British Association which had as its task an enquiry into the *Social Relations of Scientific Research*. In this task he was supported by a Leverhulme Fellowship.

Then came the war and put an end to these research activities. For some time Klingender was employed as a scientific officer in a research unit of the Ministry of Home Security, but this post seems to have left him sufficient time and energy to pursue his prime interest, the sociology of art. His first publication in this field, *Hogarth and English Caricature*, appeared in 1944, that is to say, before the end of the war. *Art and the Industrial Revolution*, a work based on original research, was published in 1947 and has recently been reprinted. *Goya in the Democratic Tradition* followed in 1948.

Some time before this (about 1934) Klingender came

under the influence of Dr. Frederick Antal (1887–1954), whose presence in London as a refugee had a profound effect on the whole direction of art studies in the country of his adoption. Antal was a Marxist, in the sense that he was applying the method of dialectical materialism to the history of art. His great work on *Florentine Painting and Its Social Background* did not appear until 1948 (the year in which Klingender was appointed Lecturer in Sociology in University College, Hull), but Antal had been lecturing at the Courtauld Institute and publishing articles (in journals such as *The Burlington Magazine*) from the time he arrived in England in 1933. One has only to compare Klingender's *Goya* (or his short monograph on Hogarth) with a work of Antal's in the same field, such as his posthumously published *Hogarth and His Place in European Art*, to be aware of the identity of the methods employed by these two scholars.

That method is clearly defined by Klingender in the Preface to the present work. The name of Marx is discreetly avoided in this definition (and was equally discreetly avoided by Antal in all his publications, though not in his more intimate contacts with his students). Goya, writes Klingender, can only be understood as an artist if we study him against his social and political background. 'Against that wider setting', he states, 'with its clash of material forces and ideas I have attempted to reconstruct Goya's own outlook from what is known of his life and more especially from his paintings, etchings, and drawings.

'I have, in other words, approached the works of Goya *primarily by studying their content*. From that content I have attempted to deduce both their theme in the narrow sense of the word and their style. I have tried to show that there is a close correlation between the wider social experience which Goya shared with his contemporaries and his own attitude to that experience on the one hand, and the formal characteristics of his style on the other; that, indeed, the many conflicting tendencies of his style development can only be interpreted as the necessarily varying expressions of as many social moods and attitudes.'

That is a clear statement of the Marxist method in art history, and it has almost everything to be said for it. It presents the work of art, not as a self-contained world of symbolic feeling, but as, in Klingender's words, a 'creative

experience fused in the crucible of life'. That is a very rhe-
torical expression, but it makes the point that what moti-
vates the artist (or at least artists of the stature of Goya)
is a participation in a dynamic social movement, in the
struggle for the integrity and freedom of mankind itself.
But obviously different artists have different attitudes in
this struggle, and not all (not Rembrandt, for example, one
of Goya's self-confessed masters, but only once mentioned
by Klingender) can be so easily identified with the political
aspects of that struggle. In other words, social sympathy
does not always imply political activity, and perhaps even
in Goya's case it is possible to exaggerate the degree of his
involvement. For example, I find the following passage in
this book (p. 173) unconvincing:

'Both Goya and Shelley belonged to that band of inspired intellectuals whose art was the clarion call of militant
democracy. But while Shelley deserted his class to join the
ranks of the revolution, Goya rose from the people. Moreover, Goya, born in 1746, grew to manhood with the tide
of bourgeois rationalism as it surged towards its revolutionary climax. Himself in the thick of the struggle, he saw his
people in action. And although he shared their defeat, he
never wavered in his militant materialism.'

This is the language of politics and not of art criticism.
The comparison with Shelley (developed at some length) is
fair enough, but though Shelley in his youth might be described as a militant materialist, there is no trace of such a
programmatic philosophy in Goya. Indeed, Goya can only
be absolved from such bourgeois characteristics as mysticism and supernaturalism by supposing (as does Klingender)
that his 'Caprichos', 'Disparates' and 'Pinturas Negras' are
expressions of some inner struggle between belief and despair within the mind of Goya (the kind of subjectivism
that is anathema to the true Marxist). In this matter
Baudelaire (whom Klingender quotes) is a better guide:
and for Baudelaire Goya was an artist of the absurd, that
is to say, of the unconscious. Baudelaire described the mind
of the artist as 'profoundly individual', and found in such
minds 'something analogous to those periodical or chronic
dreams with which our sleep is regularly besieged'—'Goya's
great merit', he said in a passage quoted by Klingender,
'consists in his having created a credible form of the monstrous. His monsters are born viable, harmonious. No one

has ventured further than he in the direction of the *possible absurd*'.* An artist of the absurd, therefore, in the sense that has been made familiar to us since Klingender's time by Albert Camus.

There is no doubt that Goya's heart was in the right place—on the side of the people and against all tyrants. But to imply that the contradictory elements in Goya (reality and fantasy) lead to the 'recreation of reality on a higher plane' is casuistic if by that higher plane is implied some new social order. 'The new reality', writes Klingender, 'resulting from the fusion of reason with fantasy has the power of a revelation. It is not the outcome of a mechanical addition. It is a new reality born of the union of two contradictory elements, a union which is creative because it is the resolution of a conflict' (p. 161). But the conflict is resolved in the mind of the artist, and remains a catharsis only uncertainly and sporadically seized by society as a whole. Goya's achievement does not differ in kind from the achievement of a tragic serenity in Sophocles or in Shakespeare, in Rembrandt or in Racine. Such achievements, though 'fused in the crucible of life', have little or no relevance to an artist's particular social background, much less to anything so specific as 'the struggles of his people'. The drama is played on the stage of the artist's inner consciousness, a stage illuminated from the front by lights reflected from 'the clash of material forces', but receding in the background into the darkness of unconscious motives and archetypal myths. No artist is a better witness to this truth than Goya.†

Nevertheless, a critic such as Klingender reminds us of truths so often neglected in the interpretation of art. An artist cannot be isolated from his environment and studied like some specimen in a laboratory. In Baudelaire's striking image, it is impossible to trace the line of suture between the real and the fantastic, between the conscious and the unconscious elements of his nature. We are in the presence of something at once 'transcendental and natural'. It is no small achievement to have traced in detail, with scientific

---

* *Trans.* by Jonathan Mayne: *The Painter of Modern Life and Other Essays* by Charles Baudelaire. London: Phaidon Press, 1964, p. 192.

† Cf. André Malraux: *Saturne: Essai sur Goya* (Paris, 1950), p. 150: 'Lorsqu'il était lié au peuple, c'était par ses passions, non par son art. Encore ne s'agit-il que de sa representation; sa fiction est autrement révélatrice. Elle n'attaque pas seulement la qualité sociale au bénéfice de la qualité artistique; elle attaque l'ordre du monde au bénéfice du mystère.'

accuracy, one of these elements, the natural, and at the same time to have admitted the troubling presence of the other element. It is, from the point of view of the dialectical materialistic, a magnanimous concession to admit that there is a higher plane of reality, and that as an artist Goya attained it. From any point of view one cannot but admire a study of an artist's development pursued with such scrupulous scholarship and such passionate sympathy.

Herbert Read

PREFACE

THE following study does not pretend to be an exhaustive appreciation of Goya's art. Its scope was purposely restricted to the task of reconstructing, as far as possible, the mental atmosphere, the moods and attitudes, and the conscious ideas he expressed in his work. Those attitudes and ideas were rooted, in Goya's case more deeply than in that of many other artists, in the struggles of his people, in the triumphs and disasters of Spain at a momentous turning point of its history. To recapture them it is necessary to examine the social background of Goya's life, and in particular the fortunes of the political movement with which he aligned himself, in detail; necessary, also, to trace the many ties which link his art both with that background and with a great tradition inherited from the past.

The method adopted in this book was, therefore, to describe the general conditions of Spanish life, economic, political, and cultural, and to define the attitude of the various strata of Spanish society to those conditions. Against that wider setting with its clash of material forces and ideas I have attempted to reconstruct Goya's own outlook from what is known of his life and more especially from his paintings, etchings, and drawings.

I have, in other words, approached the works of Goya primarily by studying their content. From that content I have attempted to deduce both their theme in the narrow sense of the word and their style. I have tried to show that there is a close correlation between the wider social experience which Goya shared with his contemporaries and his own attitude to that experience on the one hand, and the formal characteristics of his style on the other; that, indeed, the many conflicting tendencies of his style development can only be interpreted as the necessarily varying expressions of as many social moods and attitudes.

It was essential for this purpose to present these varied data as a comprehensive, yet subtle, skein of interacting forces, linked with the past and pressing forward into the future; as a combination of action, emotion, conscious

xiii

thought, and creative experience fused in the crucible of life.

Goya attained maturity only comparatively late in life. Apart from his authorship, there is little that is remarkable in any of the works he produced before he was thirty, and it is curious to reflect that his name would have been quickly forgotten had he died at the same early age as Shelley, Byron, or Géricault. Yet his creative period proper extends over almost half a century—roughly from 1780 to 1828—and it covers a sequence of phases remarkable for the contrasts both in his style and in the social problems it reflects.

It was thus impossible simply to write continuous accounts for the period as a whole, first of the social history of Spain, then of the cultural background, and finally of Goya's life and art. To preserve a sense of unity and to demonstrate the intimate interaction between life and art it was necessary to discuss the experiences which compelled Goya to change his style at various decisive moments of his development in immediate conjunction with his works themselves. The material is consequently presented in the following form:

The first chapter deals with the age of enlightened reform from about the mid-eighteenth century to the French Revolution, with the Spain of Charles III, and its supreme artistic emanation, Goya's tapestry cartoons. Both Spanish liberalism and Goya's art are profoundly national in character. It is impossible to understand either without tracing their roots in the social and cultural tradition of Spain. The relevant phases of that tradition are surveyed in rapid retrospect.

Chapter 2 is devoted to the Caprichos and the chaotic tangle of reaction, moral and political corruption, repression, and determination steeled by disillusionment mirrored in that work.

Six years of war, the horrors of the guerrilla campaign, barbarous sieges and starvation, a struggle which was both a national and a social revolution, provide the setting for the analysis of Goya's 'Disasters of the War' in Chapter 3.

Six years of dark oppression, the misdeeds of the traitor King restored to power by his people's valour, produced the agony of the 'pinturas negras' and the ' Disparates' discussed in Chapter 4.

The Revolution of 1820, defeated by disunity and intervention, and followed by an even more hideous phase of persecution, concludes the cycle of historical events encompassed in the eighty years of Goya's life. But the virile serenity of his final works reveals a spirit hardened by adversity and confident that integrity and freedom cannot be vanquished.

Thus Goya drew his inspiration from the hopes and struggles of his time. His art is linked by a thousand subtle threads with the daily life of his people. He never shirked the issues which confronted them. But by the genius of his art he made the concrete universal, and because he lived wholly and unreservedly in his time, Goya's name is immortal.

NOTE ON SOURCES

The authorities I have drawn upon for points of detail are indicated in the footnotes, but I am more particularly indebted for my general facts to the following works:

(*a*) Goya biography and art:

F. J. Sánchez Cantón, *Goya* (French edition: Paris, 1930). This first biography, in which documented facts are clearly distinguished from the fascinating legends collected by earlier writers, has been used throughout as the final arbiter in questions of dating and attribution. I have also made extensive use of A. L. Mayer's indispensable catalogue of Goya's works (*Goya*, Munich, 1923) and of more recent contributions to the standard periodicals. A comprehensive Goya bibliography up to 1935 will be found in the catalogue issued by the Bibliothèque Nationale for their Goya exhibition of that year (*Goya: Exposition de l'œuvre gravé, de peintures, de tapisseries, et de cent dix dessins du Musée du Prado*, Paris, 1935).

(*b*) General and cultural history of Spain:

Rafael Altamira y Crevea, *Historia de España y de la civilización española*, Barcelona, 1909–11.
D. Antonio Ballesteros y Beretta, *Historia de España*, Barcelona, 1929–34, vols. v-vii.
Hermann Baumgarten, *Geschichte Spaniens vom Ausbruch der französischen Revolution bis auf unsere Tage*, Leipzig, 1865–72.
C. E. Kany, *Life and Manners in Madrid, 1750–1800*, Berkeley, Cal., 1932.

A. Salcedo Ruiz, *La época de Goya*, Madrid, 1924.
A. D. Martin Hume, *Modern Spain*, London, 1899.
H. Butler Clarke, *Modern Spain*, Cambridge, 1906.

Exhaustive bibliographies on many aspects of Spanish social and cultural history are attached to each chapter in Ballesteros *op. cit.*

During three years of study I received encouragement and advice from friends too numerous to mention. My indebtedness to Dr. Friedrich Antal will be self-evident, when his great work on Florentine Painting will at last become available to the public. Dr. Enriqueta Harris most generously allowed me to use her comprehensive collection of photographs and notes on Goya.

F. D. K.

HAMPSTEAD
April 1940

Seven years' delay in publishing an essay of interpretation cannot fail to affect its author's judgements. New experiences and the study of different, though related subjects widen his perspectives and correct the distortions inevitable in all close-up studies. But although I have taken due note of such changes in revising the proofs of my book, they have not affected its main thesis. That it can now appear with its full complement of illustrations, despite post-war difficulties, is due to the generosity of Sir John Stirling Maxwell, Sr. Sánchez Cantón of the Prado Museum, and Mr. James Laver, of the Victoria and Albert Museum, who have kindly allowed drawings and prints in their collections to be photographed for this purpose. My thanks are also due to Mr. José Villanueva for checking the Spanish quotations.

F. D. K.

April 1947

GOYA IN THE
DEMOCRATIC TRADITION

Chapter 1

EIGHTEENTH-CENTURY SPAIN—
THE TAPESTRY CARTOONS

THE four-score years of Goya's life, extending from 1746 to 1828, witnessed a cycle of social upheavals which transformed the face of Europe. Goya grew to manhood with the rising tide of eighteenth-century rationalism. During the years of the French Revolution his powers had fully matured, and he continued to work with undiminished vigour for three decades, which saw the rise and fall of Napoleon, the victory of international reaction, and the first of a new cycle of revolutions.

Spanish history during this period is marked by a sequence of no less violent changes. When Goya died in exile, feudal Spain had crashed to ruins. A new era had dawned in the development of his country, and the first battles had been fought for a free people's Spain.

Goya's creative development mirrors the stormy course of the Spanish Revolution. For both, the eighteenth century was a period of preparation. Progressive Spain matured its energies for the coming struggle. Its dominant mood was one of confident exuberance. Its background, gay and colourful, is reflected in Goya's tapestry cartoons. Yet even in the eighteenth century there was no lack of sombre shadows in the Spanish scene. Though temporarily subdued, Black Spain, too, was preparing to defend its heritage. Both antagonists had their roots deep in the nation's past. We must trace those roots, if we are to understand the struggle which was the very life-blood of Goya's art.

It will be our task, in this chapter, to study the background of that struggle. First we shall muster the forces bent on the maintenance of the *status quo*, the Spain of feudal anarchy and backwardness, hugging the chains of economic and spiritual enslavement which had been forged for it by an all-powerful theocracy, and we shall trace the ascendancy of that Spain in the tragic history of the Hapsburg

1

era. We shall then survey the forces gathered for the assault on this degrading heritage: the progressive movement centred in the Bourbon court, whose policy of economic and social reconstruction could strike roots in Spain only because it aroused the dormant energies of a great democratic tradition. We shall follow the history of that tradition and of its reflection in the 'golden age' of Spanish art and literature, so vital for the cultural revival of the eighteenth century and the mother-soil of Goya's art. Next we shall study that revival and its impact on the outlook of the Spanish people, and thus conclude our survey of the complex factors which determined the character of Goya's first creative achievement, the tapestry cartoons.

THE FEUDAL BACKGROUND

The social structure of Spain on the eve of the French Revolution is illustrated by the Census made at the command of the minister Floridablanca in 1787.[1] The total population was then 10·4 millions, the adult population (16 years and over) 6·6 millions. If we omit some 47,000 inmates of hospitals, prisons, and similar institutions, the occupied male population of Spain was distributed as follows:

Occupation	No.	%
Clergy . . .	148,795 *	4·5
Nobility (hidalgos) . .	480,589	14·5
Peasants . . .	907,197	27·5
Day labourers (jornaleros)	964,671	29·1
Lawyers . . .	15,528	0·5
Officials . . .	36,465	1·1
Merchants . . .	34,339	1·0
Manufacturers . .	39,750	1·2
Artisans . . .	270,989	8·2
Servants . . .	280,092	8·5
Armed Forces . .	77,884	2·4
Students . . .	50,994	1·5
Total .	3,307,293	100·0

* Including 62,249 monks, but excluding 33,630 nuns.

[1] Censo de España, Madrid, 1787. The Census of 1797 was not accessible to me. Ballesteros, following Altamira, quotes what purport to be corresponding figures

According to these figures almost 60 per cent of the occupied population were either peasants or landless, but mainly agricultural labourers, and it is instructive to note that the latter were more numerous than the peasantry. A further 20 per cent were unproductive nobles and priests living mainly from the land. Industrial producers proper accounted for less than 10 per cent of the occupied population, and even if some of the day labourers were employed in the towns or on construction works, the total for industry cannot have exceeded 15 per cent. Personal servants were more numerous than artisans, and it is a striking comment on the impoverishment of the lower nobility that there were almost five hidalgos for every three servants. Over 270,000 out of the 480,000 hidalgos were recorded in the northern provinces of Burgos, León, and Asturias, and the whole population of the Basque country claimed noble rank. But a wide gulf separated the lower from the high nobility—the 119 grandees and 535 other *titulos de Castilla*. Only from these the great secular landlords of eighteenth-century Spain were recruited: the Dukes of Alba and Infantado who shared the whole of Upper Andalusia between them, while the southern part of that province was divided among the estates of the Dukes of Alba, Osuna, Arcos, Medinaceli, and Medina Sidonia.[1]

> For ten leagues I crossed the duchy of Medina Sidonia [writes Bourgoing[2]], which in this district consists of corn fields and pastures. In no part of them was a vestige of any human habitation. Not an orchard, kitchen garden, ditch, or tile. The great proprietor seems to reign there like the lion of the forests, by driving away by his roarings those by whom he might otherwise be approached; and both therefore alike reign over deserts.

In the first decade of the nineteenth century Canga Argüelles estimated that 51·5 per cent of the agricultural

---

for both years, but there are evident inconsistencies of definition—even assuming that the categories employed by different eighteenth-century statisticians can be compared. I have quoted individual figures for 1797 from Ballesteros *op. cit.* and Baumgarten *op. cit.*

[1] The last two had incomes of 8 and 6 million reals respectively, yet all the grandees were overwhelmed by debts and the Medinaceli estates were administered by receivers.

[2] J. F. de Bourgoing, *Nouveau Voyage en Espagne*, Paris, 1788; English ed. London, 1789. B. was secretary to the French embassy at Madrid from 1777 to 1785. Recalled in the latter year, he returned to Spain as ambassador of the Republic.

land of Spain (then amounting to 55 million fanegas) was owned by the nobility, 16·5 per cent by the Church, and 32·0 per cent by the communes and the peasantry. The state of the peasants differed widely even in adjacent provinces having similar natural conditions. Thus in the north the peasants of Galicia had been reduced to such misery by a system of sub-letting—for practically all the land was owned by the Church and the nobility—that the majority were forced to seek employment as seasonal labourers in other parts of the peninsula. But all the travellers of the time are unanimous in praising the flourishing appearance of the Basque villages where the tribal democracy of pre-feudal times had been preserved almost unimpaired. In the south there was a similar contrast between the exploited labourers of the big Andalusian estates and the fruit-growing small-holders of Murcia and Valencia. Between these coastal districts there lay the impoverished, badly cultivated up-lands of Castile, a gaunt landscape studded with deserted villages.[1]

THE CHURCH IN EIGHTEENTH-CENTURY SPAIN

In this feudal, agrarian economy the Church was the dominant institution. Owner of one-sixth of Spain's agricultural land and vested with countless privileges, it enjoyed a revenue little less than that of the State.[2] Its power over the mass of the people was still unchallenged.

In 1797 over 3,000 monasteries and convents were counted in Spain, although their number had greatly declined since the seventeenth century. They were inhabited by more than 60,000 monks—Benedictines, Bernardines, Augustines, Hieronymites, Carmelites, Carthusians, Capuchins, Franciscans, Dominicans—36 different orders in all, not counting the four great military orders, and by over 30,000 nuns belonging to 29 orders.

Yet in Catholic Spain there were almost 3,000 parishes without a priest of their own. Only 16,481 out of 91,258

---

[1] For further details cf. R. Leonhard, *Agrarpolitik und Agrarreform in Spanien unter Carl III*, Munich, 1909.

[2] According to Canga Argüelles, *Diccionario de Hacienda* ('Rentas del clero'), the net income of the Church, *i.e.* after all its taxes and other contributions to the State had been deducted, amounted to 1,101,753,000 reals, compared with a State revenue of 1,371,000,000. (To convert reals into £ at the exchange rate prevalent about 1788 omit the last two noughts from the former. This is the practice adopted by J. Townsend, *Journey through Spain*, London, 1792.)

secular clerics recorded in 1797 were parish priests, and in the country districts many of the latter were so poorly paid that they were dependent upon the charity of their parishioners.

Though the ministering clergy were poor, the wealth of the great monasteries and cathedral chapters, with their prelates, canons, prebendaries, rectors, deacons, confessors, chaplains, choristers, sacristans, and other place-holders, was fabulous. The Archbishop of Seville and his 235 subordinates at the Cathedral had a revenue exceeding six million reals, the Archbishop of Toledo alone had nine millions, while between them his 40 canons, 50 prebendaries, and 50 chaplains received four millions more. Altogether 600 people were employed at Toledo Cathedral. Its treasury contained, among other marvels, a model of the building made of pure silver and weighing 22,000 ounces; a massive gold shrine weighing 50 pounds; a shrine of the Virgin containing 1,250 pounds of silver strewn with jewels. But since the middle ages the population of Toledo had declined from 200,000 to 25,000, the number of inhabited villages in the neighbourhood from 551 to 349. Seville, with its cathedral and 30 other churches, its 84 convents, and 24 hospitals, was a city of beggars.[1]

The Church did little to justify its virtual monopoly of education. Less than 400,000 out of over three and a half million children received even a rudimentary education. The number of elementary schools in Spain was less than half that of its parishes.

The authority of the Inquisition had, it is true, received some check since the middle of the eighteenth century, and its moral prestige had correspondingly declined, at least among the intellectuals protected by the court. But the Holy Office retained extensive powers of censorship, and heresy prosecutions of leading writers and even statesmen continued throughout this period.[2]

The religious activities of the laity were organised by the guilds and brotherhoods which embraced every walk of life. In 1779, 19,024 such bodies were counted in Castile alone. At the same time the swarms of beggars in the towns

---

[1] Townsend *op. cit.*

[2] Notably those of the reform minister Count Aranda in 1770, the economist Olivarde (one of the leading agrarian reformers, who had come into collision with the clergy while in charge of the new settlements in the Sierra Morena) in 1776, the writer Clavijo in 1780, the State archivist Tomás de Yriarte in 1786, and the poets Meléndez Valdes and Samaniego in 1787. Cf. Kany *op. cit.*

—an important section of the population in the general scheme of Christian charity[1]—were wholly dependent upon the clergy, who supported them with daily doles of 'monastery soup'. In Madrid some 30,000 people, or nearly one-fifth of the population, were maintained by charity during the latter part of the eighteenth century.[2]

The power of the Church was symbolised by the obsequious reverence paid by the entire nation to the Host. If the King chanced to encounter a priest carrying the viaticum, he demonstratively gave up his carriage to him. When the viaticum was carried past a theatre, the performance was instantly interrupted, and the actors and spectators fell on their knees with every sign of devotion. Not until the doorman announced that the priest's bell was no longer audible, could the play continue.[3] The duties of confession and communion were rigorously enforced at least once a year. Certificates were issued to all who had fulfilled these duties, and anyone unable to produce such a certificate at Easter-time would get into serious trouble. As a result, a thriving traffic in these documents was carried on by prostitutes who went to communion as often as they could manage during Lent.[4]

But if hypocrisy and cant were the inevitable concomitants of formal observances meticulously enforced, the Church captured the imagination of the people with the sumptuous ceremonies and splendid processions which it staged for their entertainment during the numerous feast days of the calendar. Even on lesser occasions the various monastery and parish churches strove to outbid one another in the displays they offered to the people. In Barcelona, for example, six especially magnificent services were announced for a single Sunday in 1802: the *fiésta de la Minerva* in the church of St. Michel Archangel; the *fiésta del Monte de Piedad* of St. Joseph; a service of special solemnity in the church of San Francisco de Paula; a grand gala ceremony in San Francisco de Asis; the *fiésta* of St. John Nepomuk in the church of the Trinitarians; and a rosary festival with music in the churchyard of Nazareth.[5]

---

[1] The Council of Trent had expressly confirmed the importance of mendicancy: The poor and sick must beg in the streets to enable good Christians to practise their charity (Fra Domingo de Soto).
[2] Kany *op. cit.*   [3] Cf. J. Casanova de Seingalt, *Memoirs*, London, 1922.
[4] Bourgoing *op. cit.* and Townsend *op. cit.*
[5] Ballesteros *op. cit.* quoting the *Diario de Barcelona*.

Nothing, however, could more convincingly demonstrate the power of the Church over the emotions of the people than the fact that processions of 'disciplinantes', traversing the streets during Holy Week in the fantastic garb of the penitents, blood streaming from their lacerated backs, though prohibited by the government in 1777, had again to be proscribed in 1799, and again in 1802.[1]

THE HAPSBURG HERITAGE

The power of the Church in eighteenth-century Spain was due to the peculiar course of Spanish history during the two preceding decades of the Hapsburg era. Spain had been in the vanguard of the movement which led to the emergence of the modern nation-state. Having united the ancient realms of Aragón and Castile, and having completed the expulsion of the Moors, Ferdinand and Isabella, the 'Catholic Kings', firmly established the supremacy of the crown, with the help of the third estate, over the recalcitrant feudal lords. Although they also limited the effective but not the formal liberties of the communes, the Catholic Kings did their utmost to foster their economic development. Their reign was an era both of internal consolidation and of imperial expansion. But when in 1516 the destinies of Spain were fettered to the family interests of the Hapsburgs, the whole character of its development suffered a fatal change.

Reared at the court of Burgundy, that model of European absolutism, Charles had been imbued with a notion of kingship which was wholly alien to the traditions of Spain. He had scarcely arrived in his new realm when he alienated the affections of his Spanish subjects by his haughty manner and the greed of the Flemish courtiers, whom he placed in all key positions. When he spurned the traditional rights of the Spaniards by attempting to make them foot the bill of his election as Roman Emperor, the communes of Castile rose in defence of their ancient liberties. The 'Comunero' rising of 1520–21 was crushed. But the defeat of the commoners permanently destroyed the alliance between the crown and the middle classes, which had been the foundation of the national awakening of Spain. Although later in

---

[1] Sánchez Cantón *op. cit.* Broken glass was attached to the tips of the whips used by the disciplinantes. It was considered the height of gallantry to contrive to squirt a drop of one's blood onto the gown of one's admiring mistress (Kany *op. cit.*).

the Emperor's reign Spain's new position as a world power and the appeal of a policy, which seemed a continuation of the reconquest, stirred the imagination of his subjects, the common people never ceased to regard his reign as a disaster and to compare it with the 'good regiment' of the Catholic Kings.[1]

Charles's reversal of the Spanish crown's internal policy was most disastrous in the economic sphere. Unable to make the Spaniards bear the costs of his election, he was driven into the arms of the German and Italian bankers, who had already exploited the chronic impecuniousness of his father. The Augsburg Fugger and Welser and three Italian banking firms between them advanced the bribe of 850,000 florins for which the German Electors consented to give their votes to Charles. The Emperor's foreign policy—his interminable wars in Italy, Hungary, Germany, and North Africa, followed by Philip's crusades against the Turks and the heretics of Flanders, France, and Britain, and his conquest of Portugal, and accompanied by the ever-mounting costs of a diplomacy based on espionage and bribes—strengthened the hold of the foreign merchant princes on the finances of Spain. *Pecunia nervus belli*. In return for their ever-increasing loans Charles and Philip had to pledge an ever larger share of their Spanish revenue to the German and Italian bankers. Every device was employed to increase that revenue: a thriving traffic was organised in public offices, favours and exemptions of all kinds, and even in patents of legitimacy for the children of the clergy. Worse still: the entire internal economy of Spain was placed at the mercy of her foreign creditors. The taxes were farmed out to them and raised to the ruin of Spanish industry, commerce, and agriculture. The protective legislation of the Catholic Kings was repealed or suspended in favour of the German and Italian merchants. The flourishing silk industry of Granada and the old Spanish trade in high-grade woollens were crushed in this manner; in 1550 the stringent corn laws were suspended in the case of all the operations of the Fugger; and the administration even winked at flagrant evasions of the ban on bullion exports. (The Fugger, for example, smuggled 200,000 ducats' worth of silver out of

[1] Such was the verdict of an old peasant whom Charles, who had lost his way while hunting, is said to have asked which were the best and the worst reigns in Spanish history. *v.* R. B. Merriman, *The Rise of the Spanish Empire*, New York, 1918–34, vol. iii.

Spain in the ships in which the Prince of Asturias sailed for Antwerp in 1553.)[1] At the same time the Fugger, whose Spanish investments amounted to three million ducats, or nearly three-fifths of their total assets in 1563, took over the administration of the vast estates of the four great military orders and the exploitation of the mercury mines of Almadén. Their rivals, the Welser, exploited the Galician mines. Charles's foreign creditors even extended their hold to the Spanish-American trade. In 1526 the Emperor granted the right of colonial trade and settlement to all his subjects, including the Germans and Italians. The Welser had already established factories in Seville and Santo Domingo (the new capital of the West Indian colonies) in 1525. Three years later they contracted to carry 50 German miners and 4,000 negro slaves to America and to conquer and colonise Venezuela, where they established a régime of ruthless exploitation, based on gold hunts and slave raids.[2] Although Philip II again restricted the right of colonial trade and settlement to Castilians, the ruin of Spain's industry made the importation of foreign goods into America inevitable. Five-sixths of all cargoes shipped from Seville under the later Hapsburgs consisted of such contraband goods, while an ever-increasing proportion of the American trade fell into the hands of foreign interlopers.[3]

Subjected to such pressure, Spain's economy was unable to resist the many other disastrous blows which fell upon it: the price revolution of the mid-sixteenth century, which her foreign rivals could turn to their advantage; the change in the direction of world trade which led to the decline of Spain's most important industrial centre, Barcelona, cut off from the American trade by the monopoly of Seville; and the policy of racial persecution which, though initiated with the expulsion of the Jews in 1492, culminated under the Hapsburgs with the expulsion of the Moriscos—the best craftsmen and cultivators of Spain—in 1609.[4]

[1] *v.* R. Ehrenberg, *Das Zeitalter der Fugger*, Jena, 1896. For Charles V's economic policy *v.* Merriman *op. cit.* and J. Bernays, 'Zur inneren Entwicklung Kastiliens unter Karl V' (*Deutsche Zeitschrift für Geschichtswissenschaft*, I, 1889). This painstakingly documented review refutes the view of Konrad Habler, *Die wirtschaftliche Blüte Spaniens im 16. Jahrhundert*, Berlin, 1888, that Spain reached the height of her prosperity under the Emperor.

[2] For further details *v.* note I in the Appendix, p. 214.

[3] *v.* C. H. Haring, *Trade and Navigation between Spain and the Indies*, Cambridge, Mass., 1918.

[4] There was little racial or religious fanaticism during the heroic period of the reconquest. The first serious persecutions were instigated by the Dominicans in the latter part of the fourteenth century, but they subsided until revived for political

The expulsion of the Moorish cultivators did not, however, benefit the Spanish peasantry. This was the age of the
disastrous depopulation of rural Spain which was a constant
source of alarm to the Cortes. The dispossessed peasants
flocked first to the neighbouring towns, and later to the
coastal regions, to seek employment in the service of the
rich, to emigrate, or to swell the ranks of the beggars, who
made Seville a flagrant contrast of luxury and degradation.[1]
Coupled with the rise in prices, the ruin of the peasantry
impoverished the lower nobility, many of whom had little
but their pride to sustain them: picking his teeth in the
street to impress the onlookers as a well-fed man of substance, the hungry hidalgo became a stock-figure of Spanish
literature during the Golden Age.[2]

Such were the results of the first German-Italian penetration of Spain. But in their downfall the Spaniards dragged
their despoilers with them into the abyss. At first, it is
true, only the smaller Spanish creditors were ruined by the
ever more frequent State bankruptcies of their country.
But ultimately these disasters played such havoc with the
financial houses of Southern Germany and Italy that even
the greatest among them were driven out of business. The
Fugger, whose Spanish assets had risen to $5\frac{1}{2}$ million ducats
by 1622 (against liabilities of $4\frac{1}{2}$ millions), were forced to
liquidate their peninsular business in 1637. Thus ended the
last and most spectacular enterprise of capitalism in its
specifically medieval form based on usury and commerce.
It was defeated by the new industrial capitalism. The centre
of economic progress had shifted to the mortal enemies of
the Hapsburgs: the Dutch and British heretics and the semi-
heretical French.

Having spurned the alliance with the middle classes,
having impoverished the lower nobility, and reduced the
grandees to the rank of courtiers, the Hapsburgs could build
the foundations of their autocracy only on the support of the

---

purposes by the Catholic Kings during the Granada campaign. Merriman *op. cit.*
and H. C. Lea, *History of the Inquisition in Spain*, New York, 1906–7.
[1] On the decline of Spanish agriculture *v.* Bernays *op. cit.* and L. Pfandl, *Spanische
Kultur und Sitte des 16. und 17. Jahrhunderts*, Kempten, 1924. On the resulting
population movements: A. Girard, 'La Répartition de la population en Espagne'
(*Revue d'Histoire économique et sociale*, xvii, 1929), and 'Le Chiffre de la population
de l'Espagne' (*Revue d'Histoire moderne*, iii, 1928, and iv, 1929). The total population
of Castile declined by one-quarter between 1492 and 1541; though it recovered
by one-seventh in the next fifty years, it fell by one-half between 1591 and 1723.
Not until 1756 did it regain the 1491 level.
[2] This motive already occurs in the *Lazarillo de Tormes* of 1554.

Church. The ideal of Spanish absolutism, anticipated by the Catholic Kings and taken to its logical conclusion by the first two Hapsburgs, implied a fusion of secular and spiritual authority in the hands of the crown. After protracted negotiations with the Pope, the Spanish Inquisition had been established in 1480 to achieve that aim. In the hands of Philip II this instrument "which seemed to embody the main principles of his life" became "the strongest bulwark of the omnipotence of the crown".[1] With its help he controlled both the public and the private affairs of his subjects. When expediency demanded, he used it to support the authority of the secular courts in crushing his political opponents, and he did not hesitate to direct the power of the Holy Office even against the Primate of Spain.[2]

But after the death of the 'Prudent King' the tool became the master. More securely founded than the ephemeral power of the favourites, who ruled Spain under the third and fourth Philips, the influence of the Church in both hemispheres increased as rapidly as its wealth. Amidst the universal ruin the monasteries and great cathedral chapters emerged as the sole beneficiaries of the Hapsburg régime.

Tied to the theocratic ideals of the past, the Hapsburgs failed to create a centralised autocracy in Spain:

> In the other great states of Europe absolute monarchy presents itself as a civilising centre, as the initiator of social unity. There it was the laboratory in which the various elements of society were so mixed and worked as to allow the towns to change the local independence of the Middle Ages for the general rule of the middle classes, and the common sway of civil society. In Spain, on the contrary, while the aristocracy sank into degradation without losing its worst privileges, the towns lost their mediaeval power without gaining modern importance. . . . As the commercial

[1] Merriman *op. cit.*
[2] Bartolome de Carranza, Archbishop of Toledo, was accused of heresy before the Suprema in 1557. The Inquisition was used for political purposes after the suppression of the popular rising in Valencia in 1523 and also in the notorious case of the ex-minister Pérez, whom Philip wished to silence because he had been his accomplice in a political murder. Having escaped from prison, Pérez sought refuge in Aragón, whose ancient liberties, including a form of Habeas Corpus, had not yet been abrogated. Foiled in his attempt to make the Aragón 'Justicia' hand over his prisoner, Philip trumped up a blasphemy charge before the Holy Office. (Pérez was accused of having uttered blasphemies while suffering torture on the rack!) The Justicia complied, but the people of Saragossa, supported by a section of the nobility, rose in defence of their 'fueros' (1591).

and industrial life of the towns declined, internal exchanges became rare, the mingling of the inhabitants
of different provinces less frequent, the means of com-
munication neglected, and the great roads gradually
deserted. Thus the local life of Spain, the independence
of its provinces and communes, the diversified state of
society originally based on the physical configuration
of the country, and historically developed by the detached manner in which the several provinces emancipated themselves from the Moorish rule and formed
little independent commonwealths—was now finally
strengthened and confirmed by the economical revolution which dried up the resources of national activity.
And while the absolute monarchy found in Spain
material in its very nature repulsive to centralisation,
it did all in its power to prevent the growth of common
interests arising out of a national division of labour and
the multiplicity of internal exchanges—the very basis
on which alone a uniform system of administration and
the rule of general laws can be created. Thus the
absolute monarchy in Spain, bearing but a superficial
resemblance to the absolute monarchies of Europe in
general, is rather to be ranged in a class with Asiatic
forms of government. Spain, like Turkey, remained an
agglomeration of mismanaged republics with a nominal
sovereign at their head. Despotism changed the character of the different provinces with the arbitrary interpretation of the general laws by viceroys and governors;
but despotic as was the government it did not prevent
the provinces from subsisting with different laws and
customs, different coins, military manners of different
colours, and with their respective system of taxation.[1]

Although the Hapsburgs prevented the emergence of a
modern Spain—"under the Emperor at least its ancient
liberties were buried in a magnificent tomb. This was the
time when Vasco Núñez de Balboa planted the banner of

[1] Karl Marx, 'Spanish Revolutions'. Anonymous article in *New York Tribune*, 9 September 1854; later instalments of this brilliant series, which deals in the main with
the period 1808–10, appeared in the same paper on 20 September, 20, 27, and 30
October, 24 November, and 1 and 2 December 1854. See *Revolution in Spain*, by
K. Marx and F. Engels: Lawrence & Wishart, Ltd., London. A previous article on
Espartero and his role in the 1854 revolution had been printed on 19 August. Marx's
thesis that the Hapsburgs accentuated the feudal anarchy of Spain is strikingly
confirmed in important details by J. Klein's study of the great guild of the sheep
graziers (*The Mesta: a Study of Spanish Economic History, 1273–1836*, Cambridge,
Mass., 1920). There was also a renewed increase in the number of localities subject
to seignorial jurisdiction. Even in 1787 there were still 17 towns, 2,358 large, and
8,818 small, villages in which the feudal lords controlled the courts. *v.* Leonhard
op. cit.

Castile on the shores of the Pacific, Cortés in Mexico, and Pizarro in Perú; when Spanish influence reigned supreme in Europe, and the southern imagination of the Iberians was bewildered with visions of Eldorados, chivalrous adventures, and universal monarchy."[1] But the colossus of Spanish imperialism was founded on feet of clay. When Philip II died in 1598, its power was exhausted. The brilliant game of bluff played by its diplomats deceived Europe for another half-century. But under the last of the Hapsburgs its weakness could no longer be concealed. Persuaded by enemy agents that he was possessed of the devil, the feeble-minded epileptic Charles II was purging his deluded soul in the agony of exorcism, while the chancelleries of Europe were plotting the dismemberment of his empire.

> Money was unbelievably scarce. Soldiers on active service were forced to beg in the streets; the servants of the royal household absconded because they received neither food nor wages; more than once the cash was lacking to supply even the king's own table. The ministries were besieged by high officials and officers whose salaries were years in arrears. Urgent dispatches were held up because the king's messengers could not pay their travelling expenses. In the provinces the people had to resort to barter. The art of public finance was reduced to open fraud and robbery. . . .[2]

Her population halved, her country districts studded with the ruins of deserted villages,[3] Spain had reached the depth of degradation.

THE SPANISH BOURBONS: A NEW START

Spain's dramatic recovery during the eighteenth century is associated with the reigns of Philip V (1700–46), grandson of Louis XIV, and his two sons, Ferdinand VI (1746–1759) and Charles III (1759–88). By abolishing the privileges of the Catalans, who had sided with his opponents during the Succession War, Philip V established a centralised administration for the whole of Spain, except the small Basque territories in the north. He and his successors made a deter-

---

[1] Marx *op. cit.*   [2] Baumgarten *op. cit.*
[3] Even at the end of the reform period, when the number of inhabitants had again been doubled, 1,511 deserted villages were counted by Floridablanca's Census of 1787.

mined bid to clean up a notoriously corrupt bureaucracy. They stimulated trade and communications by building roads and canals, by reforming the obsolete system of taxation, and by restoring the maritime power of Spain. They attempted to revive Spanish industry by inviting foreign manufacturers to settle in their realm, by establishing numerous model enterprises under State control, and by encouraging technical education. They similarly sought to arrest the decay of Spanish agriculture by rescinding the abuses of the tenancy law and providing smallholdings for landless labourers, and they also settled colonies of foreign peasants in the deserted regions of the Sierra Morena.[1] The most convincing proof of their success is provided by the population figures of Spain during the eighteenth century. The total population was almost doubled and the inhabitants of the various provinces increased at the following rates between 1723 and 1787: Castile 88 per cent, Catalonia 64 per cent, Aragón 72 per cent, and Valencia 155 per cent.[2]

To restore the supremacy of the crown in the affairs of Spain, the Bourbons had to curb the excessive power of the Church. Although Philip V suffered a setback during the latter part of his reign in this respect, his sons were more successful. The Concordat of 1753, negotiated by Ferdinand VI, reduced the number of clerical appointments to be filled with papal nominees from 12,000 to 52. Charles III expelled the Jesuits from all Spanish dominions in 1766[3] and curbed the powers of the Holy Office by a series of decrees which again subjected its actions to the approval of the secular authorities.

The Spanish Bourbons thus in effect revived the policy of their French ancestors in the age of Richelieu and Colbert before the revocation of the Edict of Nantes (1685), and the principles of enlightened absolutism provided the impetus which pushed Spain onto the path of recovery at the very time when they had already become a reactionary deadweight in France.

[1] For detailed accounts of these reforms *v.* Altamira, Ballesteros, and Baumgarten *op. cit.* Bourgoing gives many interesting details concerning the State factories. The cloth factory at Guadalajara, *e.g.*, employed 3,825 weavers on 686 looms, while some 40,000 cottage labourers supplied it with yarn. In the agricultural sphere the intentions of the government were better than its achievement (*vide* Leonhard *op. cit.*).   [2] Girard *op. cit.*
[3] The Jesuits had already been expelled from Portugal in 1759 and from France in 1764. They were finally suppressed by the Pope in 1773.

But the Spanish Bourbons lacked one of the corner-stones on which the great Cardinals of seventeenth-century France had founded their policy: the support of a progressive middle class. The Spanish middle class had long become subservient to the dictates of the theocracy. A sinecure in the bureaucracy or in the service of the Church was the height of their ambition. Lawyers and officials, recruited from the 'letrados' who had received their training at the Church-controlled universities, occupied the last remaining spheres of middle-class influence in the early eighteenth century. Their material interests were so essentially identified with the existing state of legal anarchy and administrative corruption that they were little inclined, *as a class*, to welcome a policy of resolute reform. Thus the foreign kings were compelled to invoke the services of foreign advisers—foreign statesmen, financiers, manufacturers, artisans, and even peasants—in their effort to restore the vital energies of Spain.

Nevertheless—and that is the secret of their success—the Bourbons did find a powerful ally within their new realm: the democratic heritage of medieval Spain. This we must now examine.

THE MAJO

The Spanish eighteenth-century scene, and in particular the Madrid scene, was dominated by a picturesque fellow, the 'majo', whose insolence was as captivating as his gaiety. In both he was equalled, if not excelled, by his female boon companion, the 'maja'. With their gay songs, the haunting rhythm of their dance measures, their noisy brawls, but also their poise and dignity, they make every other figure on the Spanish stage appear small and insignificant. It will be worth our while to watch them a little more closely.

The majo, we are told,[1] was a boastful individual, "with a chip on his shoulder", who was always ready to pick a quarrel and took a pride in being well dressed in a manner all his own. A colourful person, he walked in the middle of the street and refused to make room for anyone, be he a citizen, a gentleman, or a policeman. He always smoked big black cigars (while smoking in any form was considered

---

[1] I am transcribing the account given by A. Hamilton, *A Study of Spanish Manners, 1750–1800, from the Plays of Ramón de la Cruz,* University of Illinois Studies in Language and Literature, vol. xi, 1926. Cf. also Kany *op. cit. v.* also Bourgoing's description in note II of the Appendix (p. 216).

vulgar by the snuff-taking upper classes of Madrid) and was, in short, the fashionable dandy of the poor with a marked dislike for honest work.

On gala occasions the maja was as elaborately dressed in the national costume as the majo. But at ordinary times she dressed as other women of the working class, for she had to earn her living, or, if she was married, to look after her home. All chestnut-sellers, orange-sellers, lime-girls, most market-women, and many servants were majas.

The relations between the majos and their majas were rigorously defined. Every majo, who was not already attached to a maja was on the look-out for one, and vice versa. They would establish their relationship by an exchange of gifts. When either party desired to dissolve the partnership, the gifts were returned. The maja would attempt to persuade her lover to marry her, and any suspicion of entanglements elsewhere would cause a violent scene. If displeased with her majo, the maja might kick him, and the majo might beat the maja if her behaviour annoyed him, but it was considered bad form to fight with her. If the maja was unmarried, she would usually keep the majo. But if, as sometimes, she was already married to an ordinary artisan, the majo would have to work for his living and to obtain the means of providing amusements and knick-knacks for his mistress. In her relations with other women the maja was as hot-tempered, proud, and quarrelsome as the majo.

The majos and majas "considered themselves as representing the pure Castilian spirit and as being superior to those of higher rank, since the latter were contaminated by alien tendencies".[1] And the upper classes conceded this claim. Bourgoing writes:

> In most countries the inferior classes think it an honour to ape their superiors; in Spain it is the contrary in many respects. There are, among both sexes, persons of distinguished rank, who seek their models among the heroes of the populace, who imitate their dress, manner and accent, and are flattered when it is said of them: He is very like a Majo—one would take her for a Maja.[2]

[1] Kany *op. cit.*   [2] *Op. cit.*

THE DEMOCRATIC HERITAGE

What was the foundation of this "pure Castilian Spirit" which made the heroes of the working class the representatives and envied models of Spanish society?

It was the indomitable pride of a people acknowledging no master, a people steeled in the eight centuries of the re-conquest, a people which only submitted to the Hapsburg yoke because its "southern imagination" had been inflamed by "visions of Eldorados, chivalrous adventures, and universal monarchy". Although the Hapsburgs had superimposed their oriental despotism on feudal Spain, they had not crushed its spirit. For feudalism, like absolutism, has a very special meaning in Spain. We have so far only considered its negative aspects, the regional diversity of habits and traditions which defied centralisation. Its positive features are even more significant. They are due to the conditions of Spanish life during the re-conquest, conditions which, on the one hand, led to the preservation of many elements of pre-feudal society and, on the other, changed the character of institutions typical of feudalism in other countries.

Serfdom, the broad foundation of feudal society, existed in its true form only in Catalonia which formed a political unit with parts of southern France during the early middle ages and had been re-conquered from the Moors by Frankish barons. The condition of the rural population in Aragón, though less abject than in Catalonia, also approached that state. But the Castilian peasantry (*i.e.* since the mid-thirteenth century the peasantry in the whole of Spain except Catalonia, Aragón, Valencia, and the Moorish kingdom of Granada) was far more independent than that of any other country in Europe. The general state of insecurity which persisted from the eighth to the thirteenth century led, in the first place, to a concentration of the people in or near fortified cities, and a considerable proportion of the Castilian peasants thus lived under the jurisdiction of the communes. In the second place, the more adventurous spirits could only be induced to settle in the exposed districts of the gradually advancing 'frontier' by the grant of especially favourable social and economic conditions. Various forms of personal dependence remained the price by which the settlers—especially those arriving after the greatest danger had passed—could purchase the protection of the powerful barons. But the burden imposed upon them was, on the whole, far less crushing than elsewhere, and a whole section of these pioneers, the so-called *behetrias de mar a mar*, were at liberty to change their masters, if they did not like them, as often as "up to seven times in one day". It is significant, moreover, that in the last two centuries of the middle ages, *i.e.* after the re-conquest had in the main been completed, the conditions of the more dependent Castilian peasants, and even those of the Catalan serfs, were greatly improved.

Even more striking was the influence of the medieval Spanish communes. It was due to the role of the towns as centres of refuge and protection during the re-conquest, but also to the fact that the cities were the natural allies of the kings in their efforts to create at least a semblance of national unity against the opposition of the anarchic nobility. Although the nobles were the mainstay of the Christian forces during the re-conquest,[1] they never hesitated to fight in the ranks of the infidels against their compatriots when it suited their convenience. They regarded the kings as equals among equals. "We who are as good as you swear to you who are no better than we, to accept you as our king, provided you observe all our liberties and laws; but if not, not"—this formula of the ancient coronation oath of Aragon defines the relations of the sovereigns to their noble subjects in all the kingdoms of medieval Spain.

Aristocratic separatism also threatened the interests of the communes, whose economic development required a measure of security and national unity. Hence the alliance between the crown and the cities, who were rewarded with important privileges. They were granted an unparalleled degree of self-government in their local 'fueros' (bills of rights), while collectively they played an increasingly important role in the Cortes. The representatives of the communes had been summoned to these national assemblies since the twelfth century, and, as the main providers of the national revenue, their influence gradually overshadowed that of the clergy and nobility. The latter ceased to attend after the great reform Cortes of 1476 and 1480 had curtailed the power of the feudal lords in Castile.[2]

---

[1] But the municipalities also provided levies for the Moorish wars.
[2] The Cortes of the Eastern Kingdom (Catalonia, Aragón, and Valencia) were in some respects more powerful than those of Castile, but the nobles and clerics never ceased

The political emancipation of the Spanish cities was a reflection of their growing economic importance. The cities of the northern pasturage area, León, Soria, Segovia, Cuenca, were the headquarters, and their inhabitants comprised the bulk of the members of the migratory sheep industry organised in the Mesta.[1] The export trade of this main industry of medieval Castile was organised from Burgos. The wool and also the products of the northern mines were carried as far as England and Flanders by the intrepid Basque navigators. While every schoolboy knows of the defeat of the 'Invincible Armada', few people realise that in 1377 the Basques, then the allies of the French, sacked the Isle of Wight, Hastings, and Rottingdean, after which they sailed up the Thames and struck terror into the hearts of the Londoners by burning Gravesend to the ground. The fame of Barcelona as a centre of industry and commerce (wool and cloth again formed the staple commodities) dates from the eleventh century. In the later middle ages it disputed the supremacy of the Mediterranean with Venice, its citizens colonised the Balearic Islands, Sicily, and even parts of Greece, while their trading posts extended from Asia Minor to North Africa and Flanders. Valencia and the Andalusian cities retained the great economic importance which they had already possessed under the Moors. After the conquest of America Seville became the sluice-gate through which the wealth of the Indies poured into Europe.[2]

Except in Majorca, where the exploitation of the rural population by the allied citizens and nobles led to a devastating peasant uprising in the 1450's, the Spanish bourgeoisie nowhere, however, attained such undisputed political power that it could have dispensed with the support of the lower classes. For when the power of the nobles was finally curbed, the citizens were confronted with the incipient absolutism

to attend them. Here middle-class support for the crown was centred in Barcelona, while the far less important towns of Aragón sided with the nobility against the king in the social struggles of the fourteenth century. The fact that King Pedro II of Aragón fought on the side of the Albigenses in the final struggle which led to their extermination in the early thirteenth century reveals the early origin of the alignment between crown and the most advanced citizens in this area.

[1] Even in the eighteenth century some 80 per cent of the 2-3 million sheep controlled by the Mesta were owned by small and medium graziers. The rest were the property of a few great monasteries (especially the Escorial) and grandees (Klein *op. cit.*).

[2] *v.* Merriman *op. cit.* On Spain's internal trade *v.* also Klein *op. cit.* and Earl J. Hamilton, *Money, Prices and Wages in Valencia, Aragón, and Navarre, 1351–1500*, Cambridge, Mass., 1936.

of the Catholic Kings. It is significant that even in Barcelona, that citadel of early capitalism in Spain, the governing body, which had originally been recruited from the privileged and most wealthy citizens, was reorganised in the mid-fourteenth century to include representatives not only of the artisans but even of the labourers. Although liberty was the watchword of all classes in medieval Spain, and although even the nobles fought under its banner (*e.g.* in Aragón), it was the alliance of the middle class and the people in the communes which was the main bulwark of Spanish freedom. The degree of independence and self-government attained by the citizens and their influence in the Cortes go far "to justify the claim that Spain was in some respects the most democratic country in mediaeval Europe".[1]

Ferdinand and Isabella laid the foundation on which their successors could transform the "still feudal monarchy of Spain into an absolute one".[2] The Catholic Kings made the first decisive inroads into the liberties of the communes, no less than of the nobility. They did not openly attack the former, however, for they required the help of the cities in order to accomplish their main task of curbing the pretensions of the aristocracy. Instead of rescinding the local fueros, they limited their effective scope by appointing or strengthening various local representatives of the central government — such as the 'corregidores' — who gradually assumed control of local affairs. They similarly reduced the power of the Cortes, after the great reforms of 1476 and 1480, by using their constitutional right of convening them only on rare occasions. But by completing the re-conquest and uniting the realms of Christian Spain; by restoring the internal security of the country[3] and raising its prosperity; by planting the banner of Castile on the shores of the Indies —the Catholic Kings turned the forces of Spanish liberty from petty regionalism to truly national aims. The spirit of exaltation with which the Spanish people embraced these aims in many respects resembled the national awakening of England under Elizabeth. In both countries the middle and lower classes supported a national effort which embodied their own aspirations, although the government in effect

[1] Merriman *op. cit.*   [2] Marx *op. cit.*
[3] Their most effective instrument for this purpose was the *Santa Hermandad*, a rural police force recruited from the cities and reviving the traditions of similar brotherhoods which had been organised by various city leagues during the earlier middle ages.

ignored their constitutional liberties. But that the spirit of Spanish independence was not extinguished is shown by the mighty rising in which the cities of Castile, united in the Holy League of Avila, sought to defend their ancient fueros against the Hapsburgs.

The *Comunero* revolt of 1520–21 and the simultaneous risings of the *Germanias* in Valencia and Majorca were the final trial of strength between Spanish democracy as it emerged from the social history of the middle ages and the new forces of absolutism. Although the 'comuneros' were hailed as their forerunners by the liberals of the nineteenth century, it is important not to overlook the conservative features which were largely responsible for their defeat. The aims of the Castilian communes, in particular, were mainly conservative: the defence of ancient rights against the foreign king and his Flemish councillors. Hence the movement was at first supported by considerable sections of the aristocracy and clergy. Only when these had deserted the cause after the first encounters with the king's forces did the *Comunero* revolt assume a more democratic aspect. Even then, however, the leadership remained in the hands of certain noblemen and priests. Though courageous and loyal to the end, their policy was doomed to failure by their fatal lack of resolution and respect for legal forms. This was dramatically revealed in the macabre scene in the castle of Tordesillas where they sought to obtain the approval of Mad Joan, queen-mother and still the legal head of Spain, for their action. They had staked the fate of their rising on the signature of an insane woman, and their failure to obtain it marked the turning point of the movement. Deserted by their allies, the commoners suffered reverse after reverse until they were finally defeated after more than nine months of struggle in the battle of Villalar on 23 April 1521. Only Toledo, the first of the Castilian cities to rise, held out for another six months under the gallant command of Doña María, the widow of the defeated leader Juan de Padilla.

The *Germanias* of Valencia and Majorca, on the other hand, were inspired from the first by democratic aims. They were militant 'brotherhoods' of artisans, labourers, and (in Majorca) peasants directed, not so much against the king as against the rich burgesses and the feudal lords. Both movements were led by commoners: both the Valencian leader Vincente Peris and the Majorcan Juan Crespi appear to have been woollen-weavers or cloth merchants. They were far more resolute and successful than their Castilian comrades, for the Valencian rising lasted three (in the country districts even four) years, that of Majorca almost two years (February 1521–December 1522). The radical character of these movements probably accounts for the fact that it did not, apparently, occur to the Castilian communes to make common cause with them, although the Valencian rising had already started in the spring of 1519 (*i.e.* some fifteen months before the *Comunero* movement which began in June 1520). Catalonia, Aragón, and most of the southern cities did not participate in any of these events. When their own time came to defend their liberties (seventy years later in the case of Aragón and in the early eighteenth century in that of Catalonia) they were easily crushed. Thus lack of unity and the age-old curse of Spanish regionalism brought about the defeat of Spain's medieval democracy. "The heads of the principal 'Conspirators' rolled on the scaffold, and the ancient liberties of Spain disappeared . . . under the clash of arms, showers of gold, and the terrible illuminations of the *auto-de-fé*."[1]

THE PICARO

Although the people bowed their heads beneath the Hapsburg yoke, they triumphed over their oppressors. This is true not only because Spanish regionalism defied centralisation, but also in a more subtle sense. Behind the glittering façade of Hapsburg Spain, behind its mystical exaltation, dreams of empire and visions of Eldorado, there lurked the sordid reality of destitution. Behind the pathetic figure of Don Quixote rides Sancho Panza—Don Quixote *is* Sancho Panza. The brotherhood of thieves and beggars, the wily 'picaros' with their thousand tricks, their laws and customs, and a language all their own, were not, as in the rest of Europe, a part of the community—in Hapsburg Spain they were *the* community. The standards of the picaro permeated and corrupted every rank, reducing all to his level. Spanish society was a society of beggars.[2] In the jungle law of low life, where "every man is Enemy unto every man", the Spaniards regained that freedom which all the

---

[1] Marx *op. cit.* For a detailed account of the risings *v.* Merriman *op. cit.*
[2] *v.* Jean Cassou, *Cervantes*, Paris, 1936.

inquisitors, alguazils, revenue guards, judges, and jailers of the autocracy could not take from them. And let us not forget that the northern provinces of the Hapsburg realm fought for their liberty under the banner of the Beggars' Wallet.[1]

The picaro of the Golden Age became the majo of Goya's time. What better proof for the change in the temper of Spanish life than this transmutation of its representative figure? The picaro with his low cunning, degraded and cynical, striving with all his wits to secure the crumbs of beggary in an age of decay—the majo with his carefree gaiety, proud of his national heritage, and the hero of the people in an age of awakening.

THE CULTURAL HERITAGE OF SPANISH DEMOCRACY

(a) *Literature.* The democratic current of Spanish society during the middle ages profoundly affected its literature and art. The earliest traces of a popular literature are to be found in the folk songs of Galicia. The romances of chivalry glorifying the heroes of the re-conquest had also had a strongly popular undercurrent. They were spread from place to place by the ballad singers (the so-called 'juglares') for centuries before they were enriched by the influence of the courtly Provençal epic.[2] In its later development that chivalrous literature, which persisted until the sixteenth century, faithfully mirrors the changing structure of Spanish society. During the fourteenth century it was adapted to the tastes of the rising middle class: in the *Mocedades del Cid*, for example, a version of the Cid story dating from the first half of the fourteenth century, that eminently feudal hero has become the son of a cloth merchant. In its last phase the literature of chivalry reflected the elation of the empire-builders. But owing to the importance of its medieval cities, Spain also witnessed the early emergence of a distinctly urban civilisation. Its development was greatly stimulated by the fact that, through their contact with the Moors, the Spaniards had obtained access to the heritage of antiquity—the product of civilisations

[1] *v.* René van Bastelaer, 'Sur l'origine de la dénomination des Gueux du XVIᵉ siècle', *Mélange Godefroid Kurth*, Liége, 1908.
[2] The earliest surviving version of the *Poema del Cid*, which is but the afterglow of a great tradition, was probably written about 1150. For the subjects discussed in the following paragraphs cf. J. Fitzmaurice-Kelly, *History of Spanish Literature*, London, 1898; and E. Mérimée, *History of Spanish Literature*, London, 1931.

which had also been essentially civic—long before any other nation in Europe. Having settled in the richest parts of Spain, the Moorish inʋaders had preserved many more elements of what Roman culture had survived the rule of the Visigoths than the mountaineers of Asturias. The culture of the Muslims and their Spanish subjects had also been enriched by the intellectual heritage of the ancients as preserved in the works of the Arab philosophers and by their frequent intercourse with Byzantium. Their Christian foes were eager to absorb not only the superior material civilisation but also the wisdom of the Orient. Since the time of Alfonso VI (1072–1109), the conqueror of Toledo, oriental texts had been systematically translated by Moorish and Jewish savants working side by side with Christian scholars under the patronage of the king. During the twelfth and thirteenth centuries—especially in the reigns of Alfonso VII (1130–50) and Alfonso X, "the Learned" (1252–84)— the Spanish philosophical schools were the most advanced centres of learning in Europe. They planted the seeds which later found fruition in the humanist renaissance.

The literature which arose in the medieval Spanish communes is characterised above all by its realism. It began with a book, worthy of the glorious tradition which it fore-shadowed: the *Libro de buen amor* by Juan Ruiz, the Arch-priest of Hita (1283?–1350?). It is a collection of ballads, legends, hymns, and disreputable stories loosely strung together by the love affairs of Don Melón and Doña Endrina as fostered by the old bawd Trotaconventos ('trot-about-among-nunneries'). Drawing freely from popular and oriental sources and from the literature of antiquity in depicting the erotic adventures of prelates, monks, and ne'er-do-wells, the archpriest painted a vivid picture of contemporary life, heightening its flavour of authenticity by the autobio-graphical technique, which remained a striking feature of Spanish realist literature.

The *Libro de buen amor* was not the archpriest's only work; he himself writes: "I composed many dance and street songs for Jewish and Moorish girls and for women of love. . . . I wrote songs for blind men to recite and for night-prowling students, and for many others who wander from door to door. As for my songs of jest and mockery, ten quires would not hold them all."[1]

<hr>

[1] Mérimée *op. cit.*

Not content with "songs of jest and mockery", Juan Ruiz championed the cause of the poor. And he did so not only against the old feudal masters, but also against the new power of wealth. In a long ballad which forms a part of the *Libro de buen amor* he denounces the magic potency of the 'dinero' which transmutes the established relations of society and subjects the world to its sway:

> Money can do anything, it's more loved than a dame,
> It makes the rogue honest, gives him a good name. . . .
>
> If you've got enough money, you'll never lack a friend.
> The Pope will give his blessing, and a happy life you'll spend,
> You can buy a seat in Paradise, and life without end,
> There's nothing like the helping hand that money can lend. . . .
>
> Money changes many bishops and abbots and friars
> Into archbishops, doctors, patriarchs, and priors.
> To the ignorant priest it gives the chances he desires,
> It turns lies to truth, and honest men to liars. . . .
>
> It sits up in court and passes wrong sentence.
> Of all crooked lawyers it is the maintenance. . . .
>
> Money breaks the links of the heaviest chain,
> And bursts prison bars with a lively disdain. . . .
>
> It robs the poor peasant of home and vines as well,
> His goods and his chattels it throws out pell-mell.
> Everywhere its leprous boils begin to spread and swell.
> But where money's judge, every wink in court will tell. . . .
>
> Money lives in great manors, the best in the land,
> Tall and very costly, painted and grand,
> With turrets and castles and estates on every hand.
> They're all bought with money, they're all at its command.
>
> It feeds on dainty meals of many a different course,
> Wears gold-brocaded robes as rich as any emperor's,
> It flashes precious jewels like a vicious whore or worse,
> And you should see the harness it puts on a rich man's horse ! . . .
>
> I've heard monks and parsons on many occasions
> Denounce the curse of money and all its temptations. . . .
> All these monks and parsons say they're serving God on high,
> But you should see them run when a rich man's going to die. . . .
>
> They stand around debating who'll have the rich man's tin.
> He isn't dead, but they start paternostering—what a din !
> Like crows around a donkey, as they peck at his skin,
> "To-morrow we shall have him, he's ours by right", they grin. . . .
>
> Money is mayor and judge, his word carries weight.
> He's the sly councillor, the cunning advocate.
> As constable and bailiff his standing is great.
> He holds the highest offices in every state. . . .

> For money the world will change its habitude.
> Through greed for it, women are wheedling and shrewd.
> For jewels and money they do what they never should.
> Money can break rocks and split the hardest wood. . . .

Having made his denunciation, the archpriest appeals straight to the people:

> Whoever listens to my song, if he can rhyme or scan,
> Is at liberty to add to it, to alter and expand.
> Only send my message flying around from hand to hand,
> As women play at ball, catch it whoever can ![1]

But as we have seen, throughout the middle ages and in fact until the early nineteenth century, the political interests of the Spanish middle classes were to a large extent also those of the poor. The bourgeoisie still had to fight the privileges of the nobility in the name of society as a whole; it could hope to break through the rigid limitations of feudal caste only by directing the dissatisfaction of the poor against the old ruling classes. Thus, it had to make far-reaching ideological concessions to the people. The democratic aspect of the social institutions in medieval Spain finds its counterpart in the popular realism of Spanish art and literature. Spanish realism, from Juan Ruiz to Goya, was an art of revolt expressing the aspirations of the people in alliance with a still progressive middle class.

The creative energies of the Spanish people culminated in their hour of defeat. The matchless brilliance of Spanish culture in the Golden Age reflects a unity of opposites. The quest for knowledge which drove the explorers across the seven seas and which inspired the daring speculations of Spain's great humanists, mystics, and heretics, no less than the achievements of her scientists, was transfused with the exaltation of knight-errantry.[2] Democracy and chivalry, the two great driving forces of feudal Spain, when severed at their roots, built for themselves a monument of enduring fame. But while the exaltation of the Christian knights was translated to the dreams of universal church and empire—

> One Fold, one Shepherd only on the earth. . . .
> One Monarch, one Empire, and one Sword—[3]

the vital realism of the people was condemned to the nega-

---

[1] A. L. Lloyd has kindly allowed me to reproduce the lines in the text from his translation of 'The Ballad on the Power of Money'.

[2] Cf. Cassou *op. cit.*

[3] Hernando de Acuña (d. 1580), quoted by H. Warner Allen in the introductory essay to his edition of the *Celestina*.

tive role of noting the pathetic contrast between aspiration and achievement. Yet it supplied the blood and tissue of Spanish creativeness. When its sustaining energies were exhausted the country relapsed into intellectual and artistic barbarism.

Popular realism marks three decisive stages in the development of imaginative literature during the Golden Age: its beginning, its central turning point, and its conclusion. In the reign of the Catholic Kings, probably not very long after the conquest of Granada and the discovery of America, a provincial lawyer, Fernando de Rojas (about 1475—after 1537), one-time Alcalde-Mayor of Talavera near Toledo and probably a converted Jew, created one of the greatest works of literary realism. The *Comedia de Calixto y Melibea*, written before 1499, is a democratic version of the Romeo and Juliet theme. For the story of the romantic lovers merely serves as the structural framework for a picture of low life, the unflinching objectivity of which has never been surpassed. The central figure pulling all the strings in a tangled skein of mercenary plots and passions is the old procuress Celestina. With profound insight into the ways of the world she contrives to enrich herself by playing on the lusts and ambitions of her prostitutes and of the rascally servants of the two lovers. But in uniting the lovers and gaining her reward, she brings death to herself and to Calisto and Melibea. Not a heroic death, however: Calisto breaks his neck by falling from a ladder as he tries to scale his sweetheart's garden wall, Melibea kills herself in grief, Celestina is murdered by the servants of Calisto, whom she has cheated of their share in the plunder. The story—which is written in dialogue form—ends on a note of deep pessimism, relieved only by the nobility of a passion (that of Melibea) which defies the law of God and man, even if death be its reward.[1]

The next half-century of Spanish literature is filled with the fantastic vagaries of the novel of chivalry, the *Amadis de Gaula* and its numerous imitations. Then, two years before Charles V retired to the cloistered solitude of Yuste,

[1] The earliest surviving edition of the *Celestina* dates from 1499, but there is reason to believe that it was not the first. An English translation was published in 1631 by James Mabbe. Modern editions of his translation: by J. Fitzmaurice-Kelly in Tudor Translations, London, 1894; and H. Warner Allen in Broadway Translations, London, n.d. The latter includes an introductory essay on the history of the picaresque novel and its imitations in England and France, with a useful chronological table.

appeared the *Lazarillo de Tormes* (1554). This work of an unknown author is the first of the picaresque novels proper. In terse and vivid prose, without a trace of sentiment or moral scruple, the *Lazarillo* recounts the tricks he played and the adventures which befell him while serving a succession of masters—a blind beggar, a miserly priest, a famished hidalgo, and others like them—from the time he left his mother when she was imprisoned for receiving stolen food from her lover, a Moor, until at last he attained the acme of human bliss—a sinecure as town crier procured for him by a priest, whose mistress he had married.[1]

Another half-century elapsed and with Philip II the heroic phase of Hapsburg absolutism sank into oblivion. In this period Spanish literature exchanged the sword for the shepherd's crook. The courtly protestations of love remained, but the giants and magicians of chivalry were replaced by the flocks and meadows of Arcady. But in the last year of the sixteenth century, one year after Philip's death, Mateo Alemán published his *Guzmán de Alfarache*, 'the Rogue'. Vanished are dreams and illusions. The knights and shepherds disappeared with them. Picaresque literature, "than which there is none more atrociously lucid or more deliberately pessimistic",[2] now reigned supreme. "All steal, all lie. . . . You will not find a soul, who is man unto man."[3] For a brief moment visionary ecstasy and realism were again united in the profound humanity of Don Quixote, then Quevedo concluded the great cycle with the agonised fantasy of the 'Sueños' and the appalling cynicism of the 'Buscón': "I am a slanderous scorpion, a proper offspring of these sandy, snake-engendering plains", was Quevedo's reply to his critics.[4]

(b) *Painting.* Equally striking is the tradition of realism in Spanish painting. For the brilliant efflorescence of Spanish pictorial art during the Golden Age was confined exclusively to the first half of the seventeenth century, the period of catastrophic disintegration, the period of the picaro. It is important to realise, however, that the triumphant emergence of a truly national style based on uncompromising

---

[1] An English translation of the *Lazarillo de Tormes* by David Rowland first recorded 1568–9. Modern edition of this translation in J. B. Trend, *Spanish Short Stories of the Sixteenth Century*, Oxford, 1928.

[2] Cassou *op. cit.*

[3] *Guzmán de Alfarache*, quoted by Cassou *op. cit.*   [4] Mérimée *op. cit.*

realism was the fulfilment of a trend which had long been maturing. The realist tendency in Spanish painting had gathered increasing momentum during the fourteenth and fifteenth centuries, until it had suffered an abrupt check with the advent of the Hapsburgs.

A detailed account of the medieval tradition is beyond the scope of this book. A few hints indicating certain outstanding phases in the development of early Spanish realist painting must therefore suffice.[1]

The first thing to note, then, is that Giotto's monumental upper middle-class style, so profoundly opposed to the hieratic formalism of romanesque painting, was already in his lifetime adopted in Spain by a contemporary of Juan Ruiz, the Catalan artist Ferrer Bassa (op. 1325, m. 1348). But it is significant that Bassa, who was not as advanced as Giotto in his understanding of pictorial space and of the organic structure of the human figure, replaced the latter's sober rationalism by a more popular emphasis on expressive features, emotional gestures, and other realistic details.[2]

During the later fourteenth century Spain followed the general European trend of gothic painting under the influence of Simone Martini and the Siena School which spread to all countries from the papal court at Avignon. This trend, represented in Spain by the work of the Serra and Borassa families for example, is characterised by a combination of both courtly and popular elements. Its renewed emphasis on ornamental splendour and elegant form persisted with extraordinary intensity right up to the end of the fifteenth century. The taste for sumptuous golden ornaments on the backgrounds, haloes, and vestments went so far that they were often raised in relief above the painted surface. Nevertheless, this barbaric ornamentalism was accompanied by an equally violent demand for realistic detail. Thus, it is not unusual to find vivid popular

---

[1] Cf. A. L. Mayer, *Geschichte der spanischen Malerei*, Leipzig, 1922; and for the medieval period C. R. Post, *History of Spanish Painting* (in progress), Cambridge, Mass., 1930.

[2] In Castile also Giotto's sober realism was adopted, side by side with the more ornamental gothic style, though at a somewhat later date. It is found, for example, in a series of panels in Toledo Cathedral which date from the later part of the fourteenth century. They are regarded by recent students as evidence that the Florentine painter Starnina worked in that city, and provide an important link between the Giotto phase of Florentine realism and its revival a hundred years later in the generation of Massaccio and Masolino. Cf. Diego Angulo Iñiguez, 'La pinture trecentista en Toledo', in the *Archivo español de Arte y Arqueologia*, vii, 1931.

types piled one on top of the other in a composition
lacking all spatial depth, while on large altar-pieces the
brilliantly characterised heads of the main figures often look
as if they were peeping through portholes in a barbaric
screen of gilt plaster (*e.g.* in the work of Pablo Vergos, m.
1495).

But side by side with this fantastic compromise there
also emerged a more consistently naturalistic style in which
realism transfuses the whole composition, instead of being
confined to isolated details embedded within a schematic,
ornamental framework. This development, which is found
in all parts of Spain, was stimulated by the now increasingly
important economic and political relations between the
Spanish courts and cities on the one hand and those of Italy
and Burgundy on the other. Characteristic examples of this
naturalistic trend are the 'Retable of the Councillors', a
close adaptation of the van Eyck's Ghent Altar produced in
1445 for the City Council of Barcelona by the Aragón court
painter Luis Dalmau (op. *c.* 1428–60); the La Sisla Retable
from the neighbourhood of Toledo (latter half of fifteenth
century, now in the Prado) which clearly reveals the influence
of Martin Schongauer; or the vivid cycle of genre scenes illustrating the story of the Dominicans—the order most closely
associated both with the upper middle class and the Inquisition (one of the scenes actually shows a contemporary
auto-de-fé and another the burning of books) painted by
Pedro Berruguete (op. 1483, m. 1503–4) for the Convento
de Santo Tomás at Avila (Prado).

This phase of Spanish realism culminated in the work of
three artists, all of whom can first be traced in Cordova
though two of them appear to have worked mainly in Catalonia. Bartolomé Bermejo (op. 1474–95), whose early paintings still show a markedly gothic elegance, has lost all trace
of gothic formalism in his moving and dramatic Pieta of
1490 (Barcelona Cathedral). Master Alfonso, of whom only
two panels of a single certain work have been preserved (the
'Martyrdom of St. Cucufas', 1473, Barcelona Museum), attained a level of objective naturalism in his landscape and
monumental figures which was not surpassed by any artist
of his generation in Europe.

The third figure in this remarkable group was Alejo
Fernandez (op. 1498, m. 1543), the leading painter of the
early sixteenth-century school in Seville, then the most im-

portant commercial centre in Europe. He obtained many ecclesiastical commissions and also designed the decorations of Seville for the triumphal entry and marriage of Charles V in 1526. But the work which most concerns us in the present context is his 'Virgen de los Conquistadores' which he painted about the same time for the chapel of the Casa de Contratación, the Spanish Colonial Ministry and organising centre of the American Trade. The Virgin stands towering on a bank of clouds above a wide expanse of sea. Under the shelter of her cloak kneel an imposing company of merchant-adventurers, some of them powerful German types reminiscent of Dürer's merchant portraits.[1] The sea below is alive with the ships that conquered a new world.

During the first two Hapsburg reigns the realist tradition of Spanish painting was interrupted by a counteracting tendency, the international movement of mannerism. Although both the Emperor and his son were patrons of Titian, and although the latter in particular also collected the best of the older Flemish realists, including the great moralities of Hieronymus Bosch,[2] the style which most affected Spanish court painting during this period was the frigidly academic mannerism emerging from Rome and Florence since the second decade of the century. In Seville, the last important centre of middle-class art in Spain, on the other hand, the rather more fantastic and therefore more popular mannerism of the Flemish Romanists was supreme until the end of the sixteenth century. The Spanish painters who adopted these styles never rose above the level of provincial imitative art. But from the last quarter of the century onwards certain Spanish artists gradually succeeded—with the help of the realistic elements which occupied a subordinate, but increasingly important, position within mannerism itself—in shaking off that lifeless academic 'correctness' which was the proper artistic expression of absolutism. Alonso Sánchez Coello (1531–88), who was inspired by his Flemish master and predecessor, Antonio Morro, perfected a

---

[1] *v.* Appendix, note I, p. 214.

[2] For an account of Philip II's eclectic and contradictory taste cf. C. Justi, 'Philip II als Kunstfreund', *Miscellaneen aus drei Jahrhunderten spanischen Kunstlebens*, Berlin, 1908. A monumental symbol of his taste is the building which was his life's ambition and which bears the stamp of his approval in every detail of its design: the gaunt pile of the Escorial rising unadorned in a desolate mountain wilderness, at one and the same time a palace, a monastery, and a tomb (1559–84: architects Castillo and Herrera).

portrait style which, however characteristic of the Hapsburg court with its stifling ceremonial, was a step towards the realism of Velazquez.[1] At the same time Navarrete, 'El Mudo' (*c.* 1526–79), who had begun as a Romanist, discovered Titian while working in the Escorial and in his later works he accentuated the Venetian's colouristic naturalism. But Venetian colourism was also the starting point for a development which at first sight appears diametrically opposed to realism. In Toledo, the ancient citadel of Spanish Catholicism, Greco's (1541–1614) expressionist art reflected all the mystic fervour of the leaders of the Counter-Reformation. Yet in his portraits and in some of his other works his intensely spiritualistic art unexpectedly assumes a character of unsurpassed realism. The same dual quality is found in the fascinating work of Luis de Morales (op. 1546, m. 1586). Philip II disliked both these artists, but it is significant that both of them produced countless replicas of their works (in Greco's case they are often workshop products of the crudest quality produced on stock) to meet an insatiable popular demand even from small provincial churches.

But the decisive impetus for the emancipation of Spanish painting came not so much from the realistic trend in this second wave of mannerism as from its culmination: the chiaroscuro realism of Caravaggio (1560/5–1609).[2] About the time when Guzmán, 'the Rogue', was published—or perhaps a little later—Ribalta in Valencia, Roelas and the elder Herrera in Seville, and Greco's friends or pupils Orrente, Maino, and Tristán in Toledo, the first representatives of the

[1] Cf. Max Dvořák, 'Spanische Bilder einer oesterreichischen Ahnengalerie', *Kunstgeschichtliches Jahrbuch der K. K. Zentral-Kommission für Erforschung und Erhaltung der Kunst und historischen Denkmale*, Vienna, 1907.

[2] This view, which is opposed by A. L. Mayer in his *Geschichte der spanischen Malerei*, is supported with a wealth of detailed evidence by Roberto Longhi, 'Un San Tomaso del Velasquez e le Congiunture italo-spagnole tra il '5 & il '600', *Vita Artistica*, 1927, ii, No. 1. In this article Longhi traces the antecedents of the chiaroscuro style both in Italy and in Spain. He shows that even such early Florentine mannerists as Pontormo and Bronzino included strikingly realistic details within their fantastic or frigidly idealistic compositions. He traces the growth of this realistic trend among the Florentine and especially the North Italian mannerists of the sixteenth century (Cremona, he says, was a "little Antwerp" and he points to the striking still lifes and kitchen pieces of Vincencio Campi—five of these, it is instructive to note, were bought by a member of the Fugger family; cf. G. Lill, *Hans Fugger und die Kunst*, Leipzig, 1908). Not only were the works of these painters exported on a large scale to Spain, but a similar trend is observable among the Italians who worked in Spain during the latter part of the sixteenth century (*e.g.* the Carduchos). The style of Caravaggio, whom Pacheco regarded as one of the greatest painters of his time and who exerted a profound influence on the Spanish realists, especially the young Velazquez, was therefore a culmination of a tendency which had been slowly maturing within a totally opposed style.

great Spanish seventeenth-century school,[1] were working in a realistic 'tenebroso' manner akin to that of Caravaggio.

To appreciate the peculiar character of Spanish painting in the seventeenth century we must remember the circumstances under which this revival of realism took place. During the middle ages the general outlook and therefore also the art of the middle classes retained a religious form, because even the most advanced centres of early capitalism remained integral—if ultimately incompatible—parts of feudal society. After the first violent struggles with the heretics, the Church rapidly learned to adapt its organisation and ideology to the needs of the new capitalists, who became its allies, while the mendicant orders deflected the spiritual demands of the restive lower classes into safe channels. There was thus no inherent contradiction between the bourgeois content and the religious form of middle-class art during the fourteenth and fifteenth centuries.

The revolutions of the sixteenth and seventeenth centuries liberated bourgeois consciousness from the leading-strings of scholastic theology. Philosophy, science, and the arts emerged as independent, secular disciplines. Except in the form of the puritan ethic—until "Locke had replaced Habakkuk"—religion could no longer provide a proper medium for bourgeois realism in art. In the main centres of mercantilism, especially Holland, religious subjects were increasingly superseded by secular genre scenes, landscapes, and portraits, while even in the absolute monarchies mythology and 'history' painting emerged as independent genres from religious art. The Church, indeed, encouraged this process of differentiation. In its last session of 1563 the Council of Trent set up a strict canon for religious art, from which all secular motives it had hitherto contained were banished. Henceforth painters of the nude had to take refuge in mythological themes with which even prelates did not hesitate to decorate their palaces, though they sometimes justified the practice with allegorical reflections on the relative merits of heavenly and secular love. Even landscape and genre motives were discouraged in religious paintings and therefore had to seek a separate existence.[2]

In Spain, however, the impoverishment and political

[1] Ribalta, 1551/5–1628; Roelas, 1558/60–1625; Herrera, 1576–c. 1665; Orrente, 1570–1645; Maino, 1586–1649; Tristan, 1586–1624.
[2] v. E. Male, *L'Art religieux après le Concile de Trente*, Paris, 1932.

impotence of the middle class prevented the emergence of a consistent bourgeois style, like that of the Dutch. The Church had ceased to be the ally of the middle class. It had become the spiritual police force of absolutism, and the Inquisition maintained a rigorous censorship for painters as well as for writers. Yet, there could be no more convincing proof that theocratic absolutism had been unable to crush the vitality of the Spanish people than the fact that the first truly national style of the Hapsburg era embodied all the realism of the defeated democracy. It did so only in its form, however. Its content remained fettered to the service of a reactionary hierarchy which could retain its hold over the destitute masses and counteract their cynical realism only by permitting an ever more sensual and opiating display of mystical elation.

Spanish mysticism has a profoundly popular as well as a theocratic root. In both these aspects it was repugnant to Philip II and his Inquisitors. Theocratic mysticism, as represented above all by the Jesuits, necessarily exalted the universal Church above the Spanish State and thus tended to support the popes in their opposition to the Hapsburgs. Popular mysticism expressed the fervent desire of the masses, and especially the lower middle class, to escape from their miseries—miseries caused in large measure by the tax collectors, alguazils, and inquisitors of the autocracy. It exalted the power of the individual to establish direct communion with God and thus revealed a suspicious affinity to heresy.[1] The victory of mysticism in both forms during the seventeenth century marks the collapse of Philip II's dream of secular supremacy and the reversal of the relations of Church and State during the second phase of the Hapsburg era. But although mysticism was the inevitable concomitant of realism in a people condemned to passive submission, both tendencies are irreconcilably opposed. Only by removing the sting of cynical realism could the Church ensure the triumph of mystical escapism among the people. Only thus could it deprive even their mysticism of its fierce spirit of independence. When the last remnant of Spain's political

[1] The popular basis of Sta. Teresa's thought—to mention only the outstanding example —is evident, if only from the overwhelming devotion which the people of Spain felt for her during the following centuries. She became as emphatically the national saint of Spain as Santiago had been during the re-conquest, and was formally recognised as such by the Cortes of 1812–14 against the embittered opposition of the higher clergy.

and economic power had collapsed about the middle of the century, the violent art of the 1620's expressing the conflict of Spanish realism and Spanish mysticism was resolved into the flamboyant emotionalism of the baroque.

The art of the early seventeenth century with which we are at present concerned still, however, expresses the full intensity of the struggle. Its realism is remorseless, and its mysticism therefore takes the form of a morbid sadism exalting the horrors of martyrdom which it displays with all the circumstantial detail of an anatomy lesson (*e.g.* in Ribera's work), or else it becomes an hypnotic obsession (*e.g.* in the monks of Zurbarán).[1] The chiaroscuro technique, with its lighting effect like that of a torch flashed into a gloomy dungeon, enhances the morbid art and sinister appeal of these works. But this was a secondary result and a perversion of its true role in the history of art. By eschewing all forms of idealisation and concentrating its spotlight on the lowest and most despised classes of society, the chiaroscuro style despiritualised art and became a stepping-stone to the objective materialism of the Dutch genre painters and of Velazquez. The process of despiritualisation began within the sphere of religious painting itself. Caravaggio, and the Spanish artists after him, placed the sacred stories in a low-life *milieu* and made beggars not only of the accessory figures but even of the holy personages. It is significant that the Church regarded Caravaggio's popular realism with extreme suspicion. Three of his pictures which had been commissioned by important churches in Rome were rejected as vulgar and irreverent: the 'Virgin with the Child crushing the Serpent' (Borghese Gallery) was rejected by the canons of St. Peter "because the scene was presented in a vulgar manner"; the 'Death of the Virgin' (Louvre) by the priests of Santa Maria della Scala because "she was merely a dead woman in process of decomposition"; and the St. Matthew (Berlin Museum) by those of S. Luigi dei Francesi because "he resembled a man of the people and vulgarly displayed his naked feet".[2] It is thus evident that the victory of realism in the religious works of the Cara-

---

[1] Ribera (1591–1652), who worked in Naples, then a Spanish dependency, since 1616, also painted a number of secular picaro themes; Zurbarán (1598–1664) worked in Seville. His more hieratic spirit was also marked in his style. Longhi (*op. cit.*) points out that his consciously tectonic and archaic style goes back to Venetian fifteenth-century art, instead of forward to realism, like that of the young Velazquez.
[2] Male *op. cit.*

vaggio school and its Spanish successors was due to pressure from below. It expressed the picaro spirit of the people, and its toleration by the Church was, at first at least, a necessary concession.

The change in the iconography of the Nativity, which occurred towards the end of the sixteenth century,[1] illustrates how the picaro spirit surreptitiously invaded religious art. The new type was a combination of the old Nativity and 'Adoration of the Shepherds' schemes. It was particularly popular in Spain, where the shepherds were represented as real picaros (*e.g.* the large Adoration in the London National Gallery formerly attributed to Velazquez, but also versions by Ribalta, Ribera, Orrente, Zurbarán, and even the gentle Roelas). In Velazquez' 'Adoration of the Magi', where the latter are, of course, aristocrats, the holy family with the baby tightly wrapped in swaddling clothes are real peasants. Spain had only just emerged from the craze for the pastoral novel, and this utter reversal in the social estimation of the 'shepherd' is a striking symptom for the changed temper of the time.

The extreme point in the reduction of religious art to the picaro level was reached in the early painting by Velazquez (1599–1660), the ostensible subject of which, 'Christ in the House of Martha', only appears as an insignificant inset visible through an open door in the background of a kitchen scene (about 1620, London, National Gallery). In thus treating his subject Velazquez was almost certainly influenced by the manner in which his father-in-law and teacher Pacheco (1564–1654) had painted the story of St. Sebastian in 1616. To quote Justi:

> The scene where the Christian soldier after his agony is sought under cover of the darkness and tended by the matron, Irene, has several times been treated by distinguished painters. The night, the dread atmosphere of persecution, the mangled body of the young martyr in a deadly swoon, the eager care of the deeply agitated women, — here was a theme worthy of a Schidone, a Spagnoletto, a Delacroix. How is it handled by our art reformer, unwarmed even by the sun of Andalusia? In a tidy spacious chamber of the Alcalá Hospital lies a man in fresh linen in a newly made bed,

[1] Male *op. cit.*

holding a soup-bowl, of a blue striped pattern. Before him stands a woman with the impassive, pale features, the wearied glance of a hospital nurse, while a little girl places some bandages on a plate. Above the settle hangs the rich uniform of an officer, on the walls are the arrows preserved as relics. Through an open window is visible the scene of the martyrdom. . . .[1]

In his pedantic respect for the proprieties Pacheco, the official art censor of the Inquisition, though carrying out the letter of his instructions, thus achieved the exact opposite of what he was appointed for. He paved the way for the despiritualisation and therefore the negation of religious art.

About this time certain Spanish artists, especially in Seville, the haven of the picaro and the last centre of bourgeois art in Spain, abandoned even the pretext of a religious subject in some of their pictures. Already Justi pointed out the evident relationship between this new type of art (of which the young Velazquez was the pioneer in Spain) and the picaresque novel. But he also made an extraordinarily significant distinction between these Spanish 'bodegones' and the contemporary Dutch kitchen pieces:

> The Dutch cabinet painters of the seventeenth century were virtuosi, who catered for a wealthy public of loose morals and refined taste. The comic element in their work rests partly on the contrast between the subject and the cleverly disguised art. But in these early Spanish pieces what at once arrests attention is their unadorned truth. Not a trace is to be seen of majolica dishes with their metallic sheen, silver ware or Art cabinets, and they are altogether much more akin to the earlier Dutch works of Brueghel, Beukelaer, or Aertsen, in which school life appears coarser and less attractive, but more direct and varied than in the later school.[2]

In other words, the Spanish bodegones are akin, not to the self-satisfied gourmet still-lifes or to the patronising, sentimental 'beggar' and 'peasant' pictures favoured by the bourgeoisie *after* its conquest of power, but to the uncompromising beggar paintings of the revolutionary phase, when the middle class still acted in the name of the people.

---

[1] Carl Justi, *Diego Velazquez und sein Jahrhundert*, 2nd ed. Bonn, 1903. I have quoted the English translation (London, 1889) of the first edition.   [2] Justi *op. cit.*

In Velazquez' youth Seville with its busy port and markets, its hosts of foreign traders and seamen, its beggars and prostitutes, was still a city of rich and independent merchants. But for the reasons which we have already discussed their influence was rapidly declining. Even more rapid was the ascendancy of the local clergy. Despite the protests of the municipality, nine new monasteries were set up in Seville during the first twelve years of the seventeenth century. This was not the soil on which the realist tendency revealed by the bodegones could come to fruition. Only one refuge remained for Velazquez, as for Quevedo: the cynical court of Philip IV, who, though totally unfit for the task of governing, had not yet abandoned the rule of a secular favourite for that of his confessors. At this court all the antinomies of Hapsburg Spain assembled: splendour and degradation, profligacy and rectitude, luxury and sordid poverty, faith and scepticism, boundless ambition and cynical accommodation. Here grandees, inquisitors, soldiers, diplomats, artists, poets, bankers, and buffoons went through their motions with all the dignity of their exalted station. But the heart had gone out of their action. In sumptuous festivals they celebrated brilliant victories leading to ignominious treaties. Slowly and imperceptibly the cynical makebelief of a boring routine replaced the stern idealism with which the play began. In its final scene the heroic tragedy of Hapsburg Spain had turned into a carnival farce in which the leading actors were the court buffoons.

In this fantastic atmosphere Spanish realism attained its culmination. Here Velazquez de-heroised courtly mythology —the picaro 'Bacchus' of 1629, the plebeian 'Forge of Vulcan' of 1630, or the sergeant-major 'Mars' of 1655–8—as he had despiritualised religion[1] in his bodegones. He painted philosophy in rags—the picaro philosophers Menippus and Aesop of 1651–60—and, almost alone among his Spanish contemporaries, he dared to display the female nude. He also painted the first objective landscapes (the two views from the garden of the Villa Medici in Rome, 1630), and the first factory picture of modern art (the 'Hilanderas' of 1655–60). In these works of his maturity the gloom of the chiaroscuro style has been replaced by a sovereign mastery of light and

[1] Only one of Velazquez' pictures shows even a trace of mysticism, and this probably due to the nature of the commission ('Christ at the Column', 1629, London, National Gallery).

motion. And could there be anything more "atrociously lucid" than the series of his mature portraits in which the degenerate Hapsburgs are abruptly confronted by the buffoons, dwarfs, and idiots of their court?[1]

The generation of Ribera, Velazquez, Zurbarán had exhausted the powers of Spanish seventeenth-century realism. When they had gone there remained only the sugary triumph of Murillo (1617–82), the *ne plus ultra* of petty-bourgeois escapism, where even the picaro has become a sentimental quietist.

We have strayed a long way from Goya and the eighteenth century. But not as far as it may seem. For the heritage of the past had entered into the very fibre of Spanish thought and feeling. And there is no more Spanish artist than Goya. Having glanced at the tradition of which he formed a link, we shall be better able to appreciate his own, unique, contribution. We must now return to the contemporary background of Goya's inspiration.

THE AGE OF ENLIGHTENMENT

Spanish civilisation during the Golden Age was characterised by the victory of exalted idealism over the realistic elements in the life and thought of the people: by the victory of the Church over the State, of mysticism over science, adventurism over practical application. In the imaginative arts realism was confined to the sphere of criticism. Its voice, like that of Cassandra, forewarned the nation of the impending doom and revealed the successive stages of decomposition with the objectivity of a clinical observer.

The eighteenth century reversed the relationship of these two elements. Realism, no longer condemned to passive criticism, could at last release its pent-up energy in deeds. Its main contribution to Spanish civilisation was the great work of economic and political reconstruction.

A small group of Spaniards had welcomed the policy of the foreign kings from the first. They formed a capable and enthusiastic vanguard of enlightenment. The series of

[1] It is not of course the *fact* that Velazquez confronted princes and idiots which is so startling—the Spanish court fools had been portrayed since the sixteenth century, and other artists (*e.g.* Rubens) also added dwarfs to famous beauties in some of their portraits—but the *manner* of this confrontation: the utter detachment which treats both groups with the same objectivity, instead of using the one to enhance the beauty or dignity of the other.

Spanish statesmen, beginning with Philip V's ministers Macanaz and Patiño, including Ensenada and Carvajal during the following reign and ending with Charles III's great ministers Aranda, Campomanes, and Floridablanca, is one of the most distinguished in eighteenth-century Europe. They were supported by an increasing (but always hopelessly inadequate) number of able administrators, jurists, and economists, who were recruited, with few exceptions, from the middle class or the lower nobility. The English traveller Townsend was struck by the fact that the most important appointments in Spain were occupied by men of low birth, while the grandees preferred an idle existence on the revenues of their estates to the ardours of education and public service. Townsend paints a vivid picture of the difficulties these men encountered in fighting the resistance of an indolent and corrupt bureaucracy. Trained for one post, they had often scarcely taken up their duties when they were hurried off to a remote part of Spain to tackle some more urgent problem. And this process was not infrequently repeated several times in succession. Under such conditions it is not surprising that many reforms remained abortive. Rather should one marvel that so much was actually achieved. This was possible only because the enthusiasm of the reformers slowly, but surely, broke down the walls of suspicion and apathy around them, because their vision of a mighty and prosperous Spain fired the imagination of the people.

At first, however, the reawakened pride of the people, that "pure Castilian spirit" embodied in the majos, unexpectedly tended to strengthen the hands of reaction and was full of danger for the cause of reform. The majos, and the common people generally, drew their inspiration from exalted notions of their country's greatness in the past, and, ignoring the true causes of its recovery, they viewed the 'foreign' innovations, ideas, and manners of the reformers with undisguised hostility. The reformers, on their part, at first also tended to misjudge the true significance of the people's new self-confidence. Deceived by its superficial aspect of conservatism—which their opponents were not slow in exploiting for their own ends—they failed to recognise the latent possibilities of a true awakening in the inarticulate nationalism of the common people. Fortunately for Spain these antinomies—the infantile disorders of a reviving nation—came to violent eruption early in the reign of Charles III before they could become an incurable cancer. An ill-advised dress reform imposed upon the Madrileños by a foreign minister provoked grave riots in the capital in 1766. Their suppression strengthened the cause of progress. One of its foremost exponents, Count Aranda, was appointed president of the all-powerful Council of Castile—he was the first layman to hold that office—and a further blow was struck at clerical reaction by the expulsion of the Jesuits.

More important than these strategic gains was the fact that the court and its supporters had been forcibly reminded of the existence of the people. They had the good sense to realise that enlightenment could strike roots in Spain only if the gulf was bridged which divided it from the people. 'Foreign ideas', in other words the bourgeois rationalism of the eighteenth century, had to be assimilated to the inarticulate tradition of Spanish democracy as it had survived since medieval times, and the people had to be convinced that the programme of economic, political, and spiritual emancipation, far from being foreign to the national heritage of Spain, was its only consistent fulfilment. That they rediscovered the democratic basis of the laws and institutions of medieval Spain and welded their own programme of reform to that tradition was the supreme achievement of a brilliant array of Spanish historians and statesmen during the later eighteenth century.

We have already made the acquaintance of the gay spokesmen of the native tradition, the majos and majas. We must now cast a rapid glance at some of the foreign innovations they regarded with such suspicion in order to appreciate the process in which these two main trends in the culture of eighteenth-century Spain were assimilated.

The first efforts of the reformers were inspired by the aim to catch up with the progress of European rationalism. The reign of Philip V is distinguished by a series of important academic foundations—the National Library was opened in 1711; the Academy of the Spanish Language, founded in 1714, published its great *Diccionario de la lengua castellana* between 1726 and 1739; the Historical Academy was established in 1738; while the Academy of the Fine Arts, to which Goya was elected in 1780, was founded by Ferdinand VI in 1752. These establishments and a host of other learned bodies set up at later dates produced their finest fruits in the second half of the century, when they sponsored the great work of economic and historical enquiry to which we have just alluded. It was then that the minister Campomanes (1723–1803) or Goya's friend Jovellanos (1744–1811), to mention only the most distinguished names, published the works which place them in the front ranks of European thought. But in the interval the spade-work of enlightenment was not neglected. Most prominent among its pioneers was the Benedictine monk B. J. Feijóo y Montenegro— one of the first of many enlightened clerics to take his stand with the reformers—who acquainted his countrymen with the main achievements of French and English philosophy in the successive instalments of his *Teatro critico universal* (1726–39) and his *Cartas eruditas y curiosas* (1742–60).

As the economic and political conditions of Spain became more settled the 'letters' of this patient publicist and others like him reached an ever wider public, and a growing section of the upper and middle classes began to support the policy of the reformers in the reign of Charles III. Gradually foreign travel began to be regarded as an indispensable element in the education of a man of fashion. Spaniards of rank entered into correspondence with the leading *philosophes* of France (according to Bourgoing there were over three hundred Spanish subscribers to the Encyclopaedia which began to circulate in 1784 in spite of the opposition of the Holy Office), and many grandees kept open house for the progressive intellectuals.

Popular education, improved methods of production, and agrarian reform became fashionable topics of conversation. Casanova, whose instinct for the fashionable foibles of 'society' in all parts of Europe can be trusted, since he made his living by exploiting them, posed as an expert on agricultural settlement when he sought to make his fortune in Spain (1768). The patriotic clubs, formed in all parts of Spain under the aegis of Campomanes to promote education and improved methods of production, were widely supported by the upper and middle classes.

These circles looked to France as the supreme arbiter of all their standards. They modelled their dress, manners, food, ideas, and amusements (except music where the Italian influence still prevailed) on those of Paris. With them francomania was as pronounced a trait as 'castiza', and all that proud notion implies, with the majos. For the intel-

lectually alert this new contact with a foreign culture was
a liberation. The walls which bigotry and persecution had
built around them were crumbling into dust. Avidly they
breathed the invigorating draught of new ideas which
swept away the cobwebs from the sleepy eyes of Spain. For
two centuries Spain's creative genius had wandered in a
maze of dreams—a sleep-walker in pursuit of a chimera.
Now at last the spell was broken, and Spain resumed its
proper place in the forward march of European thought.
But with the average nobleman or citizen the emulation of
foreign fashions was no more than a superficial veneer.
With their rigid etiquette, their jealousies and tempers, the
middle class 'cortejo' and his mistress (who was always a
married woman) were, at bottom, only slightly more genteel
editions of the majo and maja, who concealed their spontaneous vivacity behind a mask of imported conventions.
And although guests and hosts in middle-class or aristocratic 'tertulias' would stick scrupulously to their French
conversation, card games, and dances, they would sooner
or later tire of these pastimes and call in the servants to
enliven the atmosphere by dancing a native fandango or
seguidilla.

Until the death of the old king, in other words, 'majaism',
though increasingly attractive to the upper classes, was still
frowned upon as something improper, something fit for
servants and the lower orders, but not for educated people.
This is confirmed by an incident William Beckford has
recorded in his *Travel Diaries*. During his stay in the
Spanish capital in 1787 he was invited to a fashionable
reception. Having bought a gorgeous Spanish costume for
the occasion, he was surprised to find all the other guests
dressed in the latest Paris fashion. To make matters worse,
the Archbishop of Toledo smilingly suggested: since the
English gentleman had done them the honour of appearing
in their native costume, would he not further add to their
entertainment by giving a display of Spanish dancing? A
troop of majas was speedily called in and, if we can trust the
author of *Vathek*, he showed himself equal to the occasion.
Later, however, the Duchess of Osuna told him not to make
himself ridiculous any longer and carried him off to her
mother's gaming tables.[1]

In a less snobbish *milieu* the relationship between majaism

[1] *The Travel Diaries of William Beckford*, London, 1928, vol. ii.

and foreign fashions—and, incidentally, the skilful way in which the government sought to make the latter palatable to the pleasure-loving Madrileños after the 1766 riots—is illustrated by Casanova's account of his visit to a public ball in 1768. Recently introduced by Aranda, these balls were denounced as an outrageous and unheard-of innovation by the conservatives. Nevertheless they were immensely popular. Casanova tells us how the whole evening was passed with fashionable French dances until at last, at midnight, the whole assembly broke into a wild fandango, such as made even that hardened old roué "cry aloud with excitement".

Majaism with its lack of restraint was in fact becoming more and more attractive to the smart set and especially to the circle of the Princess of Asturias, whose morals were an outrage to the puritanical old king. Towards the end of the reign the nocturnal adventures of would-be majas of the highest rank were the favourite topic of the scandalmongers, and the greatest ladies of the land, the Duchesses of Osuna and Alba, were reputed to be jealous rivals for the favours of the bull-fighter Romero. Goya painted both these ladies and attended their tertulias in the later '80's and '90's, when his star as a fashionable portrait painter reached its zenith. It would, indeed, be difficult to find a better illustration of majaism than the voluminous Goya legend which would make a second Cellini of our artist. There are few among his portraits of attractive women to which the legend has not attached some piquant piece of scandal.

Morel-Fatio is certainly right in regarding would-be majaism, the frivolous imitation of the real majos and majas by the smart set, as a symptom of the *encanaillement* of the court aristocracy, who would have been wiser to conceal their degradation.[1] When on the edge of the abyss the aristocracy has a curious habit of destroying its moral defences by toying with the ideology of the enemy. Blind to the fatal implications of the bourgeois cult of nature, the French nobility applauded the milkmaid fashion of Marie-Antoinette, and the Spanish grandees were similarly heedless of the democratic roots of majaism, when they perverted its moral freedom. It is interesting that Bourgoing, writing on the eve of the Revolution, also compared the

[1] Alfred Morel-Fatio, *La Satire de Jovellanos contre la mauvaise éducation de la noblesse*, Bibliothèque des Universités de Midi, 1898. In this satire, which was published in the journal *El Censor* in 1787, Jovellanos ridicules both the superficial aping of foreign manners by the aristocracy and its would-be majaism.

fashion of majaism with the shepherd cult of contemporary France. Speaking of the 'gitanos' and 'gitanas', the rural or vagabond versions of the Madrid majos and majas, whose representation on the stage "renders vice familiar by concealing its deformity under a gay exterior", he continues: *"They are, if I may say so, the shepherds of the Spanish stage*, certainly less insipid, but at the same time less innocent than those of ours. Their tricks, plots, and amorous intrigues, suited to their manners, are the subjects of several sainetes and tonadillas, and probably serve as lessons to some of the spectators." Thus majaism, the symbol of the national awakening of Spain, became the poison of its ruling class, who in a former age had degraded the virile democracy of feudal Spain to the level of the picaro.

ISLA AND CRUZ

The assimilation of foreign innovations to the native tradition is reflected in the literature and art of eighteenth-century Spain. Indeed, it may be doubted whether this synthesis, which made liberalism a living force in Spanish history, could really have been achieved without the imaginative appeal of art. This aim could not, however, be attained by the didactic 'satires' and tragedies fashioned after French and Italian academic models with which many worthy reformers, including Jovellanos, sought to revive the creative genius of their country. It required a living art expressing the genuine experiences of the people. Just as the new liberalism had to strike roots in the democratic heritage of Spain, so its artistic revival could draw vital sustenance only from the soil of Spanish realism.

It was therefore of great significance that the learned Jesuit, José Francisco de Isla (1703–81), chose the form of the picaresque novel when he—perhaps unwittingly—aided the cause of the reformers by attacking the pretentious ignorance of the vulgar mendicant friars. The *Historia del famoso predicador Fray Gerundio de Campazas, alias Zotes* (1758) did more to discredit clerical obscurantism than any more formal indictment could have done. Its publication caused a literary scandal which culminated in its suppression by the Holy Office in 1760. Later Isla also translated *Gil Blas* into Spanish—that great book in which the lucid objectivity of the picaresque novel is transfused with the spirit of enlightenment without loss to either—and his ironical pretence of having discovered the original Spanish manuscript which Le Sage had, he claimed, merely translated, was taken at its face value by many Spaniards (Isla's translation appeared posthumously in 1783).

More important even than Isla's novel was the revival of the Spanish theatre which began in the 1760's. Important, because it arose without any didactic or controversial afterthought straight from the soil of majaism. The Spanish stage had reached a sorry state of decay. The hack adapters of the seventeenth-century dramatists, who still provided the majority of the plays, had reached stalemate in ludicrous hyperbole and braggadocio. On the other hand, the lifeless copies of French neo-classical models which the reformers tried to foist upon the public had proved disastrous failures, especially with the pit, whose reception made or marred a play, although, as Bourgoing tells us, the pit or "patio for the most part contains the meanest of the people, who sufficiently display their vulgarity, ignorance, and rags". In this dilemma the Spanish stage was saved in a manner, which is as significant as it is unexpected, by the Madrid petty official Francisco Ramón de la Cruz Cano y Olmedilla (1731–94). Like so many of his fellow authors, Cruz had started his career with uninspired translations and imitations of French and Italian plays.[1] But he restored the vitality of the Spanish stage when he turned his attention to the playlets, often enlivened with songs and dances, which had been performed since the earliest days of the Spanish theatre in the interludes between the acts of the main piece. These trifles had always been distinguished by their popular flavour, calculated to please the pit. The 'pasos' by Lope de Rueda (1510?–65), whom Lope de Vega called the father of Spanish comedy, are brief episodes drawn from the everyday life of the people. Later writers developed this form in the pieces known as 'entremeses'. Cruz now infused a new vitality into this ancient tradition by drawing the material for his *entr'acte* playlets, which were called 'sainetes', from the streets and maja-haunts of contemporary Madrid. Form and plot of the sainetes were as simple as those of the longer plays were involved, and their insertion between the acts of the main piece helped to make the audience lose the thread

---

[1] He was also, incidentally, the first Spaniard to translate Shakespeare—he translated Hamlet from the French version of Ducis in 1772.

of its labyrinthine plot altogether. Bourgoing's statement
that the theatre was often deserted after the second interlude is not, therefore, surprising. But although Bourgoing
is very scathing in his remarks about these main plays and
the stilted manner in which they were performed, he writes
of the sainete:

> The manners and character of the inferior classes
> of society, and the petty interests which associate and
> divide them, are therein represented in the most strik-
> ing manner. It is not an imitation but the thing itself.
> The spectator seems to be suddenly transported into a
> circle of Spaniards, where he is present at their amuse-
> ments and little cavillings. The manner and dress is so
> faithfully copied that he is sometimes disgusted. He
> sees porters, flower girls, and fishwomen, who have all
> the gestures, manner, and language of those he has
> seen a hundred times in the street. For these kinds of
> characters the Spanish comedians have an admirable
> talent. Were they equally natural in every other they
> would be the first actors in Europe. The composition
> of these little pieces, however, required no great talents.
> It might be supposed the author was afraid of going
> too far, and only waited for an expedient to withdraw
> himself from his embarrassment. He opens the door of
> a private house, and presents, as by chance, some of the
> scenes which most commonly pass in it; and as soon
> as he thinks the spectator's curiosity satisfied, he shuts
> the door and the piece concludes.

Cruz was as prolific as the scene from which he drew his
inspiration.[1] More than four hundred of his sainetes have
been preserved, and they retained their popularity until
long after their author's death. Altamira asserts that he
was the first Spanish author who put on the stage a serious

[1] For detailed appreciations *v.* Hamilton and Kany *op. cit.* Cf. Cicero's reference to
the Roman mime (he discusses a story put forward by Clodia): "Its conclusion is not
like that of an ordinary play; it is like the conclusion of a mime (*mimi ergo est iam
exitus, non fabulae*), in which, when no end can be found, the actor escapes from
the hands of those who are holding him; the signal is given for the end of the piece,
and the curtain rises for the next play" (*Pro Coelio*, lxv, quoted by Allardyce Nicoll,
Masks, Mimes and Miracles, Studies in the Popular Theatre, London, 1931). Nicoll
comments: "In all probability the mimes had no such exact structural forms as
appeared in comedy or in tragedy. No rules fettered the mimographs, and the
actors were free to express themselves as they cared. The only thing which dominated the mimes was the desire to please; for one hour, for two hours, they jested
merrily and uttered their lines of proverbial wisdom, and then, just as life shuts
itself off from the eyes of the individual spectator, so they, having played their
appointed space, with a final jest rang up the curtain on the new piece—the comedy
or the tragedy—which was to follow their representation" (p. 128).

play about the lower classes of Madrid. His subjects were all taken from the lives of the lower and middle classes of the capital. He himself defined the secret of his appeal when he prefaced his collected plays with the words: "Truth dictates, and I write".

Ever since J. Somoza (1781–1852) compared the sainetes with Goya's tapestry cartoons their similarity has been regarded as a commonplace. One need only glance at Cruz's titles to confirm the parallel: 'El Prado por la noche', 'Manola', 'La maja majada', 'Las tertulias de Madrid', 'Las castañeras picadas', 'La Pradera de San Isidro'. . . . But the differences between Cruz and the Goya of the tapestry cartoons are no less significant. In the latter Goya achieved a true synthesis between new ideas and old traditions, while in his sainetes Cruz made himself the mouthpiece of the majo's naïve conservatism.

> Cruz does not deal with the two classes—the middle and the proletariat—in the same way [writes A. Hamilton]. His manner towards the proletariat is one of sympathy tinctured with mild amusement. He disapproves strongly of most of what the middle class does, thinks, and says, and he shows it. A thorough reactionary, he believed that in the past, and only in the past, lay the greatness of Spain, and therefore that all the customs of the past were excellent, and all changes and innovations of his own day were *ipso facto* to be condemned. Especially was this true of such innovations as had their source on the north side of the Pyrenees.

Yet this staunch old die-hard rendered yeoman service to the cause of progress. His ascendancy more or less coincides with the suppression of the 'autos sacramentales' by Aranda in 1765. Until that date those ancient miracle plays had been performed on the Madrid stage much in the same way as the secular pieces. After describing the performance of an auto, the English traveller Clarke continues:

> One of the actresses immediately unbound Christ [who had just died on the cross], divested him of his crown and scarlet robes; and when he had put on his wig and coat again, he immediately joined the other actors and danced a seguidilla.[1]

It is a striking symptom for the changed temper of

[1] E. Clarke, *Letters concerning the Spanish Nation*, London, 1763.

Spanish society since the seventeenth century that the reformers clamoured for the prohibition of these plays, not in order to attack religion but, on the contrary, in order to protect it from ridicule. The publicist Clavijo (1726–1806) wrote in his paper *El Pensador*:

> To see, as I have seen, a man, who in the interlude was dressed as a ruffian smoking a cigar, become, in the auto, one of the Holy Trinity, is just as offensive to reason and nature as to see an actor who takes the role of the Eternal Father in the auto called *Los alimentos del hombre* transformed later, for the sainete into a gate-keeper, stationed at one of the city entrances where goods are examined, making indecent remarks to a girl who in the auto had taken the part of an angel.[1]

Bourgoing, writing in a similar strain, speaks of the autos "in which angels, saints, and virtues, personified, were exhibited, to the scandal of religion and common sense; ridiculous pieces, in which Calderón had displayed all the extravagance of his imagination".[2]

That Cruz supplied the Spanish stage with a medium, as acceptable to the common people as the autos had been in former days, but wholly directed to their earthly lives and not their transcendental fantasies, that he saved the stage for the people and thus prepared the ground for its revival in the following generation—therein lies his undying contribution to the cause of Spanish freedom.

THE ART POLICY OF THE BOURBONS

The Bourbons attacked the political pretensions of the Church and sponsored a policy of enlightenment in Spain only because that policy was dictated by the needs of absolutism. As soon as the Church accepted the secular supremacy of the crown, the Bourbon kings were eager to demonstrate their loyalty to the Catholic faith and to reinforce the authority of the clergy over the people. Nor would the Bourbons have countenanced an attack on the principle of aristocratic privilege in the name of enlightenment.

This situation is reflected in the preference of the first two Bourbons for the baroque style and in its persistence,

---

[1] Quoted by Kany *op. cit.*
[2] In another passage, however, Bourgoing expresses his admiration for Calderón, whom he regards as the greatest Spanish play-writer.

even in court commissions, until the third quarter of the eighteenth century. The French baroque style, with its emotional emphasis on the pomp and majesty of royalty, was represented at the Madrid court by the painters Michel-Ange Houasse, Jean Ranc, and Louis Michel van Loo. Its influence was merged with that of the Italian baroque, which still reigned supreme in decorative and ecclesiastical painting.[1] Both tendencies were far closer in spirit than classicism to the only native style which still retained a semblance of vitality in the early eighteenth century. It was then that the Spanish version of the baroque, the ornamental style known descriptively as 'churriguerismo' (after the architect José de Churriguera, 1665–1725), attained its flamboyant apogee.

During the 1760's, however, when the movement of reform was about to enter its most brilliant phase, the equivocal position of the Bourbon court was dramatically reflected in its art policy. Within nine months of each other both Giovanni Battista Tiepolo (1696–1770), the last of the great Venetian baroque painters, and Antón Rafael Mengs (1728–79), the friend of Winckelmann and the foremost exponent of neoclassical 'simplicity' in painting, were called to Madrid. Mengs arrived first, in the summer of 1761, and stayed until 1768, returning for another three years in 1774–7; Tiepolo spent the last eight years of his life, from 1762 to 1770, in the Spanish capital. A fierce battle of intrigues ensued, in which the reform party supported Mengs, while the old king favoured the Italian master. Things came to a head when Tiepolo had finished his vast decorations in the Royal Palace at Madrid (1762–6) and was ordered by Charles III. to supply six altar-pieces for the palace-church of San Pascual at Aranjuez, then in course of

---

[1] A. M. Houasse (*c.* 1680–1730), in Spain shortly after 1707; Jean Ranc (1674–1735), a pupil of Rigaud, called to Madrid as court painter in 1724; L. M. van Loo (1707–71), a younger member of a well-known family of artists, appointed court painter in succession to Ranc in 1736, he was co-founder and director of painting of the Academy of San Fernando in 1752, but returned to Paris in the following year. The most important Italian decorative painters active in Spain during the first two Bourbon reigns were: the Neapolitan baroque virtuoso Luca Giordano (1632–1705), who was known as 'Fa presto' from the incredible speed of his work, appointed court painter by Charles II in 1692, left Spain in 1702; the Venetian Jacopo Amigoni (1675–1752), who, after having worked for long periods in Bavaria, London, and Paris, became court painter to Ferdinand VI in 1746, a position which he retained until his death; and Corrado Giaquinto (*c.* 1699–1765), one of the last noteworthy representatives of the Neapolitan school, who went to Madrid in 1753 as successor to Amigoni, and left Spain in 1761 reputedly from pique at the appointment of Mengs.

construction. The partisans of Mengs, headed by the king's confessor (who had just triumphed over his enemies, the Jesuits), were anxious to obtain this commission for their own favourite. They adopted delaying tactics and succeeded in preventing the submission of the finished panels to the king until after Tiepolo's death in 1770. Although these last works of the great Venetian were eventually installed in San Pascual on the insistence of Charles III, they were taken down again and replaced by works of Mengs, Bayeu, and Maella at some date before 1787.[1]

Since Tiepolo was incomparably the better artist and since his influence on Spanish painting, and especially Goya, was in the long run at least as profound as that of Mengs, it is insufficient to explain this turn of events merely as a change of fashion or as the result of intrigues. Some of the principles Mengs was fighting for had, in fact, already emerged as increasingly powerful undercurrents within the opposed style of the baroque itself. Of the French painters working at Madrid, Houasse, for example, had painted an altar-piece of St. Francis de Regis (Madrid University) which is reminiscent of Le Sueur's sober classicism, but in which the people participate in an even more realistic manner in the actions of the saint. It was to one of the panels of this altar-piece that Goya later went for the composition of his own 'St. Francis of Borgia at the Deathbed of an Un-believer', as Sánchez Cantón has shown. In 1730 Houasse also painted a series of small panels for La Granja, the subjects of which, including 'A Game of Blind-Man's-Buff', 'A Picnic', 'A Ball Game', anticipate the tapestry cartoons. By this time the influence of Watteau was evidently affecting even such distant outposts of French culture as the Bourbon court at Madrid, and Watteau was, of course, not only the father of the courtly shepherd idyll, but also, with his paintings of soldiers, comedians, and other characters from low life, the link between the Le Nain and Chardin. Another symptom of this undercurrent in baroque art are some portraits of Spanish intellectuals painted by van Loo in the 1740's. They lack the flamboyance of the contemporary court portraits and are little removed from the Mengsian ideal of simplicity.[2]

[1] Cf. F. J. Sánchez Cantón, 'Los tiépolos de Aranjuez', *Archivo Español de Arte y Arqueologia*, Madrid, vol. iii, 1927.
[2] Cf. illustrations in Sánchez Cantón's *Goya*.

The growth of naturalism in decorative painting during this period has been studied in detail by Dvořák in a brilliant article devoted to the baroque ceilings in Vienna.[1] Dvořák shows how the unity of architecture and painting, which marks the true climax of the baroque in Italian seventeenth-century works, was gradually replaced by a consummate stagecraft aiming to translate the spectator into an imaginary sphere beyond all material space. In that fairyland not only saints and angels (or, in secular buildings, nymphs and goddesses), but also courtiers, natives of exotic countries, travellers, sailors, artisans, and ordinary street crowds move about so naturally that the spectator feels himself one of them. The original purpose of this illusion was to suggest the reality of the supernatural miracle or apotheosis which occupies the centre of the composition. Gradually, however, the groups of spectators who fill imaginary terraces, balconies or landscapes in the margins of the design, absorbed more and more of the spectator's interest, until they became almost independent illustrations of real life, disrupting the former unity of the monumental baroque style.

As the heir of the Venetian tradition of naturalism Tiepolo was, of course, particularly susceptible to this trend. Indeed, his work at Würzburg largely influenced the later development of decorative design in Vienna. But Tiepolo's naturalism appears even more dramatically in some of his late religious works. The storm-swept view of Este and the dead mother and child in the altar-panel of 'Sta. Tecla freeing the Town of Este from the Plague' which he painted just before coming to Spain, in 1759, suggest Goya in his most macabre mood, and there were similar passages in some of Tiepolo's paintings for Aranjuez.[2] The continuity of this naturalist trend is most convincingly demonstrated, however, by the development of Domenico Tiepolo (1727–1804). Up to 1770 Domenico's style is indistinguishable from that of his father, whose assistant he was; but after he had returned to Venice in 1771 his art assumed an ever increasing resemblance to Goya's work during the period of the tapestry cartoons.

[1] *Entwicklungsgeschichte der Barocken Deckenmalerei Wiens. Gesammelte Aufsätze zur Kunstgeschichte*, Munich, 1929.
[2] Cf. Sánchez Cantón *op. cit.*, and 'Bocetos y dibujos de Tiépolo', *Archivo Español de Arte y Arqueologia*, vol. v, 1929. A sketch for the Este altar-piece was in the Collection Boix at Madrid.

The victory of Mengs over Tiepolo in Spain was therefore historically inevitable. In 1760 the ideal of sentimental classicism was more progressive than the authoritarian principle of baroque design, because it enabled the new trends which were welling up in all spheres of thought and feeling, including baroque painting itself, to develop more adequate forms of expression.[1] Considered purely as a period fashion, neoclassicism was as short-lived as the decorative baroque style. But from a long-term point of view its influence coincided with that of the naturalist undercurrent in Tiepolo's art. The ideals of naturalness and simplicity advocated by Mengs formed the bridge which led the artists of bourgeois enlightenment back to the mainspring of Spanish realism: "What justness, what true distribution of clair-obscure, in the works of Velazquez", Mengs wrote in 1776 to Don Antonio Ponz, the secretary of the Academy of San Fernando and author of a famous travel-survey of Spain's art treasures. "How well he understood the effect of light in showing the distances of objects one from another, and what a school for an artist to improve himself in studying the works of this great man." Mengs considered the works of Velasquez as the best examples of what he called the 'natural style'. According to Mengs the natural style, like the comic muse in poetry, aims to attain the most perfect imitation of nature with all her faults and blemishes. This distinguishes it from the 'sublime style'—in his view the highest category of art—which idealises nature by means of selection and simplification. In this latter style Mengs considered that the Greeks had never been equalled, although of all the 'moderns' Raphael had approached most closely to their perfection. But although he rated the natural below the sublime style, Mengs again and again expressed his admiration for Velazquez as a painter: "Whoever wishes to find a more perfect solution (of aerial perspective) than is to be observed in the works of Velazquez, may see it in nature herself; but its principal parts he will always find in the works of this great master". That Mengs himself was profoundly

---

[1] Mengs is not the only case in which an artist whose reputation has proved to be ephemeral nevertheless played an important and progressive role in his own time. The part played by de Loutherbourg at the same period in England is curiously similar to that of Mengs in Madrid. But in de Loutherbourg's case it was his superbly skilful baroque stagecraft which helped the English landscape school to advance beyond the objective classicism of the topographical draughtsmen to imaginative romantic painting.

influenced by his study of these works is shown above all in his portraits. Those he painted in Spain approach closer to the realistic bourgeois portrait type than any of his earlier ones.[1]

Mengs soon became the acknowledged leader of the younger generation of Spanish artists. Of these Goya's brother-in-law and teacher, Francisco Bayeu (1734–95), was the most talented and successful, until his star was obscured by his pupil.

GOYA

Francisco José Goya y Lucientes was born on 30 March 1746, in the village of Fuendetodos in Aragon. He was educated in near-by Saragossa, where his grandfather had been a notary and his father followed the trade of a gilder. When his father died in 1781, the registrar certified that "he had made no will, because he had nothing to bequeath".

At the age of fourteen Francisco Goya was apprenticed to the Saragossa painter José Luzan y Martinez (1710–85), a busy church decorator in the Italian baroque tradition. In 1763 Goya first went to Madrid where he probably entered the studio of Francisco Bayeu. His career began when he returned to Saragossa after a brief visit to Italy in 1771. The next decade was a period of struggle for Goya. He was working partly at Madrid and partly at Saragossa, where he was employed, with a number of other artists, on the decorations for the new cathedral of Nuestra Señora del Pilar under the general supervision of Bayeu (in 1771–2 and 1780–81). But by the latter date he had already reached a stage of development where he could no longer tolerate the narrow limitations of that type of commission. After a violent rupture with the cathedral authorities and with Bayeu he abandoned the work and returned to the capital. He had, indeed, already found his proper *milieu*: in 1776 he had been commissioned to paint cartoons for the Royal Tapestry Factory of Sta. Barbara at Madrid.

During the '80's Goya established his position in the

---

[1] After defining the basic principles of his conceptions of art, Mengs proceeds to describe the main paintings in the Royal Palace at Madrid in this letter. It was written at the request of Ponz, who wished to include a contribution by the famous painter in his *Viaje de España* (1772–94), where it was originally published. I have used an English translation by Sir John Talbot Dillon, published in London in 1782 under the title *Sketches on the Art of Painting with a description of the Most Capital Pictures in the King of Spain's Palace at Madrid in a letter from Sir Anthony Raphael Mengs Knt to Don Antonio Ponz.*

art world of the capital. He was elected a member of the Academy of San Fernando in 1780. About the same period he began to paint portraits and within a few years he became a fashionable society painter. For a period of more than twenty-five years his portraits provide us with a gallery, not only of the court and its grandees, but also of the most distinguished statesmen, artists, and intellectuals in Spain.

Goya's outlook in those years was carefree and exuberant. After the penury of his youth he rejoiced in a style of living appropriate to his success. He had married, at some date between 1773 and 1776, Josefa Bayeu, the sister of his teacher and compatriot, who bore him many children. He now kept a carriage and spent much time in the salons and on the country estates of his wealthy patrons. He was spirited and vivacious. Even when he was eighty he boasted that, sword in hand, he, who had spent many hours in the bull-ring, feared no one. For many years after his death fantastic tales of his adventures in his youth and early manhood were current in Spain. Tales of bull-fights, amorous exploits, abductions, encounters with the police, hair-breadth escapes, and a dare-devil ascent over Michelangelo's dome to the cross of St. Peter's. Matheron, Goya's first biographer, collected these stories in the 1850's. His account, which is dedicated to Delacroix, reads like a picaresque novel.[1]

THE TAPESTRY CARTOONS

The Royal Tapestry Factory of Sta. Barbara at Madrid was founded in 1720 as one of the new economic and cultural enterprises of the crown. It was administered by a Flemish expert, J. van der Goten, who had been called to Madrid for the purpose. His son, Cornelius van der Goten, was still in charge of the establishment when Goya began to work for it.

During the first half-century of its existence the tapestries produced by the Madrid factory did not greatly differ in type from those of similar establishments elsewhere. Following the usual programme it produced convention-alised 'peasant' scenes after Teniers (until 1727); then followed a series illustrating the story of Don Quixote after designs by the Italian baroque painter Andrea Procaccini

[1] L. Matheron, *Goya*, Paris, 1858.

(1671–1734) and a parallel series by M. A. Houasse illustrating Fénelon's *Télémaque*; and finally a number of tapestries after miscellaneous models depicting mythological and 'historical' subjects. It was therefore a decisive innovation, indicative of the desire of the Spanish court to bring its artistic programme into line with the taste of the people, when these conventional mythological, literary, and 'peasant' models were replaced, under the supervision of Mengs, by popular scenes in a contemporary and definitely Spanish *milieu*.

Goya, who received his first commission from the factory in June 1776, was only one among several young painters employed for this new programme of cartoons. The others were Francisco and Ramón Bayeu, J. de Castillo, and Manuel Napoli. For Goya this appointment was of vital importance. At the age of thirty he was given his first real chance to escape from the narrow sphere of provincial ecclesiastical commissions, and he was employed on a programme of work which identified him with the reform party not only by conviction, but also professionally. The course was set for one of the most heroic careers in the history of art.

During the next fifteen years Goya's style developed from the conventional manner of a provincial baroque decorator, through Mengsian naturalness and the technical discipline of Tiepolo, to a new conception of realism derived from a study of the older Spanish masters. The subject-matter of all Goya's cartoons is provided by the people and, in particular, the people of Madrid. But his conception of this theme underwent a development similar to that of his style. He started from majaism, that is to say, from an idealisation of the people: or perhaps better from the people in their Sunday-best and at play, and he proceeded to a more and more truthful differentiation between the various classes and social types, showing the people at work, and suffering and not merely amusing themselves. The series as a whole is still pervaded by the aesthetic feeling of the later eighteenth century, with its emphasis of tonal harmony and delicate colouring, and the dominant mood throughout reflects the optimism of the Spanish reform movement.

We must now follow the various stages of this development in detail. Goya delivered his first thirty cartoons to the tapestry factory between 1776 and 1780. The tapestries for which they were designed had been commissioned for the decoration of the apartments occupied by the Prince of Asturias in the Pardo Palace. Their range of theme is indicated by the following table:[1]

No.	Subject	Date of Delivery
1	The Picnic on the Banks of the Mazanares .	1776
2	The Dance near San Antonio . . .	1776
3	The Brawl at the New Inn . . .	1777
4	Maja and Muffled Majos . . .	1777
5	Man Drinking	1777
6	The Sunshade	1777
7	Flying a Kite	January 1778
8	The Game of Cards	January 1778
9	Children with a Balloon. . . .	January 1778
10	Children plucking Fruit. . . .	January 1778
11	The Blind Guitarist	March 1778
	Revised version	October 1778
12	The Madrid Junk Market . . .	January 1779
13	The Valencia Crockery Stall . . .	January 1779
14	Officer and Lady.	January 1779
15	La Acerolera ('Brave Girl'—a market scene).	January 1779
16	Children playing at Soldiers . . .	January 1779
17	(Children with toy cart) . . .	January 1779
18	The Game of Pelota	July 1779
19	The Swing	1779
20	The Washerwomen	Painted July 1779
21	La Novillada (bull-fight) . . .	Del. January 1780
22	(Youths with Dog)	Painted 1779?
23	(Three Men at a Spring) . . .	Painted 1779?
24	The Tobacco Excisemen . . .	January 1780
25	Child with Tree	January 1780
26	Child with Bird	January 1780
27	The Woodcutters	January 1780
28	Ballad Singer	January 1780
29	The Rendezvous	January 1780
30	The Doctor	January 1780

The cartoons placed in brackets have been lost. No. 30, 'The Doctor', is now in the Scottish National Gallery at Edinburgh; all the others are in the Prado.

In these cartoons Goya was feeling his way towards a less schematic manner, but his first steps towards naturalism were still somewhat hesitant. Large-scale figures, generally grouped rather self-consciously, dominate the compositions. Trees, buildings, and other landscape elements merely serve as foils for them. The colouring is often rich and full of contrasts. At first majo and maja scenes predominate, and

[1] This table and that on p. 60 are taken from A. L. Mayer, *Goya*, Munich, 1923.

there is sometimes even a touch of caricature in their treatment (fig. 1). But even among the earliest cartoons there are some which recall Tiepolo by their graceful charm, as, for example, the 'Sunshade' of 1777 (fig. 2).

In 1777 and 1778 Goya made a profound study of the older Spanish pictures in the royal collection. He discovered Velasquez and made a series of etchings after his works. It was perhaps one of the immediate results of this study that in the cartoons delivered from 1779 onwards definite social types based on direct observation appear in ever-increasing numbers. In the crowded street scenes of 'The Blind Guitarist', 'The Madrid Junk Market', and 'The Valencia Crockery Stall', for example, middle-class and society people, servants, street vendors, and beggars are clearly differentiated by their costumes, gestures, and facial types[1] (fig. 4).

Goya did not of course abandon his favourite majos or slightly idealised servant and maja types. They are as gay as ever in the coquette servant girl ('La Acerolera'), the 'Game of Pelota', 'The Swing', 'The Washerwomen', and the bull-fight scene ('La Novillada') of 1778–9. But in the last cartoons delivered in 1780 there is a wide range of subjects, from the two designs with children to the grim 'Excisemen' and the Edinburgh 'Doctor' with his scarlet cloak and gold-trimmed hat, warming his hands at a brazier before a deep-blue landscape background (fig. 3).

During the six years which intervened between the completion of the first set of cartoons and his permanent appointment as painter to the tapestry factory with a salary of 15,000 reals, Goya established his social position in the capital. It was a period of consolidation also from the point of view of his creative development, a period in which he assimilated and gradually mastered the various influences he had received in previous years.

Having returned to Madrid in 1781, Goya entered a competition for the altar-pieces of the church San Francisco el Grande. It was a scheme of considerable importance for the Mengs school, since it was a challenge to the younger Spanish artists to demonstrate their capabilities on a large scale. The unveiling of the seven pictures in the presence of

---

[1] This is also the case in some of the contemporary cartoons by Goya's colleagues and especially in many popular prints, topographical views, etc., of the period. At this stage Goya was merely the most advanced representative of a general movement.

the king in 1784 was a great social event, and Goya's success on this occasion—he had painted 'The Sermon of St. Bernardino of Siena before King Alfonso of Aragon'—greatly enhanced his fame in society circles.[1]

More important for his artistic development were his first essays as a portraitist. His earliest dated portrait is that of the director of the tapestry factory, C. van der Goten, of 1782, but others probably preceded it, including his first self-portrait. In these early works he closely followed Mengs, so much so that it is often difficult to attribute them with certainty. He even attempted to break with the baroque tradition in a large group portrait of the minister Floridablanca (1783), who is standing at a table with his secretary and looking at a picture which is held up for him by the artist himself. By 1785–6 Goya had mastered his problem and welded the influences he had absorbed into a new, intensely personal style. On the verge of maturity, he had now entered his "hour of optimism" which is reflected in the "brilliant and luminous" works of the next few years.[2] But before setting out on the course dictated by his personal inspiration he publicly proclaimed his indebtedness to the great master of Spanish realism: the portrait of 'Charles III as a Hunter' (1786) is an act of homage to Velazquez. Later in life Goya acknowledged three masters: Velazquez, Rembrandt, and, above all, Nature.[3] About the time we are now discussing, Goya honoured Rembrandt in the same way as he had honoured Velazquez. The portrait he painted of himself working in the half-light of his studio (Coll. Villagonzalo, Madrid, 1787–8) as clearly reveals his admiration for the great Dutchman as the hunter-portrait his gratitude to the Spaniard. And Nature? All his life Goya worshipped Nature, not by imitation, but by following the guiding star of truth.

Goya's development in the 1780's is no less evident from the style of the second group of cartoons which he painted

---

[1] Thus he received several commissions for paintings with religious themes from prominent people during 1784 and 1785, among them the Duke of Medinaceli (the 'Annunciation') and Jovellanos (four pictures now lost). Goya's friendship with Jovellanos started in 1783.

[2] Sánchez Cantón *op. cit.* It is interesting that among the portraits of 1787–8 were those of Cabarrús and the other directors of the newly founded Bank of San Carlos, the most important economic foundation of the reform period.

[3] This statement, reported by Matheron (*op. cit.*), is confirmed by a deposition of Goya's son found among the papers of the Spanish painter Carderera and reprinted in the *Archivo Español de Arte y Arqueología*, vol. vii, 1931.

between 1786 and 1788.[1] Their subjects are:

No.	Subject	Date of Delivery
31	Spring (Las Floreras) . . .	Painted early in 1786
32	Summer (harvest scene) . . .	Painted in mid-1786
33	Autumn (La Vendimia—vintage scene)	1786
34	The Wounded Mason . . .	Painted end of 1786
35	Poor Family at the Well . . .	Early 1787
36	Winter (The Snow Storm) . . .	Early 1787
37	The Marriage . . .	1787
38	Girls carrying Water . . .	1787
39	Los Gigantillos (children at play) .	1787
40	(The See-Saw—children playing) .	1788
41	Juego de Zancos (majos on stilts with musicians)	1788

Goya had now mastered the lessons of the Venetians, Watteau and Mengs. These eleven cartoons and certain other pictures related to them are bright and graceful and full of atmosphere. They are similar in their delicate naturalism to some of Fragonard's open-air genre scenes. As a rule the landscape is much more important in them than in the earlier cartoons, and the figures fit harmoniously into their natural setting. From the point of view of subject-matter three groups can be distinguished among these cartoons. Each illustrates a different element in the outlook of the Spanish reformers, then at the height of their power.

The first group is represented by the two paintings of 'Spring' and 'Autumn':—flowers and vintage. Exquisite landscapes bathed in light and radiant with joyful colour harmonies, they are peopled with aristocratic families abandoned to the delights of country life. It was probably in 1786 that Goya had made the acquaintance of the Duchess of Alba. He visited the Duke and Duchess on one of their estates, and the picture of 'Autumn', if not painted during that visit, may well have been inspired by it. Both these pictures breathe the spirit of Rousseau and reflect the philanthropic interest of certain enlightened aristocrats in the ideas of progress (fig. 5).

The second group is composed of happy anecdotal scenes. The figures are realistically observed, although somewhat idealised, lower middle-class, peasant and majo types,

---

[1] These tapestries were destined for the bedroom of the Infante Don Gabriel Anton in the Escorial.

while two of the cartoons show children at play. Gaiety is the keynote of the harvest scene with its rejoicing peasants, no less than of the majos on stilts, the maja servants carrying water, and the wedding procession. At times the attitude is moralising and sentimental in the eighteenth-century middle-class sense. This is particularly true of the wedding picture, which embodies the spirit of the group to perfection. Enclosed within an exquisite elliptical composition, rounded by the bridge above and the converging steps below, the marriage procession contains the humorous stock types of the pretty young bride, the ugly old husband, the smug curate, and the hypocritical father. Admiring maidens and happy urchins complete the assembly (fig. 6).

The last group of three cartoons is wholly distinct from the others. Benevolence and moral anecdote are replaced by a stirring social appeal. The types depicted are real workers and peasants, and the veil is drawn from the agonies of poverty and labour: frost-bitten mule drivers are crossing the desolate, snow-covered Sierra with their mangy dog and their beast of burden; a poor widow and her shivering children are standing at a well in a bleak winter landscape; a mason, who has fallen from his scaffold, is carried helpless from the scene by his comrades (figs. 7-9).

Seven genre pictures which Goya painted in 1787 for the Duke of Osuna's country seat, the Alameda, further illustrate this phase in his development. They are similar in spirit to the 'aristocratic' and 'anecdotal' cartoons which we have just discussed. The aristocratic mood is embodied, perhaps with an undercurrent of irony, in a picture known as 'The Accident'—a lady has fallen from her mule—and in another showing brigands robbing a diligence, but especially in a second version of 'The Swing' ('La Gitana'). The other paintings showing picadors with bulls, an ox-cart taking a large stone to a construction job, a may-tree and a village procession, are middle-class anecdotes or majo scenes.

There is also a further example of Goya's objective realism, although this time in a happy mood: the exquisite landscape view of Madrid with the festive scene on the banks of the Mazanares in the foreground. Goya's 'Pradera de S. Isidro', painted in 1788, links the landscapes of Velazquez with French impressionism (fig. 10).

The stage of Goya's development represented by the tapestry cartoons culminated in 1788. The events which

occurred between that year and 1791, when he completed
the series, profoundly affected Goya's life and outlook. His
last four cartoons were painted under protest, since he no
longer regarded the cartoon as a satisfactory medium for
his aims. Two of them show children (Nos. 43 and 45), the
other two fashionable amusements: a game of blind-man's-
buff (the 'Gallina Ciego') and four girls tossing a dummy
(the 'Pelele').[1] A new element of tension, latent in the
'Gallina', becomes apparent in the grotesque limpness and
rouged mask of the 'Pelele'. The reasons for this change in
mood will be discussed in the following chapter.

GOYA'S POSITION IN 1788

In the section of his book in which he describes the state
of the arts in contemporary Spain Bourgoing cites Maella
and Bayeu as "the present principal supporters of the
Spanish school", and then continues: "Don Francisco de
Goya merits also by his talents an honourable mention; he
portrays, in pleasing style, the manners, customs, and games
of his country". Had Goya's career stopped short in 1788 or
in 1791, when he was forty-five years old, posterity would
have found little to add to this verdict. With his tapestry
cartoons Goya expressed the outlook of the progressive
intellectuals patronised by the court. The three 'social problem' subjects, which are so incongruous in the context of
the series, suggest that his sympathies lay with the more
radical rather than with the more conservative members of
the group. But if a few portraits are omitted (especially
those in which he was consciously imitating Velazquez and
Rembrandt), his art did not differ notably either in content
or style from that of other contemporary painters who
expressed the spirit of eighteenth-century rationalism in
Spain and elsewhere. His own great genius had not yet
revealed itself.

The parallel, already noted, between Goya's work and
Domenico Tiepolo's underlines this point, especially if it is
remembered that Domenico was nineteen years older than
Goya. Domenico's own considerable talent did not develop
freely until after the death of the elder Tiepolo in 1770; it
may be studied at its best in the frescoes he painted after
his return to Italy and up to 1793 in the Villa Zianigo, a

[1] These tapestries were designed for the study of Charles IV in the Escorial.

small country-house near Venice that had belonged to his father.[1] A scene from Tasso and some religious subjects had already been painted by father and son in 1749, but the rest of the decorations are Domenico's work from the later period. Their spirit is well defined by the terms *Capricci e Fantasie scherzose, carnevalesche*, in which they are described by Lorenzetti. These include fauns and satyrs, centaurs and romantic warriors, but they mostly show masked pagliacci and carnival crowds:—the Venetian equivalents of Goya's majos and majas. There is one design, however, that goes far beyond anything in Goya's cartoons. It is called 'il mondo novo' and dated 1791. A whole wall of a long, but comparatively low, room is taken up by the rear view of a crowd of life-size people eagerly pressing forward to watch some street performance invisible to the spectator. There is an element of satire in this painting (and also in two other panels in the same room and in a number of contemporary drawings of Venetian street scenes) which suggests Rowlandson or Fuseli. But Domenico was a more penetrating observer than either of these artists. The days of the ancient merchant republic were counted and Giandomenico Tiepolo, its last noteworthy painter, felt the chill which the dawn of a new world had cast over the carnival at Venice. The 'mondo novo' is the immediate precursor of Goya's *Caprichos* (fig. 11).

The significance of Goya's contact with the Tiepolos was therefore more far-reaching than appeared at first sight. During the period of the tapestry cartoons it was mainly the Venetian artists' approach to Nature, their impressionist vision of colour and atmosphere, that was important for the young Spaniard, since it helped to guide him to Velazquez. But the *scherzi* and *capricci* and the romantic landscapes, which Giovanni as well as Domenico Tiepolo produced on occasion, belong to another tradition in Italian art, the source of which had influenced even the great Velasquez himself. Caravaggio and visiting Flemish realists of the sixteenth century, including Pieter Brueghel the Elder, had created a taste for romantic low-life themes treated, now in a realistic, now in a fantastic manner. The popular genre

[1] Cf. P. Molmenti, 'La Villa Zianigo e gli affreschi di Gian Domenico Tiepolo', *Emporium*, vol. xxvi, 1907, and G. Lorenzetti, *Ca' Rezzonico*, Venice, 1936. The decorations of the Villa Zianigo are now housed in the Palazzo Rezzonico at Venice with the rest of the eighteenth-century collections of the Civico Museo Correr.

pieces of Cerquozzi in the seventeenth or Crespi in the eighteenth century, but also many engraved series of 'trades' and 'street cries', are typical of the one trend; Salvator Rosa's landscapes with bandits, Callot's caprices or, in the first half of the eighteenth century, Magnasco's spooks and devilries, of the other.[1] But many artists, including Domenico Tiepolo, used either tendency with equal facility according to their needs. How important this whole imagery was to become for Goya did not appear until conditions had changed and there was no more reason for the carefree optimism he had expressed in the tapestry cartoons.

[1] Cf. the masterly survey of the whole trend by L. Planiscig, 'Alessandro Magnasco und die romantisch genrehafte Richtung des Barocco, *Monatshefte für Kunstwissenschaft*, 1915, and numerous articles on individual artists in the Italian periodical *Dedalo*, 1920–21 to 1931–2.

Chapter 2

THE CAPRICHOS

SPAIN'S modern history is a succession of violent changes, a panorama painted in glaring contrasts of light and shade. The period of enlightenment, which seemed to have shattered the foundations of clerical totalitarianism in Spain, was followed by a sudden reversal of conditions. Deserted by the crown, the progressive party lost control of the levers of power. The patient work of reconstruction was wantonly reduced to ruins. Reaction, profiting by the discomfiture of its opponents, regained its foothold as the only solid force in the country. Despondency and a sudden realisation of the immensity of their task now replaced the confident exuberance of the reformers, and the people lost their carefree gaiety as they sullenly acquiesced in the renewed misrule of their oppressors.

The contrast between these two periods is heightened by a peculiar personal symbolism. History was singularly kind to Charles III in allowing him to die, at the age of seventy-two, in December 1788, a few months before the French Revolution exposed the inherent contradiction between enlightenment and absolutism. Thus he remained the symbol of his country's rehabilitation in the eighteenth century, and the odium of a reversal of policy which was inevitable has fallen with unrelieved severity on his successors.

When the Third Estate of France shattered the political and legal forms which hampered the free development of capitalist society, and the figure-head of Bourbon absolutism rolled on the scaffold, there could be no doubt of the course which family ties and tradition imposed upon the Spanish Bourbons. Under the aegis of Floridablanca, the minister whose policy most consistently embodied the ideas of the old King, the revolution in France was immediately answered by fierce reaction in Spain. In proscribing all

things French Floridablanca attempted to sever the roots
of the Spanish intellectual movement, of which he himself
had until then been a distinguished member. One by one
the leading reformers were banished or imprisoned.[1] A
rigid censorship of all printed matter was imposed. Not only
was the importation of revolutionary literature from France
prohibited, but a ban was placed on all the main works
of eighteenth-century rationalism—on the Encyclopaedia,
the works of Voltaire, Rousseau, Montesquieu, Tamburini,
Gibbon, Bourgoing, and many other writers. The patriotic
and reform clubs which were so prominent in the preceding
decade were suppressed or muzzled. Every manifestation of
dissatisfaction or criticism of the administration was regarded as a symptom of sedition and treated accordingly.
By 1791 all newspapers except the official *Diario de Madrid*
and the police list of 'Articles Lost and Found' had been
prohibited. The intellectuals were dismayed; reaction and
bigotry again raised their heads in the hope of a new lease
of life for a system which had seemed doomed only yesterday.

SPANISH SOCIETY IN THE AGE OF THE FRENCH REVOLUTION

Few countries in Europe offered such apparently fool-
proof opportunities for the restoration of unenlightened
absolutism as did the Spain of Charles IV and Maria Luisa.
There was no question as yet of a bourgeois economy having
outgrown the forms of 'paternal' control by the State to
which it owed its revival. Apart from the enterprises established by foreign capitalists, most of the important factories
set up in Spain during the eighteenth century were run—
regardless of their persistent unprofitableness—by the
State, some even by the Church. Except in Catalonia and
Valencia, Spanish private enterprise was in the main confined to commerce—especially colonial commerce—but even
the wealthiest merchants did not abandon their ancient
guild organisation, nor could they have survived without
their monopoly privileges.[2]

Because there was little or no independent capitalist
development in Spain there was also no industrial proletariat
in the proper sense of the term. The independent artisans

[1] *E.g.* Count Cabarrús was arrested in June 1790, Jovellanos was banished to Asturias two months later, and in the following spring Campomanes was dismissed from office.　　[2] *v.* Appendix, note III, p. 216.

in the towns remained subject to the restrictions, but also to the protection of their guilds and fraternities. The largest factories were situated in the countryside and often combined an extensive employment of cottage labour with factory production proper. Above all, there could be no 'free' labour market, as long as the poor in the towns could rely on their daily ration of monastery soup without having to sell their labour power. On the other hand, the peasants and landless labourers in the country districts were so isolated from one another, and their conditions presented such extreme contrasts, that there was little solidarity between them.

Thus the poor in town and countryside retained their traditional conservatism. Their representative figures—the picaro in the seventeenth and the majo in the eighteenth century—passively reflected the general temper of the lower classes, but could not give direction to their dissatisfaction or to their spirit of independence. On the contrary, the more the masses suffered, the more fanatical did they become in their loyalty to Church and crown, which they associated with their memories of a better life in the past.

The nobility of eighteenth-century Spain was, as we have seen, sharply divided between a handful of immensely wealthy grandees, who spent most of their time at Madrid and rarely visited their estates, and an overwhelming majority whose economic status was often but little better than that of peasant proprietors. Although their poverty made the lower nobility inclined to side with the reformers on many issues, they were, as a class, resolutely opposed to any restriction of the system of entail, which they regarded as the only safeguard of their economic security. But the abolition, or at any rate severe restriction, of entail was one of the cardinal points of the reform programme, for it was recognised that the capitalist transformation of Spanish agriculture could only be achieved under the stimulus of free competition on the real estate market. This fundamental opposition overshadowed the notable services which many enlightened nobles rendered to the cause of reform, and as soon as the progressive party did in fact abolish entail (in the revolution of 1820–23) the lower nobility, as a body, turned to the side of reaction. During the period with which we are concerned in this chapter, however, the attitude of the lower nobility to the reformers had not yet taken any definite shape. Many intelligent members of this class sympathised with, or even participated in the movement—Jovellanos, for example, was an Asturian hidalgo,—but the great majority of these patriarchal squires were probably as much under the influence of the clergy as their peasants.

The greatest landowner in Spain, the Church, was as fundamentally opposed to the agricultural policy of the reformers as the nobility. But its enmity to the progressive movement was accentuated by the temporary setback it had suffered as a political institution during the reign of Charles III. The Church therefore eagerly exploited the opportunity which now presented itself for regaining its political influence and isolating the reformers from the mass of the people.

Thus the ideas of the reformers were far in advance of the actual conditions in Spain at the time of the French Revolution. Instead of reflecting the immediate, practical interests of a definite class in contemporary Spanish society, they were drawn from the general stream of European enlightenment on the one hand, and from the democratic tradition of medieval Spain on the other. For this reason also the reformers themselves were not a homogeneous group but a motley assembly of bourgeois lawyers and officials, aristocrats and clerics, united only in their patriotic enthusiasm. When the crown turned against them, they were utterly isolated. Yet they represented the future of Spain. Their programme of democratic reforms, when purged of its subservience to the interests of absolutism and fused with the native tradition, expressed the deeply rooted aspirations of the people which only a century of economic changes and political revolutions could render articulate.

PILLARS OF ABSOLUTISM

The real, if intangible, power of the progressive movement in the reign of Charles IV (1788–1808) is shown, above all, by the fact that it could not be crushed. Indeed, its influence paralysed the very power which could have crushed it. If old King Charles III had been the incarnation of enlightened absolutism, his daughter-in-law—for she alone counts in the new reign—was living proof that absolutism and enlightenment could no longer be united under the conditions created by the French Revolution. That in attempting to do so she corrupted both was the tragedy of

Queen Maria Luisa. While still Princess of Asturias, she and her husband had avidly supported many new ideas and fashions—including Goya's art—which the old King had viewed with suspicion. When the ruling classes of Europe recoiled in horror from the implications of enlightenment, as revealed in France, Maria Luisa could not wholly abandon the outlook and habits she had previously assumed. Torn between her resolution to defend the absolute power of the crown and her progressive inclinations, she could neither submit to the personal discipline—the show of piety, the moral cant, the haughty isolation, and the musty ecclesiastical atmosphere—befitting a Spanish queen, nor could she give free rein to her emancipated outlook. Her absolutism thus took the form of a capricious petticoat régime, while her enlightenment could find an outlet only in a cynical contempt for moral conventions. By making her personal conduct the scandal of the market-place, she rapidly succeeded in discrediting the very principle of hereditary monarchy and exposing to ridicule every sanction on which its claims are founded.

> How carols now the lusty muleteer?
> Of love, romance, devotion is his lay,
> As whilome he was wont the leagues to cheer,
> His quick bells wildly jingling on the way?
> No! as he speeds, he chants "Viva el Rey!"
> And checks his song to execrate Godoy,
> The royal wittol Charles, and curse the day
> When first Spain's queen beheld the black-eyed boy,
> And gore-faced Treason sprung from her adulterate joy.[1]

A half-wit king content to renounce the cares of State for the pleasures of the hunt; a queen, intelligent and unscrupulous in the exercise of her unlimited control over both king and country; an incompetent playboy raised to the dignity of Prime Minister at the age of twenty-four after a brief career as a guardsman, at one and the same time both the Queen's lover and the King's favourite—these were the guardians of the divine right of kings at a time when the principle of legitimacy was challenged by an ex-corporal dethroning half the monarchs of Europe. The poison of 'dangerous ideas' expressed in the fashion of majaism was destroying the old moral order at its roots, even before the new forces were strong enough to replace it.

---

[1] Byron, 'Childe Harold's Pilgrimage', Canto I, stanza xlviii (written towards the end of 1809, first published 1812).

'APRÈS NOUS LE DÉLUGE'

It is difficult to imagine a government more cynically corrupt than that of Maria Luisa and her minion Manuel Godoy. The Queen lost no opportunity of enriching the favourite, and she invested him with all the trappings of spurious magnificence. In April 1792 he was granted one of the most lucrative crown estates. Eight days later the Queen saw fit to mark the occasion of her first visit to church after the birth of her thirteenth child by raising its reputed father to the dignity of a grandee of the first class with the title Duke of Alcudia. Three months later Godoy was appointed member of the Royal Council, and in another four months Foreign Minister and head of the administration. In 1793 his combined salaries as minister, councillor, captain-general, and captain of the guards totalled 803,176 reals. Disastrous wars, the cessation of the American revenues, a policy of reckless inflation, and a series of bad harvests followed by epidemics reduced Spain to a state of economic prostration. But Manuel Godoy continued his meteoric career of aggrandisement. He increased the ever-growing list of his titles and emoluments by obtaining such sinecures as Grand Cross of all the four military orders, Secretary to the Queen, General Superintendent of Roads and Postal Services, President of the Royal Academy, the Natural History Cabinet, the Botanical Garden, the Chemical Laboratory, and the Astronomical Observatory. His income, which included a rental of one million reals from crown estates, finally exceeded that of all the judges in the realm of Spain added together. His fortune at the time of his fall was estimated at 40 million reals.

Favouritism and all that it implies was nothing new in the annals of Spain, or of any other absolute monarchy. But a queen prepared to tamper with the usage governing the legitimate succession, in order to secure her own position and that of her lover, at the very time when France was declared a republic—this was surely an innovation symptomatic of the spirit dominating the Spanish throne in the age of the Caprichos. Although that plot was foiled, it was repeated at a later date, and these intrigues were the real reason why the Spanish court was split into two viciously hostile cabals headed respectively by the Queen and the Prince of Asturias. Either party sought the support of

Napoleon for their plots and thus, ultimately, brought about the downfall of both.

Like master, like man. The bureaucracy, scarcely cleansed of the corrupt practices traditionally associated with the Hapsburgs, speedily relapsed into its former state of indolence and graft. Nepotism again became the order of the day. Multiplication of sinecures and fantastic salaries at the top were balanced by cuts and incredible arrears of pay in the lower ranks of the civil and military services. Between May and December 1799, for example, the latter received only three months' pay, and even that only in depreciated State securities. Godoy and his creatures had reduced the art of promotion to a system in which appointments, contracts, and other favours were bestowed on those whose causes were pleaded by the most attractive wives or daughters.

The results of this system are demonstrated by the number of place-holders who thronged the higher ranks of the armed forces. To celebrate the marriage of the Prince of Asturias in 1802 no less than 26 lieutenants-general, 57 field-marshals, and hundreds of colonels were newly created in a time of peace. At the end of the régime, when the navy had been allowed to rot until its effective force was reduced to scarcely more than 15 ships of the line and frigates, its higher command consisted of one Grand Admiral (Godoy), 2 admirals, 29 vice-admirals, 63 contre-admirals, 80 captains of ships of the line, and 134 captains of frigates. The corresponding complement for the army, which nominally counted 120,000 men, but in reality did not exceed 50,000 to 60,000 effectives (including 16,000 cavalry without horses), was one generalissimo (Godoy), 5 captains-general, 87 lieutenants-general, 127 field-marshals, 252 brigadier-generals, and 2,000 colonels.

ECONOMIC AND POLITICAL COLLAPSE

Under such conditions the structure of economic reform carefully raised during the preceding period of necessity collapsed. The public debt, which amounted to 2,693 million reals at the beginning of the reign, had risen to 7,204 million at its conclusion. Reckless inflation,[1] the sale of offices and privileges, increased taxation and the mortgaging of future

[1] The first steps down the slope of inflation had already been taken, however, during the last years of Charles III's reign. The budgetary balance achieved by Ferdinand VI had been upset by Charles's costly war with Britain, and an attempt was

revenues—all the old expedients of Hapsburg finance, and many new ones besides—could not arrest the headlong rush of Spain's economy into the abyss. When all had failed there was even a half-hearted attempt to apply some of the remedies long advocated by the reformers, such as the suppression of superfluous sinecures or the mobilisation of the property of the dead hand (1797–8). But the privileged classes raised such an outcry that the only result of these projects was confusion worse confounded. The true measure of the Spanish government's degradation is provided by a scheme it launched in 1799—little more than a decade after the death of Charles III. Despairing of its ability to cope with the tangle of its financial affairs, the State decided to hand over the administration of the national debt to the Church. It called upon an ecclesiastical junta under the presidency of Canon Juan Antonio Llorente, secretary of the Inquisition, to prepare a scheme for the execution of that proposal. This junta offered to raise the annual contribution from the Church to the State from 60 to 150 million reals, without any additional burden to itself, merely by taking the collection of its taxes into its own hands. In exchange for the privilege of raising its own taxes the Church would also be prepared to guarantee the interest and sinking fund of all State securities issued to the public. As soon as this offer became known the bonds appreciated 13 points (they were then 40 per cent below par), but the scheme was foiled by the opposition of the Madrid guilds.

Plague, famine, and the costs of war increased the miseries of the Spanish people during the last years of the reign. But this did not prevent the court from flaunting its corruption before its starving subjects in sumptuous festivals to celebrate the 'victory' of the favourite in the inglorious 'War of Oranges' against defenceless Portugal (May-June 1801) and the marriage of the Prince of Asturias (October 1802).

The economic difficulties of Spain were accentuated by the disastrous course of its foreign policy. Although violently opposed to the French Revolution,[1] the Spanish government did not join the interventionist coalition until

made to meet the deficit by means of State securities issued by the new Bank of San Carlos. But until the times of Charles IV inflation did not assume any serious proportions.

[1] Strictly speaking, this applies only to the time ending with the dismissal of Floridablanca. The few months of the Aranda régime saw a definite improvement in the relations between Spain and France, until the trial and execution of Louis made all friendly contact impossible.

after the execution of Louis XVI in 1793. The rout of the Spanish armies in the following year left the country at the mercy of the regicides who had occupied its northern provinces. When Spain escaped almost without territorial concessions at the Peace of Basle (1795), there was universal astonishment and rejoicing, and Manuel Godoy was rewarded with the official title of 'Prince of the Peace'.

But the peace which shed its lustre on the favourite destroyed the independent status of Spain in the affairs of Europe. Henceforth the Catholic Monarchy became the vassal of the Heretical Republic. Bound by the Treaty of San Ildefonso (October 1796) to support France with men and subsidies, Spain was drawn into the wars against England. These shattered its naval power and eventually led to the disintegration of its overseas empire. The last years of the reign were filled with plots of the camarilla to make Napoleon assure the future of Manuel Godoy by means of a principality in Portugal.

DAY-TO-DAY VACILLATIONS OF POLICY

The decline of Spain during the age of Maria Luisa and Manuel Godoy appeared, on the surface at least, as a sequence of violent oscillations. These we must examine if we are to understand the attitude of the reformers to the events of their time.

We have already noted that the crimes of the Queen and her favourite were as monstrous from the standpoint of absolutism as from that of bourgeois progress. Their administration aroused the hostility of the clerical party and of the masses under its control no less than the hatred and scorn of the intellectuals. To maintain their position the Queen and Godoy had to play off the one party against the other. Their régime, therefore, presented itself from day to day as a rapid succession of contradictory phases in which periods of overt reaction alternated with sterile attempts at reform.

The period began, as we have seen, with a consistent bent towards reaction in defence of absolutism under the guidance of Charles III's old minister Floridablanca. From the first, however, the efforts of that stern disciplinarian to maintain the integrity of the administration were foiled by the intrigues of the Queen. Deprived of his control of State

finance from the beginning of the reign and of the Ministry
of Justice in April 1790, he was dismissed and banished,
when, in February 1792, he attempted to enlighten the
King concerning the part played by Manuel Godoy. With
consummate skill the Queen then exploited the discontent
of the reformers by substituting for the man whom they
naturally regarded as a renegade, his traditional rival, the
francophile Count Aranda. There followed a period of
apparent liberal government. The censorship was relaxed,
and Spain adopted a more conciliatory attitude towards
France (March to December 1792). But from the first
Aranda had merely served as a cover for the real designs of
the Queen: the exaltation of her favourite, who replaced him
in November 1792.

The spring and summer of 1793 witnessed an outburst
of reactionary fervour to avenge the death of Louis XVI.
Spain at last joined the allied interventionists, but the incompetence of the government in conducting the campaign
quickly damped the enthusiasm of the Spaniards. Military
humiliation and dissatisfaction with the malpractices of the
government strengthened the appeal of liberal propaganda
from France to certain sections of the Spanish middle class,
the bureaucracy and the officers' corps. When old Count
Aranda was imprisoned in March 1794 for protesting against
the policy of Godoy, his confiscated papers revealed the
existence of a widespread agitation to remove the favourite.
Already in June a new plot was discovered, demanding
peace with France, the dismissal of Godoy, administrative
reforms, and the convocation of the Cortes. There followed
another spate of mass arrests and prosecutions, and it now
appeared that the clergy as well as the bourgeoisie were
working for a change of policy, for the Grand Inquisitor—
a strange companion for the liberal intellectuals—was among
those implicated in the proceedings. Wild demoralisation
followed the occupation of Northern Spain by the armies of
revolutionary France, and the latter part of 1794 and the
first months of the following year were filled with rumours
that the royal family were preparing to fly from the capital.

Then, suddenly, abject gloom turned to jubilation, and a
spirit of benevolence replaced the atmosphere of persecution, when, in July 1795, the terms of the Peace of Basle
became known. In the first flush of his new glory the Prince
of the Peace extended the policy of peace to all men of good-

will, even to the suspect Spanish reformers. The prosecution pending against Floridablanca was quashed, Aranda was released from jail, and so was Cabarrús, who was used for negotiations with France through his daughter, Mme. Tallien. Even Jovellanos was pardoned, and his fundamental treatise on the Agricultural Law—the charter of Spanish liberalism throughout the first half of the nineteenth century[1]—was published at State expense. Everything seemed transformed. Schemes for the regeneration of Spain, such as those contained in the open letters of Cabarrús to Jovellanos, were the general topic of the day.

But the brilliant outlook proved deceptive. By the middle of 1796 the real significance of 'the Peace' became apparent. War with England, which came in October, was its inevitable outcome. Humiliating defeats, the cessation of colonial tribute and trade,[2] and financial collapse followed by increased taxation for all classes, led early in 1797 to renewed intrigues against the government both from the right and from the left. It was the right wing which now engendered the most dangerous and certainly the most spectacular conspiracy. The clergy were genuinely alarmed at the new French sympathies and liberal aspect of the government. A plot was hatched by the Queen's confessor, the Grand Inquisitor, and the Archbishop of Toledo to arraign Godoy before the Holy Office. Even the Pope wrote to the Grand Inquisitor to support the scheme. But this letter and other incriminating documents fell into the hands of Napoleon,[3] who forwarded them to his new ally. As a result the three Spanish prelates were forthwith banished to Italy on the plea that they should "console the Holy Father in these trying times" (March 1797). But in the autumn pressure from the right was reinforced by the second bulwark of reaction, the upper bureaucracy organised in the Council of Castile, which addressed a strongly worded protest against a decree of the government to the King.

In this situation Godoy considered it expedient again to

---

[1] Its full title is: *Informe de la Sociedad Económica de esta Corte al Real y Suprèmo Consejo de Castilla, en el Expediente de la Ley Agraria. Memorias de la Real Sociedad Económica*, Madrid, vol. v, 1795.
[2] Even coastal shipping and the fishing industry were paralysed by the impotence of the Spanish navy to protect them against the British after the defeat of San Vicente in 1797.
[3] Napoleon was then on his Italian campaign which led, in the following year, to the sacking of the papal palaces, the arrest of the Pope, and the establishment of a republic in the former papal domain.

seek support from the left. So the surprised country awoke one morning in November 1797 to find that the esteemed leader of the reformers, Don Gaspar Melchor de Jovellanos, had been appointed Minister of Justice, and Don Francisco de Saavedra, another progressive intellectual, Minister of Finance. From the first, however, the new ministers found themselves in violent disagreement with Godoy, and the financial threats to feudal privilege which we have already discussed, and Jovellanos' projects for juridical and educational reform, caused such an outburst of opposition that the feeble hopes of progress were speedily dashed to the ground again. After repeated attempts had been made to poison them, both the reform ministers disappeared from public life in August 1798. Jovellanos retired to his native Asturias. Saavedra was too ill to attend to his duties; he was formally dismissed in the following February.

Nothing could be more characteristic of the reign than the situation which now followed. The opposition of both parties in Spain, and pressure from France, had compelled Godoy ostensibly to resign his position as Prime Minister in March 1798. Just then his infidelities had caused a temporary estrangement between him and the Queen, but when they had made up their quarrel he was able to exert an even more powerful influence from behind the scenes. On the surface, however, the dismissed reform ministers were replaced by two men representing the two parties in Spain at their most violent extremes. The resulting deadlock is described in the following terms by Baumgarten:

[Jovellanos was succeeded by a man] of whom it is no exaggeration to say that he desired to restore the evil days of the Hapsburg Philips with all their fanatical despotism. This minister, Don José Antonio Caballero, had made his career by marrying a lady-in-waiting of the Queen. He is described with rare unanimity by all Spanish historians as a compound of fulsome flattery, lack of character, implacable hatred for all men of principle and intelligence, shameless greed and unblushing despotism. Since he possessed every vice required at this court to the highest degree, he maintained his position as the evil demon behind the throne until the storm broke which swallowed up this Sodom in the floods of revolution. [But] at the same time when Caballero entered the Ministry of Justice, Don Mariano

Luis de Urquijo took up his duties as deputy for Saavedra in the departments of Finance and Foreign Affairs. This Urquijo was as passionately opposed to the power of the Church, and he shared the contempt of the Paris radicals for all traditional institutions with the same fanaticism which Caballero displayed in defence of every abuse. His elevation was not, however, due to these convictions, but to the fact that, personally, he was a worthy compère of Caballero, that he was to the highest degree unprincipled, arrogant, and immoral. Historians of every shade claim that he attained his position solely on account of his splendid figure and the impression it made on the Queen, who at that time was rivalling Godoy in promiscuity. Thus the chaotic vacillations of Spanish policy lead us back to the source which determined all its other features: protagonists of the most conflicting tendencies might well share the highest offices in the state, if only they were united in depravity and absolute submission to the whims of the Queen. It did not matter if in other respects the one was for, the other against Rome, the one for, the other against the Inquisition. Both could follow opposed aims with equal success, or else alternate in exercising the predominant influence. Neither attained any fundamental advantage for their respective policies; but both were in the highest degree successful in their common efforts to disrupt the power, honour, order, and prosperity of Spain.[1]

The clash between the tendencies supported by these rivals culminated after the death of the Pope in the autumn of 1799, when Urquijo re-established the old principle of the independence of the Spanish Church from Rome. A violent struggle followed, especially between the progressive, nationalist section of the clergy and the ultramontane reactionaries. But since the details so far recounted suffice to indicate the atmosphere of Spanish life in the age of the Caprichos, we can rest content to note that the last years of the régime witnessed one final swing of the pendulum in either direction.

The swing to the right lasted from 1801 to 1805. Urquijo having been dismissed in December 1800, Godoy was again supreme (though he still remained behind the scenes until 1802), and he now unreservedly supported the clerical party.

[1] *Op. cit.* vol. i.

A vicious campaign of political persecution began in March 1801. Many intellectuals, some aristocrats, and even three bishops were implicated, and the attack culminated in the arraignment of Jovellanos before the Holy Office (he remained imprisoned and suffered great hardships until the fall of his persecutors in 1808). But in the later years of this phase the military and economic disasters of the renewed war with England caused such a resurgence of popular hatred for the favourite that he made a final effort to curry favour with the left.

In 1806–7, the last two years of his administration, Godoy went out of his way to pose as a protector of the sciences and of general enlightenment. He suddenly evinced an intense interest in the humane principles of education advocated by Pestalozzi, and with a blaze of publicity he founded a Pestalozzi School in Madrid. (Goya had to paint him as protector of education with the new school and its pupils in the background.) He then decreed a surprisingly advanced reform of the Spanish Universities, and there were even renewed attempts to legalise the sale of certain properties of the Church and the nobility. But for our purposes the most important action of Godoy during this his last 'liberal' period was that he sanctioned the first official publication of Goya's 'Caprichos' by the Royal Chalcography (1806).

THE INTELLECTUALS UNDAUNTED

In many periods the cultural revival initiated by a vigorous economic and political advance did not attain maturity until the movements prompting it had been crushed by a temporary victory of reaction. Many great works of art and literature which mark outstanding stages of human progress do not, therefore, reflect the youthful enthusiasm of their authors, but a nostalgia which only their grim realism can preserve from resignation. This was the sequence of events in the earlier history of Spain, and the tragedy was repeated in the eighteenth century. Spanish science, political economy, history, literature, and the arts achieved their greatest triumphs after the movement which had sponsored them had collapsed and the hopes of the reformers had expired in a shambles of iniquity and corruption. Persecution, far from silencing the progressive intellectuals, steeled their convictions and enabled them to cast off the superficial optimism which had tended to cloud their vision in happier days. Moreover, the government itself made their task easier for them by its vacillations. The brief intervals of professed enlightenment at the palace enabled the reformers to publicise their views.

The prevailing chaos quickened the efforts of the Spanish intellectuals to apply the spirit of European rationalism to the specific problems of their country. Their intense preoccupation with history is evidence of a desire to understand the origin and nature of those problems. An historical approach colours every sphere of creative thought at this period. The History Academy counted the greatest figures of the time among its members. A critical study of Spain's past in all its aspects—economic, political, legal, social, and cultural—replenished the intellectual arsenal of the reformers and inspired them in their struggle for a better future.

Their outlook was given poetic form in an impassioned Ode which the young writer Manuel José Quintana (1772–1857) addressed to Juan de Padilla, the leader of the Castilian comuneros of 1520–21. This ode was written in May 1797, the year in which Goya first planned to publish the 'Caprichos'. Its argument may be summarised as follows:

When Padilla succumbed, through "shameful discord", the Spanish genius was abased. In vain six centuries of struggle to free the country from the Moorish foe: for now another, "more perfidious and tyrannous oppressor" fastened the yoke of slavery to the neck of Spain. Impoverished, ignorant, and fanatical, the Spaniards became the tools of despots who devastated Europe and made a desert of innocent America. "Three hundred years have passed", Padilla, breaking the silence of the grave, calls to the people of Spain, "and still you are bearing the chains of enslavement. . . . Tyranny and superstition have slowly devoured your very name. What use is now your pride? The world no longer trembles before you. Vile slaves—it derides you! But look! The chains of tyranny are falling before the fury of the nations. Will you, sunk in shameful dreams, be the last to join the noble cause? . . .

> No: que en violenta
> Rabia inflamada y devorante saña
> Ruja el león de España
> Y corra en sangre á sepultar su afrenta.
> La espada centellante arda en su mano,
> Y al verle, sobre el trono

Pálido tiemble el opresor tirano.
Virtud, patria, valor: tal fué el sendero
Que yo os abrí primero:
Vedle, holladle, volad: mi nombre os guie,
Mi nombre vengador à la pelea:
Padilla el grito de las huestes sea,
Padilla aclame la feliz victoria,
Padilla os dé libertad, la gloria!"

The last lines of Quintana's poem may roughly be translated:

No: May the Spanish lion
Roar in anger
And rise in rage to bury his dishonour
The flashing sword blazing in his hand—
And when he sees him, the pallid tyrant
Will tremble on his throne.
Virtue, patriotism, valour: that was the trail
I was the first to tread:
Follow its course: my name will guide you,
My name, the avenger in battle:
Padilla be the cry of the hosts,
Padilla will acclaim the joyous victory,
Padilla will give you liberty and glory!

Later in the same year, 1797, Quintana greeted Jovellanos' rise to power with another ode, and in 1805 he wrote
a patriotic play, 'Pelayo', which deals with the legendary
hero of that name, whose resistance to the Moors in the
Cave of Cavadonga, in the remote Asturian mountains (A.D.
718), was glorified by the Spanish chroniclers as the beginning of the re-conquest. Quintana's poem celebrating the
revolution which put an end to Godoy's power, 'A España,
despues la revolución de Marzo' (1808), will be found in
Menendez y Pelayo's anthology *Las Cien Mejores Poesias
de la Lengua Castellana*.

The message of Quintana's ode to Padilla had already
been expressed in a pamphlet entitled *Pan y Toros* (*Bread
and Bulls*). On 12 June 1792 Jovellanos had written to his
friend the historian, D. José Vargas Ponce (1760–1821),
suggesting that the latter should compose a dissertation on
the subject of bull-fights in which he should examine their
political, moral, and economic significance. It is probable
that Vargas Ponce delayed the final execution of the project
until 1796, for this date is given in the majority of early
manuscript and printed copies of *Pan y Toros*, which is
there described as "An Apologetic Oration on the Flourishing State of Spain in the Reign of King Charles IV, delivered
in the Plaza de Toros, Madrid, by Don Gaspar Melchor de

Jovellanos".[1] Numerous manuscript copies of the pamphlet circulated secretly among the progressive intellectuals during the next twenty-five years. The first printed edition was issued in Madrid in 1812 in the few months of liberty between the second and last occupations of the city by the French. The second edition was published during the following year in Cadiz, and several others were printed in various Spanish cities in 1820. In other words, whenever, throughout Goya's lifetime, the liberal revolution was victorious, *Pan y Toros* was issued in printed form to the public. It must therefore be regarded as one of the most important documents of that revolution, and it is particularly revealing for the outlook of Goya and his circle at the time when he was working on the Caprichos.

The first part of *Pan y Toros* is a bitterly satirical survey of Spanish life and Spanish institutions. Coming to Madrid, the author informs us he found the nation in all stages of development from infancy to senile decay. He found Spain "without population—without industry—without riches—without a patriotic spirit—and even without any acknowledged government: its fields waste and without cultivation; its villages immersed in ruin".

Its people were "without instruction, without knowledge; a brutal mob; a nobility which boasts of its ignorance; schools without principles; universities, the faithful depositories of the prejudices of the barbarous ages".

In appearance the country was "full of martial spirit . . . a body of generals, sufficient to command all the armies of the world; and, were there but soldiers in proportion, who might conquer all the regions of the universe"; but the military are only good for "curling their hair, bleaching their uniforms, regulating their paces to the tune of a country dance . . . and oppressing their fellow citizens".

He found Madrid "a metropole with more churches than houses; more priests than laymen; more altars than kitchens: nay in the dirty gateways, and in the meanest wine-houses may be seen pasteboard puppets, images of wax, fonts of holy water, and sacred lamps. . . . There is no corner of it but is covered with advertisements of novenaries, in which they never fail to give accounts of miracles as credible as the metamorphoses of Ovid."

As for the arts and sciences: "Philosophy is simplified

[1] *v.* Appendix, note IV, p. 217.

by the artificial abstracts of Aristotle, and, clearing it from the tedious observation of nature, they have made it the slave of sophistry. Morals . . . but slightly tinge the minds of those amongst us, who, forsaking philosophy, dabble in the law, until they fancy themselves legislators. . . . Poetry is despised as a symptom of insanity; and oratory as the trifling of idleness. . . . All professional men say that the studies of physics are folly and nonsense; and that a treatise *De Decisionibus curiae de Magistratibus*, or any such work, for the benefit of mankind, will never proceed from beyond the crucibles."

Even worse is the state of Castilian legislation which "recognises for its origin an age of the greatest ignorance and turbulence; an age in which the sword and the spear were supreme law, in which the man who had not the strength to lay low three or four at a thrust, was accounted infamous and little less than a beast; an age in which bishops commanded armies, and, instead of sheep, nourished wolves and leopards".

Then "the great Philip II in the palace of the Escorial" placed Spanish law on a new foundation: to him it owes "that despotic exterior with which it has been invested . . . the impregnable bulwarks of such numerous councils, whose forms are changed oftener than Proteus' . . . the many inexhaustible springs which from day to day have enriched it with more judges than laws, and more laws than human actions . . . that powerful phalanx of literary men, who, armed with their pens and enveloped in perennial wigs, overcome all in their way and trample down everything before them. . . . A new law is enforced in the twinkling of an eye, whilst the observance of an old one costs the dispute of a century . . . tribunals which hang twenty citizens in a day, and afterwards debate for twenty years on unharnessing the mules from a carriage."

Philip also gave to the political economy of Spain "its indefinable system and its astonishing regulations, which until now no one has understood . . . its singular sagacity in augmenting the royal revenues by increasing the contribution from the people . . . the happy thought of monopolising commodities, by which, through the simple oppressive system of buying cheap and selling dear, and preventing at the same time a too numerous assembly of sellers, all that you wish is at once gained. . . . Customs and excise are a most wonderful source of commerce and industry: independent of these, commodities would be sold at one-third cheaper, and the price of labour would be of some use in stamping their intrinsic value. . . . But for these duties of excise the kingdom would be without that astonishing multitude of counsellors, administrators, and mediators . . . custom-house officers and registrars . . . those most useful troops belonging to the royal revenue which form a numerous army of idlers and gossips; nor would treason and espionage be rewarded as a virtue. . . ."

In addition "every village possesses its municipal code, its municipal contributions, and its statutes, which are the basis of public happiness. It is a great satisfaction . . . to arrive, pierced with cold and wet, at an inn, and there to have to look for a dinner from the monopolisers of wine, oil, meat, salt, and other necessaries of life; to procure a fanega of barley, and to go to the corregidor to have it measured; to purchase a pellejo of wine, and to pay the price of a permit for taking it out of town; not at all to know whether you shall sleep in your own bed or a gaol, because the alcalde has the power of making you pass a miserable night there, without assigning any reason. . . ."

The writer then defines his attitude to religion, one of the key problems of the Spanish liberal revolution:

"Thousands of bishops Spain has seen, who, encumbered with civil and forensic forms, have never fulfilled the object of their mission, which was no other than to preach the Gospel to all the world, directing men by ways of peace, and not by that of legal process. The holy Scriptures, the daily bread of faithful souls, has been denied to the people, as a deadly poison; and puerile meditations and fabulous stories have been substituted in their room. The great influx of friars has made the dreams and deliriums of some foolish men and women pass for revealed truths, and disfigured the eternal edifice of the Gospel with temporal and corruptible supports. . . .

"The plain simplicity of the word of God has been obscured by the artificial commentaries of men. That which the Lord hath spoken, that all may understand it, has been thought hardly intelligible, but to one or two doctors, who, by torturing the meaning of the clearest expressions, have made them subservient to their purposes for creating upon them the idol of tyranny.

"The church has been constantly labouring to banish

from the faithful the prejudice of the particular virtue of images; and the ecclesiastics have never been weary in their endeavours to establish it.

"Religion is reduced to mere externals . . . we confess every month, yet remain in vice all our lives; we are Christians in name, but worse than Gentiles in our customs; in fine, we have a greater dread of the dungeon of the Inquisition, than of the tremendous justice of Jesus Christ!"

Only at this stage the author turns to the ostensible subject of his peroration. But in describing the bull-fights—"the links of our society, the food for our patriotism, the seminaries of our political manners"—he scales the heights of passionate accusation: "tavern-keepers and grandees, barbers and dukes, courtesans and matrons, laymen and clergy . . . the licentious fop who inflames the incautious damsel by indecent words and gestures; the base husband who places his wife by the side of her gallant; the coward majo who musters up all his insolence; the impudent manola who makes boast of her effrontery; ecclesiastics glad of the excuse for spending amongst sinners the price of their sins . . ."—all are crowded together, without reserve, "in this august amphitheatre . . . where luxury, profligacy, shamelessness, libertinism, stupidity, and, in short, every vice which disgraces human nature, hold their court".

The most striking feature of this section of the pamphlet, and one which is equally evident in the 'Caprichos', is the changed evaluation of majaism. In the sainetes and the tapestry cartoons majaism appeared as an exuberant manifestation of popular virility, in *Pan y Toros* and the 'Caprichos' it has become a symbol of national degradation —the majo has again become a picaro.

After comparing the "festive Spaniards" with the "grave English" and the "volatile French"—the "Idolators of freedom, who think a single link of servitude intolerable"— the author of *Pan y Toros* concludes:

O happy Spain!—O my happy country! thus distinguished from all other nations of the world! Happy ye, who shutting your eyes to the cavillings of philosophers, only open them to the wise sophistry of your own sages! Happy ye, who content with your own estate, envy not that of others; who accustomed to govern nobody, obey all! Happy ye, who knowing the just value of letters patent, prefer it to merit and virtue!

Happy ye, who have discovered that merit and virtue are entailed upon the nobility, and that it is impossible to possess either without the appellation of 'Don'.

Pursue these enlightened maxims—continue in this prosperity—and be (what indeed you are now) the *ne plus ultra* of the fanaticism of the ages.

Despise (as you have hitherto done) the idle babbling of envious strangers—abhor their turbulent maxims—condemn their free opinions—prohibit all their books which have not passed the 'holy table'— and sleep in peace, lulled by the hisses that deride you!

THE CAPRICHOS

It was in 1797, one year after the probable date of *Pan y Toros*, that Goya first intended to publish the Caprichos.[1] A drawing for the plate which he then proposed to use as the frontispiece bears the inscription: 'Idioma universal dibujado y grabado p^r Fr^co de Goya, año 1797', and on the lower margin the further words: 'El autor soñando. Su yntento solo es desterrar bulgaridades perjudiciales y perpetuar con esta obra de Caprichos el testimonio sólido de la verdad' (Universal language drawn and etched by Francisco de Goya in the year 1797. The artist dreaming. His sole intention is to banish harmful vulgarities and to perpetuate with this work of the Caprichos the solid testimony of truth). What these 'vulgarities' were he explained when he announced the publication of his work, as finally completed, in the *Diario de Madrid* of 6 February 1799:

"Convinced that the criticism of errors and vices, though primarily the function of rhetorics and poetry, may also serve as the subject matter for painting, the artist has selected from the extravagances and follies common to all society and from the prejudices and frauds, sanctioned by custom, ignorance, or interest, those which seemed most suitable for ridicule and stimulating as images."[2]

The commentary, which Goya later added to explain these 'extravagances and follies, prejudices and frauds' in detail, seems at first sight commonplace. It consists of brief moral sentences, like popular proverbs and 'refranes', and, no doubt, often taken from them. But the corresponding

[1] Goya began to work on the Caprichos towards the end of 1793; cf. *infra*, pp. 102, 103.
[2] It is sometimes claimed that not Goya, but his friend the art-historian Cean Bermúdez, was the author of this announcement. But even if Bermúdez was responsible for its phrasing, Goya obviously endorsed its substance.

etchings belong to 'the most inspiring inventions of the human spirit'.[1] What is the reason for this discrepancy? All the passion of a great artist living fully and unreservedly in his time is concentrated in the engraved image. The concrete events of the day, that succession of follies, injustices, and oppressions summarised earlier in this chapter, and the emotions of indignation, hatred, revolt, which they aroused, when recollected in the reverie of creation, assumed the shape of universal symbols.[2] To those who had lived through the same events—and to a generation like our own, whose experiences have been so similar—Goya's symbolism contains few riddles. A hint suffices to evoke its meaning. That is the function of the captions, which are terse and often subtle, and also of the later commentary, which is commonplace, because really superfluous.[3] Nevertheless, captions and commentary together make it easier to grasp the rhythmic sequence of ideas which determined the pattern of the whole cycle, and the following analysis is therefore largely based on them.

[1] Cf. Dvořák, *Eine illustrierte Kriegschronik. Gesammelte Aufsätze zur Kunstgeschichte*, Munich, 1929. This article, one of the most profound appreciations of Goya ever written, was first published in 1916. It is, unfortunately, marred by the fact that Dvořák took von Loga's interpretation of Goya's career (*Goya*, 1903) at its face value. Loga claimed to have based his view on documentary evidence—a series of letters Goya had written to a former school friend employed at the cathedral of his native Saragossa, first published by F. Zapater, *Noticias biographicas*, 1868—but he failed to appreciate the special nature of that evidence and to correlate it with the changing conditions of the time. *E.g.* the main document quoted to establish Goya's devotion to the king is undated; Zapater attributes it to 1800, but Sánchez Cantón has proved from internal evidence that it cannot have been written later than 1791; hence it proves nothing about Goya's attitude during and after the period of the Caprichos. But to describe Goya, without any qualification, as a devout churchman and loyal servant whose whole happiness consisted in pleasing his royal masters, is as fantastic as to picture him, with the romantics, as a sinister stage-revolutionary and nihilist.

[2] The violent aversion which the Victorian critics felt for the Caprichos is as typical as the profound influence the series exerted over their contemporaries in France. In 1872 Ruskin, it seems, accomplished what the Inquisition had been foiled in doing: he and his bookseller Ellis burnt a fine set of the Caprichos with all due ceremony. On this and on P. G. Hamerton's similar attitude cf. H. Stokes, *Goya*, London, 1914. On Goya's influence in nineteenth-century France cf. the essay by Jean Adhémar in *Bibliothèque Nationale*: 'Goya, Exposition de l'œuvre gravé', etc., Paris, 1935.

[3] Each of the Caprichos has a descriptive caption of slogan-like terseness. At a later date Goya himself wrote a brief commentary expanding these slogans. The passages quoted in the text are taken both from the original captions and from Goya's own commentary, which is now preserved in the Prado. The excitement caused by the Caprichos is shown by the fact that there are a number of contemporary commentaries of unknown authorship which are far more radical and, above all, more personal in their interpretation. The most interesting of these, written by someone evidently aware of Goya's own commentary, was reprinted by the Comte de la Viñaza (*Goya*, Madrid, 1887), and partially by Paul Lefort (*Gazette des Beaux Arts*, 1867, 1868) and P. d' Acchiardi (*Les Dessins de F. Goya au Musée du Prado*, Rome, 1908). I have quoted some of its identifications in the text.

The 'Caprichos' are divided into two main parts having different, though overlapping, themes. Each part is introduced by a self-portrait. The first, comprising the etchings from plate 2 to plate 36, expounds the follies and extravagances of private life as exemplified by the relations between the sexes in a class society: "They say yes and give their hand to the first who comes". "What sacrifice! As is often the case, the bridegroom is not exactly desirable, but he is rich, and the liberty of an unhappy child must purchase the maintenance of a starving family. That is the way of the world." "There have been many disputes whether men or women are worse. The vices of both come from their bad education. Where custom demands that the men shall be perverse, the women will be the same." "The world is a masquerade. Face, clothing, voice, all are put on. All wish to appear what they are not, all deceive and no one recognises his fellow" (figs. 12-18).

Illicit love with all its passions and miseries, marriages of convenience, secret assignments, nocturnal adventures, flirtation, abduction, adultery, and prostitution provide the leading theme of this part of the 'Caprichos': it is the theme of majaism, but of majaism unmasked and deprived of its gaiety, the theme of love perverted and brutalised by the overriding laws of a society which turns everything sacred into a commodity of the market-place. ". . . et puis toutes ces blanches et sveltes Espagnoles que de vieilles sempiternelles lavent et préparent soit pour le sabbat, soit pour la prostitution du soir, sabbat de la civilisation!"[1] wrote Baudelaire.

The cup of human misery is emptied to its dregs. From time to time the tension rises to breaking point. Thus in plates 5 to 10 three different flirtation scenes are abruptly followed by a terrifying kidnapping picture (fig. 16), and the sequence reaches its climax in plate 9, a man in despair holding the lifeless body of a woman; and plate 10, the man mortally wounded in a duel sinking into the arms of his anguished mistress. Or, to take another example, the prostitution sequence: 'All will fall'—birds with men's heads are decoyed and plucked by the girls (No. 19); 'Already they are plucked'—they are swept from the house with brooms (No. 20); 'How one plucks them'— the girls in turn are

---

[1] Charles Baudelaire, 'Quelques caricaturistes étrangers'. First published in the periodical *Le Présent*, 15 October 1857; reprinted in the volume *Curiosités esthétiques* in the collected edition of 1868, vol. ii, pp. 426 *et seq. v.* also Appendix, note VI, p. 220.

plucked by lawyers with cat's faces (No. 21); 'Poor little ones'
—the macabre scene of their arrest (No. 22); and as a culmination the two frightful Inquisition scenes ('From this
dust', No. 23, and 'No remedy', No. 24) (fig. 17).

Interspersed between the successive variations of this
theme there are other follies and extravagances of private life:
the miser (No. 30); bad education (Nos. 3, 4, and 25: 'The
child is naughty and the mother cross—which is worse?');
gluttonous monks (No. 13); the drunkard whose house is on
fire (No. 18); brigands (No. 11); or the quack dentist[1] (No.
33). And again there are points at which the dramatic tension rises to a climax: the horrifying 'Hunt for teeth' (No. 12:
"The teeth of a hanged man are most effective for the arts
of sorcery. Without this ingredient nothing can succeed. A
pity that the people believe such trash" (fig. 14)); and the
two stirring prison scenes (No. 32, 'Because she was too
yielding'; and No. 34, 'They are overcome by sleep: Do
not awaken them. Sleep is the only consolation of the
unfortunate' (fig. 18)).

That certain plates in this first part of the Caprichos
were identified by Goya's contemporaries with particular
pieces of scandal is not surprising in view of the character
of the régime. To the Madrileños No. 5, for example ('Birds
of a feather', a lady and her beau with two old women
crouching in the background (fig. 12)), would naturally
recall the story which the poet Southey picked up on a brief
visit to Spain in 1796:

> About two years ago the washer-women of Madrid
> were possessed of a spirit of sedition, and they insulted
> her Majesty in the streets: "You are wasting your
> money upon your finery and your gallants—while we
> are in want of bread!" . . . The ringleaders were con-
> demned to perpetual imprisonment. The Queen, how-
> ever, has never entered Madrid since. . . .[2]

Nor need one attach too much weight to Goya's own
claim when he wrote in his announcement, already quoted,
in the *Diario de Madrid*: "Since most of the subjects
illustrated in this work are purely fictitious, sensible people
should be lenient with their failings". Nevertheless, Baudelaire was perfectly justified in claiming that even someone

---

[1] The drunkard and the quack dentist are also, of course, obvious political symbols.
[2] *Robert Southey, Letters written during a Short Residence in Spain and Portugal,*
Bristol, 1797.

who knows nothing of the historical background of the Caprichos, a simple lover of the arts who has never heard of Godoy, King Charles or Maria Luisa, cannot fail to be deeply moved by Goya's designs. This he attributed to Goya's originality, to the fullness and rightness of his means of expression and to that fantastic atmosphere in which he bathed all his subjects. What distinguishes these etchings from ephemeral caricatures, even though they are, as it were, 'suspended' over particular events, what gives them the quality of a universal language (of '*le comique éternel*' instead of *le comique fugitif*), is, Baudelaire says, their resemblance to those recurring dreams which haunt our slumbers periodically.[1]

This observation is particularly convincing in the light of Goya's drawings (which Baudelaire never saw). The first versions of several Caprichos (as well as some ideas for them which he later discarded) are contained in a sketchbook Goya used during a visit to Sanlúcar, one of the Andalusian estates of the Duchess of Alba. To this estate she retired after her husband's death in June 1796, and Goya accompanied her. Fragments of two separate sketchbooks he used during this visit, which probably lasted until the spring of 1797, have survived. They contain idyllic 'maja' episodes in the spirit of the later tapestry cartoons, as well as some intimate subjects, such as a lady at her toilet, stepping out onto the balcony in her nightgown after rising, holding her siesta, dressing, or receiving guests. The features of the Alba (whose most splendid portrait Goya also painted at this time) are unmistakeable in several drawings of both groups, and she also appears in some Capricho-like paintings, two of which are, however, dated 1795. But surprisingly enough, precisely the most intimate drawings reappear, completely transformed in mood and with altered features, as some of the brothel scenes of the Caprichos. The sinister print of a girl pulling up her stocking (Capricho 17, fig. 13) is a case in point.[2] Moreover, the Duchess also appears in the last symbolic part of the series. In No. 61, 'Volaverunt' (fig. 21), she floats through the air borne by three crouching witches, a splendid apparition with butterfly-wings attached to her

---

[1] Cf. Appendix, note VI, pp. 220-21.
[2] Cf. H. Rothe, *Francisco Goya, Handzeichnungen*, Munich, 1943, and Sánchez Cantón *op. cit.*, who identifies a second, younger woman, probably a servant of the Duchess, in some of the Sanlúcar drawings (in 1797 the Duchess of Alba was thirty-five years old, Goya fifty-one).

head. In a further plate, which Goya suppressed when he published the Caprichos, this figure reappears (fig. 22). Her head is winged as before, but it is double-faced. With one face she caresses the forehead of the artist himself, who is fervently clutching her right arm. The other face looks back to a second lover who cowers behind her and raises a finger to his lips in a gesture of secrecy. Her left hand is placed in the hand of this rival by her servant, another two-faced woman. A castle-in-the-air fills the background. In the foreground a grinning mask resting on two money-bags appears as a hideous sexual symbol. Before it a viper hypnotises a frog.

The secret of Goya's power can now be more closely defined. He did not castigate the vices and follies of his fellow-men abstractly as a moralist. But he experienced them in his own life, as an enjoying and suffering human being. His was a time when age-old patterns of behaviour were rendered obsolete by new forces reshaping the material conditions of life. In majaism the ancient barriers between the classes seemed, for a moment, swept aside. And in his own passion for the Duchess of Alba Goya himself seemed to have realised that new, ideal relationship, where men and women would meet as human beings, and no longer as master and servant, noble and commoner. But in both cases the ideal proved to be an illusion. What began as a beautiful dream ended as a hideous farce. The new conditions of life created even greater barriers between men than those they had destroyed. From Goya's own most intimate joys and sorrows there thus arose those nightmare images which made his soul a mirror of his time.

It is not difficult to conceive how inflammatory such a portrayal must have been in a society ruled by the court of Maria Luisa. But 'vices and follies' only represented a part of the character of that society. To complete his picture Goya had to add its 'prejudices and frauds'. Both sides were combined in the contemptible figure of the 'Prince of the Peace'. He is therefore the hero of the six plates, Nos. 37 to 42, which form a link between the first and last parts of the Caprichos, and in which he appears, significantly enough, in the character of an ass.

The sequence begins with a plate showing a young donkey being taught the A B C by an old ass (No. 37). Goya's own caption and commentary are as follows: 'Does the pupil know more' (than his teacher?)—"It is difficult to tell whether he knows more or less. But in any case the teacher could not be more grave." The commentary published by Viñaza runs:

> It is clear that Plate 37 can only allude to the Prince of the Peace during his earliest period of favour. Destined from the beginning for the elevated role he was later to play, his political education was entrusted, first, to Acuña, now the archbishop of Santiago, shortly afterwards to Barradas, and finally to Mollinedo, an old clerk in the department of Foreign Affairs, whose long service was taken as proof of great knowledge and who must have been greatly astonished when he was called upon to teach what he most certainly never knew."

In the following design a monkey sings and plays the guitar to another old ass with an expression of fatuous admiration, while two men behind his back applaud mockingly: "Bravissimo! If ears suffice to hear, no listener could be more intelligent. But it is to be feared that he applauds what has no sound" (Goya). Godoy, now a monkey, flatters the old ass, his king.

It is the next plate (39) which establishes the correctness of this interpretation beyond doubt. A young ass in human clothes is sitting at a table and looking at a large book containing illustrations of many other asses. Goya writes: "Back to his grandfathers.—This poor animal has been turned insane by the genealogists and heraldry experts. He is not the only one!" The second commentator informs us that a genealogical tree had been faked for Godoy, according to which he was descended from the Gothic kings and related to the reigning family by numerous ties (fig. 23).

Godoy the quack, the bane and ruin of Spain (a theme already implicit in the quack of No. 33), is exposed to the full force of Goya's scorn in plate 40, the ass-doctor at a deathbed asking: 'Of what illness will he die?'—"The doctor is excellent, thoughtful, meditative, pensive and grave. What more do you want?"

And the excellent, meditative, and reflective donkey must naturally find a monkey who will paint his image in the shape of a lion (No. 41). "No more, no less.—He did well to have his portrait painted. For thus those who neither knew nor ever saw him will know who he is."

But even in this sequence Goya, it seems, wished to emphasise that it was not the personal character, however contemptible, of the favourite which really mattered, but the whole corrupt system which produces his kind. For he concluded this transitional series with a design in which two men representing the people are groaning under the weight not of one, but of two donkeys. And he chose as his caption the first words of a popular refrain which runs: 'You who are unable to bear the load, carry me on your shoulders' (No. 42).

The function of these designs as a connecting motive is expressed not only in their content but also in their form. The style of the first part of the 'Caprichos' is predominantly realistic. The element of caricature is relatively subdued. Symbolic images only appear sporadically, as in the birds of the prostitution sequence. In the transitional Godoy designs symbolism is used throughout, but it is rendered realistically and confined to two images: the ass and the monkey. But in the concluding part of the 'Caprichos' symbolic meaning and grotesque imagery are fused in a wild turmoil of fantastic visions.

This last sequence begins with a separate frontispiece, the design already mentioned, which Goya apparently intended to use in 1797 as the initial plate of the whole set (figs. 25, 26). Again the artist appears himself. But now he has fallen asleep at his desk. In the darkness behind him there arise the nightmare visions of his dreams: owls, bats, giant cats, and other monsters. One has picked up a pencil and is holding it towards the prostrate artist. But the original inscription has been replaced in the etching by the caption:

'El sueño de la razón produce monstruos'

(The sleep of reason produces monsters).

And Goya explained this statement by adding:

"La fantasia abandonada de la razón, produce monstruos imposibles: unida con ella, es madre de las artes y origen de sus maravillas."

(Fantasy abandoned by reason produces monsters: united with reason she is the mother of the arts and the source of their marvels.)

What are these monsters that assail the artist when

reason sleeps, monsters that must "vanish at the break of
dawn" (plate 71, fig. 34)? Passion guided by reason inspired
the finest deeds of the Spanish people, produced the marvels
of Spanish art. But abandoned by reason, faith, selfless devotion, loyalty, heroism, the search for truth, and the passionate love of freedom are turned into their evil negations:
superstition, bigotry, selfishness, base flattery, cowardice,
heresy-hunting, and servility. By the arts of black magic an
army of parasitical monsters, witches, and sorcerers have
converted what was noble and generous into what is base
and degrading. To support their own indolence, they have
forged the simple faith of the people into a chain which
enslaves them. 'They spin fine, and not even the devil can
unravel the plots they contrive' (No. 44). 'It seems that
man is born and lives only to be sucked dry' (No. 45:
"There is much to be sucked"). Who are these devils, Goya
asks, and he answers: *Devils are those who do evil, or prevent
others from doing good, or those who do nothing at all"*
(No. 78).

Countless are the disguises and expedients of these
monsters—prelates and friars, spies and inquisitors, bureau-
crats and petty officials, noblemen and usurers, sycophantic
place-holders high and low—who plot to suck the people
dry. In the artist's nightmare their fantastic shapes assume
the fleeting uncertainty, the quality of rapid change and
varied impersonation, the dim vagueness alternating with
sudden precision, which are common to all dream images.
That is why it is unnecessary to unmask every one of the
numerous species participating in this wild sabbath of
witches: the spinners, suckers, blowers, the 'nice and harm-
less little gnomes', the chinchilla rats, 'Fat Mama' and the
'Grand Master of the Seminary of Barahoma'. But many of
them are clearly identified. For instance, the 'blowers', for
the Spanish word 'soplones' means stool pigeon, spy, as
well as blower: "The blowing witches are the most disgust-
ing of the whole pack of devils and the least intelligent in
their art; if they knew anything, they would not be blowers"
(No. 48, fig. 27).

Or take the 'Chinchilla rats' of plate 50: Two limp
figures are shown, one lying on the ground, the other apparently leaning against a wall. Everything about them
betrays indolence and utter indifference to their surround-
ings. Their arms seem clamped to their sides, their eyes are

closed and huge padlocks cover their ears. All their mental
and bodily faculties seem bent on the sole task of opening
their mouths so that they may be spoon-fed by a man with
ass's ears who is himself blindfolded: 'Those who hear
nothing, know nothing, do nothing, belong to the numerous
family of the Chinchillas, which was never good for anything' (fig. 28). In one of the preliminary drawings for this
etching the strange garments of these 'Chinchillas' are even
more clearly marked with armorial bearings than in the
print. Moreover, Goya provided a further key to the meaning of this design through the curious title which he chose
for it. It is taken straight from Le Sage's *Gil Blas*, where
the pathetic representative of the old nobility is Captain
Don Hanibal de Chinchilla.[1] It will be remembered that that
old hidalgo "valued himself, above all, on being delicate in
point of honour". Nevertheless, he finally obtained his long-
sought-for pension through the intervention of the seductive
Señora Sirena, "a nightingale of Aragon" whom the first
secretary to the Duke of Lerma kept "in a cage near the
court". Unlike Goya's Chinchillas, Don Hanibal had, however, rendered real service to his country, and the picture
which Le Sage draws of him is much more sympathetic
than Goya's savage satire. This is a good example of
Goya's method of conveying a meaning which could not be
openly expressed under the prevailing conditions of censorship. It also illustrates the intimate fusion of design and
caption, of pictorial symbol and literary allusion, in the
Caprichos.

'Las Chinchillas' are not the only gibe at the expense of
the nobility in the Caprichos: the theme of the *mariage
à la mode* is embodied in the cruel satire of No. 57, 'The
Filiation' (*i.e.* register of descent): "The aim here pursued
is to coax the wealthy bridegroom by showing him by means
of executors' deeds who were the parents, grandparents,
great-grandparents and great-great-grandparents of the
senorita. And who is she? Later he will see her as she really
is." And it is difficult to conceive of a more savage attack
on Rotten Row snobbery than the plate with the two
composite monsters (one a man with the head and talons of
a vulture, the other a ferocious-looking old brute with ass's
ears) who ride on creatures half bear, half donkey, gravely

---

[1] Book VII, chapter 12. Isla's Spanish translation of *Gil Blas* had first appeared in
1783; another edition was issued in Valencia in 1791–2.

parading their importance before an enthusiastic multitude (No. 63). Goya's own caption and commentary are: 'Look, how grave they are!'—"This print shows that here are two witches of rank and authority who have gone out on horseback to take a little exercise" (fig. 29). The last illustration of this theme is the pompous 'Blimp' of plate 76, who exclaims: 'Your excellency is . . . ahem, as I was saying . . . egad! Mind you! Or else . . .'—"His stars and batons have made this fool believe that he is a superior being, and he abuses his office by annoying all who know him; arrogant, vain and insolent with his subordinates, knavish and vile to those who are more competent than he" (fig. 30).

The game of legal robbery and extortion is not a peaceful one. The monsters fight over its spoils. ". . . friendship is the daughter of virtue; the wicked can be accomplices but never friends", Goya wrote in his commentary to No. 62, which Baudelaire described in the following terms:

> . . . un paysage fantastique, un mélange de nuées et de rochers. Est-ce un coin de Sierra inconnue et infréquentée? un échantillon du chaos? Là au sein de ce théâtre abominable, a lieu une bataille acharnée entre deux sorcières suspendues au milieu des airs. L'une est à cheval sur l'autre; elle la rosse, elle la dompte. Ces deux monstres roulent à travers l'air ténébreux. Toute la hideur, toutes les saletés morales, tous les vices que l'esprit humain peut concevoir sont écrits sur ces deux faces, qui, suivant une habitude fréquente et un procédé inexplicable de l'artiste, tiennent le milieu entre l'homme et la bête[1] (fig. 33).

Often the lesser demons are the victims of a mightier devil. The gambler's destiny raises its favourites to the heights amidst fireworks and smoke, only to abase them as rapidly again (plates 56 and 77).

Worse than all the other evils which haunt the artist's nightmare are superstition and its exploitation by a sycophantic rabble.[2] Priests and monks—"moines bâillants, moines goinfrants, têtes carrées d'assassins se préparant à matines, têtes rusées, hypocrites, fines et méchantes comme des profiles d'oiseaux de proie"[3]—throng the latter pages of the 'Caprichos'. "Will you swear to obey and respect

[1] Baudelaire *op. cit.*
[2] The international scope of anti-clericalism at that time is confirmed also by the publication, in 1796, of Diderot's *La Religieuse* (written in 1760) and of Lewis's *Monk* in 1795.　　　　　[3] Baudelaire *op. cit.*

your masters and superiors? to sweep their attic, to spin tow, beat tambourines, howl, scream, fly, cook, grease, suck, bake, fry, to do everything whenever it is demanded?" ask the two arch-sorcerers, invested in all the insignia of obscurantism, in the etching entitled 'Devota profesión' (No. 70). And with all the meekness of blind faith the figure seated on the shoulders of an ass-eared monster replies: "I swear it". To which the masters answer: "It is well, daughter, you are a witch now. Congratulations."

In his hatred for the enslavers of his people Goya occasionally drops the mask of elaborate symbolism and returns, for a fleeting instant, to the crystalline clarity of his realistic style. This happens even in the second part of the Caprichos, in three prints which show the suffering people themselves, and not their exploiters: The first is the design (No. 73) showing an idle girl standing in front of an old couple who are winding wool (fig. 37). This picture illustrates the remarkable text: 'If he who works hardest has the least enjoyment, he is quite right: it is better to be idle'. One is reminded of the traditional 'cartagenera':

> Obrero, por qué trabajas
> si para ti no es el producto;
> para el rico es la ventaja,
> y para tu familia el luto.
>
> (Labourer, why do you work,
> if the fruits are not for you;
> the profit is for the rich man,
> and for your family, only sorrow.) [1]

The next plate, but one, in the 'Caprichos' (No. 75) is an impassioned exposure of the misery caused by the clerical ban on divorce: a man and a woman, tied to one another with a strong rope (the feet of the woman being shackled as well), are struggling violently to free themselves, while a monstrous, bespectacled owl hovers above them: 'Is there no one who will untie us?' (fig. 36).

Lastly, there is the young woman with the child and the old people in the background kneeling devoutly before an empty monk's cowl which is spread menacingly over the trunk and branches of a dead tree. "Such is superstition that a whole people tremblingly reveres a piece of wood which wears the costume of a saint!" is the comment of the Viñaza manuscript on the plate which Goya

[1] Lloyd *op. cit.*

entitled 'What a tailor can do!' (No. 52, fig. 35).[1]

Another literary allusion was most probably the source of Capricho 58 (fig. 38). It represents a scene reminiscent of the Boccaccio novel (No. III, 8) in which a wretched husband is kept in a monastery dungeon under the delusion that he has died and is suffering the torments of purgatory, while the prior is seducing his wife. In Goya's print the husband is kneeling on the ground, clasping his hands and looking in terror at a vicious monk who is approaching with a clyster-pipe to give him a purge. The victim is surrounded by three other, equally repulsive friars, one of whom is holding a light which picks out the five faces and the cowl of the foremost monk in ghostly white from the surrounding darkness. Hidden in the gloom to the left of the main group is a veiled woman. In the background two ogres, one with monstrous horns, are dimly discernible. The contrast of terror and brutal mockery, the obscene laughter echoing through the musty stillness of the vault, the atmosphere of vice triumphant over dumb credulity—make this design a flaming protest against the frauds and insults with which a cynical minority maltreats the people. And the whole bitterness of the design is concentrated in its caption: 'Trágala, perro' ('Swallow it, dog!').

Twenty-one years after the first publication of the Caprichos the Spanish people hurled the same insult back at their oppressors. 'Trágala, perro' is the refrain of one of the most popular songs of the 1820 revolution:

> Dicen que el trágala es insultante
> pero no insulta más que al tunante

Original as was Goya's conception in this design, it was nevertheless anticipated in a surprising manner by the frontispiece to an English pamphlet entitled *Mumbo Chumbo: a Tale. Written in the Antient Manner, recommended to Modern Devotees.* This pamphlet was printed in 1765 for T. Becket and P. A. De Hondt, near Surrey Street, Strand, London. The frontispiece is signed "S. Wale del. C. Grignion. Sculp." and is described as follows, under No. 4136, in the British Museum Catalogue of Prints and Drawings, Division I, *Political and Personal Satires*, vol. iv, p. 366:

"An engraving showing a huge, disproportionate idol of quasi-human form, wearing a clerical gown only, standing on a wooden pedestal which is furnished with concealed wheels. This effigy has an expression of fury on the face, emits fire and smoke from its mouth, and stretches forth its hands to take an infant which is offered as a sacrifice to it by a young mother. Four other women are kneeling before the figure in abject terror or extreme supplication. Two clergymen stand behind the figure and seem to prompt its movements.

"This design was intended to illustrate 'Mumbo Chumbo', as above, a poem which professes to display the superstitious and wicked conduct of 'Juggling Priests' in imposing on the women of an Arabian tribe. To appease their consciences the women of the tribe are represented as offering their children to the monster. These proceedings are denounced as anti-Christian, and opposed to the goodness of God."

Y mientras dure esta Canalla
no cesaremos de decir trágala.
Trágala, trágala, trágala, perro
trágala, trágala, trágala, perro.

(They say that "trágala" is insulting
but it insults none but scoundrels
And as long as this Canaille survives
we shall not cease to say "trágala".)

To appreciate the full significance of this song, one must take the text in conjunction with its melody. There could be no greater contrast. For gay exuberance the tune of 'Trágala, perro' is unsurpassed in the rich folk-song tradition of revolutionary Spain. We shall see at a later stage why that is so. But although at the moment of liberation the people are swept off their feet by their joy, rather than by their urge for revenge[1] their enemies were struck to the quick by the revolutionary implications of 'Tragala perro'. Not only the defeated reactionaries, but also the more respectable right-wing liberals were outraged by this song. Riego and his friends caused a political scandal by singing it after their triumphal entry into Madrid. Even the sober Baumgarten loses his usual restraint when he speaks of the "infamous Tragala". Yet it survived in the tradition of the people, and, fortunately, it has been recorded with other songs of the Spanish Republican Army, for *Chant du Monde* ('La Voz de España', No. 1001).

There can be little doubt that a thorough study of the incomparably rich treasure of contemporary 'refranes', 'coplas', and other popular ditties would throw an equally revealing light on many other Goya prints and drawings which still remain obscure. An artist so profoundly in tune with the moods and aspirations of his people could not help transposing those topical snatches of doggerel, which provided the texts for the haunting songs and dances of Spain, into his own medium. And it is precisely the quality of vivid topicality, that forceful imagery so truly reflecting the mood of the people, which the Caprichos share with the folk-songs of their time.

---

[1] The first lines of the 'Trágala', repeated three times in the course of the song, are:

"Tu que no quieres lo que queremos:
la ley preciosa puesta en bien nuestro."
"What you don't want, we want:
the precious law [*i.e.* the Constitution] which is our
salvation." .

When Goya was composing his grand and so truly 'universal' indictment, the Spanish people were still, however, far from that awakening which made them fling their oppressors' insults back into their teeth. Therefore the message of the 'Caprichos' as a whole is summarised, not so much in the 'Trágala' design as in the following plate (No. 59). An immense slab of stone, tilted on edge and bearing down upon a group of figures beneath it, fills almost half the surface of the print. One of the figures is lying asleep, almost touching the stone that is about to crush him, others are quarrelling or sitting in dumb resignation. The frightful load is supported with desperate effort by the gaunt, emaciated figure of a man, while an old woman, worn out by toil, wrings her hands and watches him with an expression of indescribable horror: 'And still they won't move!' (fig. 39).

The 'Caprichos' end with a picture of vile-looking monks yawning and stretching themselves. Below it is written the menacing call: 'The hour has come' (fig. 41).

THE CONFLICT OF REASON AND FANTASY

The Caprichos are Goya's first truly personal inventions. Their style differs entirely from that of his earlier work. Each plate resembles a darkened stage in front of which one or two actors are picked out by the footlights. The background, produced by the coarse-grained aquatint medium of which Goya made such original and masterly use, varies from deep black to a modulated grey. Sometimes it resembles a dark cloud suspended menacingly over a glowing horizon; occasionally a tree or part of a building is hinted at, or else the shadowy outlines of mysterious figures appear in the gloom. The nightmare atmosphere of these designs culminates in the final sequence. The young girl, for example, who is running away from vile monsters in Capricho 72 (fig. 20), is, clearly, glued to the spot. But the more realistic appearance of the figures in the first part is also deceptive. Those seductive girls and terrifying hags, those sinister plotters whispering together, are not creatures of flesh and blood: they are phantoms, born in the artist's mind, to concentrate and intensify reality. For this kind of art the 'natural style' Goya had acquired with the help of Mengs in the period of the tapestry cartoons was useless.

He himself wrote in a prospectus he drafted for publication with the Caprichos:

> The artist begs the public to be indulgent with him, because he has neither imitated other works, nor even used studies from nature. The imitation of nature is as difficult as it is admirable, if it is really perfect. But an artist may also, surely, remove himself entirely from nature and depict forms or movements which to this day have only existed in the imagination. . . . Painting, like poetry, selects from the universe whatever it considers most suitable for its purposes. It unites qualities and characters which nature has scattered among different individuals and concentrates them in a single fantastic being. Thanks to this creative combination, the artist ceases to be a mere copyist and acquires the title of an inventor.[1]

It is interesting to compare this statement with the following passage from Mengs' letter to Ponz:[2]

> Painting imitates every visible thing in nature not exactly as it is, but according to outward appearances, or might be; the intention being principally to instruct in giving pleasure. This would not happen if nature was copied closely; for the same or greater difficulties would occur to comprehend the productions of art than those of nature: so that the expression given by art is to furnish a clear *idea* of what nature has produced; and such works will be so much the more valuable, as the idea conveyed will be perfect, distinct and clear.
>
> Everything which art produces exists already in nature . . . [but] the art of painting may in general be said to out-do nature, because it unites those perfections which in nature are dispersed, or else disencumbers her from such attributes as may not be necessary to a chosen subject . . . from whence it happens that the invention may often yield more delight than the original. In consequence of this I must add that imitation in painting should not be servile, but *ideal*; that is it should imitate those parts of natural objects which give us an idea of the thing we perceive. . . . This

---

[1] This draft prospectus has never been published in full. Carderera, then its owner, published extracts from it in the *Gazette des Beaux Arts* in 1860. It was exhibited by Maggs Brothers at the Bibliothèque Nationale show of 1935. The passage quoted is taken from **Mayer** *op. cit.*   [2] *Op. cit.*

line of beauty is therefore called *ideal*, as not to be found in the common course of nature; from whence many have supposed that the ideal has no reality. A perfect piece of painting should always have something ideal. . . .

It is curious to note how literally Goya—or, possibly, his friend Cean Bermúdez—adopted certain words of his predecessor, while defining a diametrically opposed conception of art. Mengs selects from Nature in order "to instruct in giving pleasure"; he rejects imitation for *idealisation*. Goya's principle of selection is not ideal beauty, but *truth*. He goes to Nature for his details, which he fuses into a fantastic whole in order to reveal the *substance* of reality, and not "its outward appearances, or as it might be".

Baudelaire (who did not know Goya's statement) brilliantly defined the formal features of Goya's style, though not its underlying purpose, when he wrote:

> Le grand mérite de Goya consiste à créer le monstrueux vraisemblable. Ses monstres sont nés viables, harmoniques. Nul n'a osé plus que lui dans le sens de l'absurde possible. Toutes ces contorsions, ces faces bestiales, ces grimaces diaboliques sont pénétrées d'*humanité*. Même au point de vue particulier de l'histoire naturelle, il serait difficile de les condamner, tant il y a analogie et harmonie dans toutes les parties de leur être; en un mot, la ligne de suture, le point de jonction entre le réel et le fantastique est impossible à saisir; c'est une frontière vague que l'analyste le plus subtil ne saurait pas tracer, tant l'art est à la fois transcendant et naturel.[1]

The "removal from nature" of which Goya speaks does not imply a removal from reality. The basis of artistic creation, as he defines it, is observation: the study of Nature in all its manifold variety. But that is only the beginning of the artist's task. Its essence is selection and concentration, the recreation of reality on a higher plane. The new reality resulting from the fusion of reason with fantasy has the power of a revelation. It is not the outcome of a mechanical addition. It is a new entity, born of the union of two contradictory elements, a union which is creative because it is the resolution of a conflict. Reason and fantasy were ceaselessly at war in Goya's mind. From the first Capricho

[1] *Op. cit.*

sketch to his last pencil stroke, every one of his works was an offspring of that struggle. No two of them contain both ingredients in the same proportions. In times of fierce reaction, when the light of reason battled in vain to penetrate the gloom of an apparently hopeless situation, the fantastic monsters, born of reason's weakness, assailed it with a fury which could only be withstood by a supreme effort. It is Goya's greatness that he was never overpowered by them. He did not run away from them. He was not afraid to let loose the furies of hell that tormented him. But he never submitted to the narcotic enticements of morbid satanism, eroticism, or mysticism, as did so many other artists during the counter-revolution and restoration periods.[1] Even in the most terrifying of his later nightmares Goya invariably retained control over the creatures of his imagination. For even in times of the deepest depression he never lost his faith in the ultimate victory of freedom.

Velazquez inspired Goya's realistic portrait style. Goya's new programme of imaginative realism was conceived under the influence of an artist no less important in the history of Spanish culture. The fusion of realism with fantasy, "forms and movements which exist only in the imagination", "single figures combining the qualities and characters which nature has scattered among different individuals"—where are these to be found, if not in the art of Hieronymus Bosch? Bosch, like Goya, lived in a world labouring in the birth-pangs of a new social order,[2] in a world of conflict the essence of which is embodied in his works. Combining the bourgeois naturalism of the Van Eycks with the demonic imagery which had vegetated for centuries in the popular tradition (*e.g.* in gargoyles, choir-stool carvings, or popular prints), Bosch made his disturbing and elemental art the mirror of all the 'vices and follies' of his time. That explains the paradox of his influence during the sixteenth century. He directly inspired Brueghel, the painter of beggars, at a time when the insignia of mendicancy had become the symbol of the Flemish national revolution. And he was a favourite painter of the arch-enemy of that revolution,

---

[1] *E.g.* Romney, Fuseli, Barry, and even to some extent Blake among the English painters, or Girodet and some later romantics in France. For literary examples *ad nauseam* cf. Mario Praz, *The Romantic Agony*, Oxford, 1933.
[2] Bosch died in 1516 on the eve of the Lutheran Reformation. The turbulent state of fifteenth-century Flanders—a veritable chronicle of wars and revolutions—is described by M. H. Gossart, *Jérôme Bosch*, Lille, 1907.

Philip II, sword-arm of the Counter-Reformation. The critique of human vanity, created as a weapon of the Flemish people in their struggle against the worldly ambitions of the Church, could also assist the militant Counter-Reformation in its revival of spiritual universalism in opposition to the new bourgeois order. Philip II thus filled the Escorial with all the paintings of Bosch he could lay his hands on, and with few exceptions all the most important works of that master which have survived are still, or were in Goya's time, in Spain.[1]

But Philip's taste does not reflect the main reason for the appeal of 'El Bosco' to the Spaniards. In his synthesis of reason and fantasy the accent rests on the democratic, popular elements. Fantasy serves to enhance and to render elemental the moral satire of Bosch's realism. Therefore his art could only be tolerated during the first, heroic phase of the Hapsburg régime. After the death of Philip II, Bosch, the painter of devilries and 'absurdities', was attacked as a dangerous heretic. In his capacity as art censor to the Holy Office, Pacheco warned the Spanish painters against the error of regarding the extravagant fantasies of El Bosco as profound mysteries. As time went on the critics became more and more violent, although the Flemish artist was defended by certain sections of the clergy, and especially the monks of the Escorial, who could not countenance the censure on their founder which these attacks implied. Two quotations from this controversy will explain better, perhaps, than a lengthy description could do, why this painter of 'dreams' could exert so profound an influence on Goya.

In the third part of his *Historia de la Orden de San Gerónimo*, published at Madrid in 1606, Fray José de Sigüenza, prior of the Escorial, included a long digression on Hieronymus Bosch[2] which has remained to this day one of the most penetrating appreciations of that artist's work.

[1] Cean Bermúdez recorded sixteen paintings by Bosch in the Spanish royal palaces and in Valencia (this list excludes copies, but it includes Brueghel's 'Triumph of Death', now in the Prado, and there may have been other wrong attributions. Carl Justi traced references to thirty-eight Bosch paintings in Spanish seventeenth-century documents. Cf. his important article, 'Die Werke des Hieronymus Bosch in Spanien', *Jahrbuch der königlich-preussischen Kunstsammlungen*, 1889. On Bosch cf. also, apart from Gossart *op. cit.*, F. v. Schubert-Soldern, 'H. Bosch und P. Brueghel', *Beiträge zur Kunstgeschichte F. Wickhoff gewidmet*, Vienna, 1903; H. Dallmayer, 'H. Bosch und die Darstellung der vier letzten Dinge', *Jahrbuch der kunsthistorischen Sammlungen des allerhöchsten Kaiserhauses*, Vienna, 1898; and the most recent study by C. de Tolnay, *Hieronymus Bosch*, Basle, 1937.
[2] It is quoted in full, together with references to Bosch by other Spanish sixteenth- and seventeenth-century writers, by Tolnay *op. cit.*

Defending Bosch against the charge of heresy, Sigüenza writes that his works, far from being 'absurdities', are a profound moral sermon. Moreover, "while others have aspired to represent the external appearances of man, he alone has dared to paint man as he is within". The monsters, demons, and composite beasts which haunt the pictures of Bosch (Sigüenza is referring in particular to the Escorial 'Hay Waggon') are the embodiments of man's own vices and evil impulses. It was Sigüenza who was quoted by Ponz[1] and by Goya's friend Cean Bermúdez,[2] when they discussed Bosch in their art-historical works published during Goya's life.

The second quotation comes from the 'Dreams' ('Sueños') of Quevedo (1627), who was himself attacked as a "pupil and second edition of the atheist painter Hieronymus Bosch". In this work El Bosco appears as one of the condemned souls in hell, and when he is asked why he made such a 'hash' of us in his 'Dreams' he replies, "because he never believed in the existence of devils".[3]

Goya, who had made an inventory of the royal collections in his capacity of Painter to the Royal Chamber, was, of course, intimately acquainted with some of the best works of Bosch. But he had been prepared for this influence ever since his early studies in Madrid. The fantastic element which the Tiepolo expressed in their 'Scherzi' and 'Capricci' had come to them, by way of Brueghel, Callot and their followers, from Bosch. But while the influence of Bosch's great moralities on the conception of the Caprichos is self-evident (even the arrangement of the set seems to reflect that of the Escorial 'Garden of Delights' with its profound opposition between sensual pleasure and the torments of hell), Goya could nevertheless truly claim that he had not imitated any existing models in the style of his work.[4] He

[1] A. Ponz, *Viaje de España*, Madrid, 1772–94. Bosch is mentioned in volumes ii and iv, where Ponz describes the art treasures of the Escorial and Valencia Cathedral respectively.

[2] J. A. Cean Bermúdez, *Diccionario de los más ilustres profesores de las bellas artes en España*, Madrid, 1800. Cf. the article 'Bosco'.

[3] I am quoting from Justi's article.

[4] Certain formal similarities may be discovered between the strongly caricatured heads in some of Bosch's paintings and in a vast number of prints directly or indirectly inspired by his work (including the 'Heads of Peasants' attributed to Brueghel and illustrated in Nos. 235-78 of van Bastelaer's catalogue) on the one hand, and the heads in certain Caprichos, in the 'Betrayal of Christ' (Toledo Cathedral, 1798), and in a Goya drawing with sixteen caricatures (also 1798, cf. the illustration in F. Boix, *Exposición de dibujos originales 1750–1860*, Madrid, 1922) on the other. But such similarities are insufficient to prove direct derivation.

achieved an entirely new synthesis of reason and fantasy, as adequate both in content and form to the age of the French Revolution as that of Bosch was to the Reformation era.

Goya's new style, as first embodied in the Caprichos, placed him beyond the reach of his most advanced contemporaries. The Spanish painters of his own generation adhered to the Mengs tradition. The younger artists, born in the 1770's and working from about 1800, adopted the more rigorous classicism of the David school, and, indeed, the most talented among them were sent to Paris by the Spanish government to be trained in the studio of that master.

GOYA'S CAREER, 1789–1806

The social upheaval which was the ultimate cause of the revolution in Goya's style has been described in the earlier parts of this chapter. Fortunately, however, the facts which are known of Goya's life at this time enable us to obtain a closer view of this change as it occurred in his own experience.

The new régime, which was to cause dismay to Goya as a progressive intellectual and to bring persecution for many of his friends, started propitiously for his professional career. In April 1789 a long-standing desire of his was at last fulfilled when he was appointed Painter to the Royal Chamber, and this mark of official approval further enhanced his prestige as a fashionable artist. A number of duties arising from his new position were added to his busy routine during the next few years. He made his inventory of the royal collections and painted the King, and in 1791, the year of the fiercest repression, he produced his last four tapestry cartoons. As we have noted in the previous chapter, they already show signs of strain arising, perhaps unconsciously, from the conflict between his social loyalties and his personal success. That strain must have reached breaking point towards the end of the following year, the year 1792 which began with the fall of Floridablanca and the change to a more liberal régime under Aranda, only to

The same is true of the curious 'conceit' of the girls with chairs on their heads (Capricho No. 26) which may have been inspired by the figure with a chair on his head in the 'Wrath' segment of the 'Seven Deadly Sins' (Escorial). Goya was too great an artist to copy, even when he was inspired by the work of a predecessor. When he did adopt a certain formal detail, he completely remodelled it to fit his own aims. It should be noted, however, that this is not true of some of the religious works Goya painted on commission.

close with the incredible appointment of Godoy as head
of the government (November). It is known that Goya
attended academy meetings in Madrid in March, May,
June, August, and early September, and he must still have
been in a tolerable state of health when he set out soon
afterwards for Cadiz; for there he painted the admirable
portrait of his friend, the lawyer D. Sebastian Martinez.
But then—*i.e.* probably in the last few weeks of the year—
he suffered a complete physical and mental breakdown. For
almost a year he was incapable of working, and he remained
stone-deaf for the rest of his life.

During his slow recovery Goya painted certain small
compositions which he described, in a letter of 4 January
1794, to D. Bernardo Yriarte, Protector of the Academy.
He stresses as their particular merit that in them he was
able to " make *observations* it would have been impossible
to make in commissioned pictures which leave no scope for
fantasy and *invention*". 'Observación', 'capricho', and 'in-
vención', these are the basic elements of the creative programme to which Goya remained faithful for the rest of his
life. And what were the themes he selected for the paintings in which he first embodied his new conception of
art? They were, in his own words, "various popular diver-
sions"—a haunting madhouse scene, a procession of flagell-
ants, a village bull-fight, a scene before a Tribunal of the
Inquisition, and the uncannily horrifying carnival scene
known as the 'Burial of the Sardine'![1] The crisis which
buried the Goya of the tapestry cartoons had transformed
not only his style, but also his conception of life.

The pictures announced in this letter and exhibited
shortly afterwards at the Academy were in fact painted
Caprichos. While he was painting them Goya was also
making his first designs for the etchings themselves. These
occupied him during the following years, and in 1797 he
was able to announce the forthcoming publication of the
'Caprichos' as a set of seventy-two plates. They were not,
however, published until February 1799, when their number
had been increased to eighty. They must have caused a
scandal, for they were withdrawn from public view after

[1] It is not certain whether the five pictures now in the Madrid Academy are the ones
referred to in Goya's letter. Mayer has some doubts regarding the madhouse
picture and also attributes the 'Burial of the Sardine' to a later period. Sánchez
Cantón identifies four of the Academy pictures, including the 'Burial of the
Sardine', with those of which Goya wrote.

having been exhibited only for a few days.[1] According to
Goya's own statement he was subsequently threatened with
a prosecution by the Inquisition, and there can be little
doubt that it was this danger which induced him, in July
1803, to offer the plates and the remaining 240 sets of the
first edition to the King in exchange for the grant of a
pension to his only surviving son. We have already noted
that a new edition was prepared by the Royal Chalcography
with the permission of Godoy in 1806.

That Goya escaped unscathed from so perilous a situation was probably due to the fact that he attained the
zenith of his career as a court and society painter just at
this time. He had been appointed Director of Painting
in the Academy after the death of Francisco Bayeu in
1795, and within a few months of the withdrawal of the
'Caprichos', in October 1799, the liberal minister Urquijo
obtained for him the remunerative post of First Painter to
the Royal Chamber.

During the same years Goya was employed as a decorative artist both by Godoy (three allegorical panels for his
palace, 1797) and the King (wall and ceiling paintings in the
church of San Antonio de la Florida near Madrid, 1798).
His royal portraits culminated in the family group of 1800.
It is one of the most remarkable portraits of all times.
Fourteen figures, including the artist himself at his easel
in the background, are standing in three informal groups,
dominated by the Queen in the centre, in a room of the
Palace of Aranjuez. The group to the right is led by the
King, pompous in his gorgeous uniform; prominent in the
left group are the Prince of Asturias and the Infante Don
Carlos. Maria Luisa, Ferdinand, Don Carlos—names which
are written in blood in the annals of Spain! Here they are
assembled, like a bourgeois family gathering, to pose for
their picture, "todos juntos", as Charles wrote to Godoy,
from the witch-like maiden aunt to the baby-in-arms. And
this vast canvas, filled with faces more repulsive than the
royal models of Velasquez, is made resplendent by a craftsmanship which has woven sumptuous silks and sparkling
jewels into an iridescent veil of brilliant hues.[2]

[1] Goya himself later stated that they were withdrawn after two days, but Sánchez
Cantón concludes from contemporary advertisements that they were more probably
on sale for twelve days. Twenty-seven sets were sold.

[2] In 1800 Goya also produced a sketch for an equestrian portrait of Godoy and a
picture of his official wife, the Countess of Chinchón, and he painted two more

Goya's numerous portraits of the 1790's are uniformly brilliant in quality. The effect of his personal crisis can be sensed mainly in the greater simplicity and profundity of the works after 1792. But the essential elements of his new portrait style had already been established in the last years before the crisis.[1] After 1800, however, there is an increasingly marked difference between his official or representative portraits, in which he made numerous concessions to fashion,[2] and the intimate portraits of his friends or of other intellectuals.[3]

We must, in conclusion, briefly glance at some of the more important imaginative works which Goya produced after the Caprichos. Outstanding among them are the paintings, already mentioned, in the small Madrid church of San Antonio de la Florida (1798).[4] It is no exaggeration to describe them as Caprichos in an ecclesiastical setting. The figures which crowd the cupola of the church, watching the saint restoring a dead man to life as if he were performing a conjuring trick at a fair, are women and their admirers from the streets of Madrid, familiar to us from the first part of the 'Caprichos'. And the brilliantly painted female angels in the pendentives might have come from the same source. But the mood of the whole work is a happier one, as befits the decoration of a sanctuary in a pleasure retreat. In this work Goya once again appears as Tiepolo's disciple. With San Antonio de la Florida the long line of splendid baroque church ceilings ends. Here architecture and painting still form an organic whole, united by one of those views up-

portraits of the favourite during the last 'liberal' phase of the régime: one shows Godoy as 'generalisimo', the other as founder of the Madrid Pestalozzi School.

[1] The brilliant portrait of the Countess del Carpio is dated 1794–5 by Mayer, but 1791 by Sánchez Cantón. Among the best society portraits of the period 1794–9 are various pictures of the Duchess of Alba and portraits of the Marquis of Bondad Real, the Marquise of Lazán, and the Marquise of Santiago. Outstanding among the portraits of intellectuals are those of Jovellanos, Saavedra (both painted while they were ministers in 1798), Martin Zapater, Melendez Valdés, Moratin, B. Yriarte, the famous singer Lorenza Correa, and the second, full-length, portrait of the actress La Tirana (Goya's first portrait of La Tirana dates from 1791, as does that of Cean Bermúdez).

[2] *E.g.* the portrait of the Marquis of San Adrián (1804) or the Girodet-like picture of the Marquise de Santa Cruz, reclining on a bed in a posture reminiscent of Mme. Récamier and holding a lyre in her hands. In 1807 Goya also painted the reactionary minister Caballero.

[3] *E.g.* the portrait of Vargas Ponce (1805) or those of D. Antonio Porcel and his wife (the latter: National Gallery, London), and especially that of the famous actor Don Isidoro Maiquez (1807).

[4] In Goya's time the Hermitage of San Antonio de la Florida was situated in the royal hunting estate known as the Casa del Campo. The church had been reconstructed in 1792.

wards into a sunlit sky which Tiepolo painted so brilliantly. But at the same time the disruption of the baroque style by naturalism and popular story-telling, which began with Tiepolo and the Vienna ceilings, is here completed.[1] And, curiously enough, just as Tiepolo's naturalism could also assume a macabre form, akin to nineteenth-century romantic painting (for example, in the Este altar-piece), so Goya, too, painted a sombre 'Betrayal of Christ' (Toledo Cathedral) in the same year, 1798, in which he was decorating San Antonio de la Florida.[2]

Six small panels which Goya painted about this period for the Osuna family (and of which one, 'The Bewitched', is now in the National Gallery in London) recall the fantastic Caprichos, while a more personal note is struck by the Capricho-like genre pictures already mentioned which show the Duchess of Alba and her Dueña, and the Dueña with two Negro dwarfs (Collection Braganza, Madrid). The fact that these pictures are dated 1795 shows that Goya already belonged to the Duchess's intimate circle for some years before their journey to Sanlúcar. He painted splendid portraits of her in 1795 and 1797, and of her husband in 1795, and he designed murals for her tomb after her death in 1802, but they were never carried out.

The torment which this relationship entailed for him and which he expressed in the unpublished print of the double-faced woman, also coloured the mood of two of Goya's most famous paintings, the Majas nude and clothed (Prado). First mentioned in the inventory of Godoy's personal effects of 1808, they were probably painted about the turn of the century. One need only compare these brilliant, but profoundly disturbing pictures with the proud goddesses of the Renaissance or with the Venus of Velazquez, on the one hand, and on the other with the piquant rococo nudes for which Mlle. O'Murphy or some other farmer-

[1] H. Rothe has published a series of photographs of details of these paintings (*Las Pinturas del Panteón de Goya*, Barcelona, 1944) which make them appear almost as broad and expressionist in their treatment as the Caprichos or even the later murals in Goya's house. But this is necessarily so if details intended to be seen only from a distance are reproduced in close-up view. These photographs therefore give a misleading impression of the festive atmosphere of the ceiling as a whole, however interesting they are in other respects.

[2] The allegorical panels for the palace of Godoy (1797) and a few similar pieces—*e.g.* the 'Time and History' of 1798—are clearly concessions to the prevailing fashion of classicism. They have remained without importance in Goya's development (even within this so alien sphere Goya's realism, however, could not be wholly excluded: the 'Industry' panel in the Godoy set shows a realistic spinning scene).

general's mistress sat as the model, in order to appreciate how much more complex the artist's approach to sex had become in Goya's time.

The maja motive recurs in a less enigmatic form in the 'Majas on the Balcony', which dates from the early years of the century. The girls are sitting behind a banister and looking down into the street, while two sinister figures, wrapped to their eyes in their cloaks, are lurking in the gloom of the background. It is the first of three separate versions Goya painted of this theme.

Goya's interest in topical events with the popular appeal of a street ballad is shown by six small panels which are collectively entitled: 'The Capture of the Famous Bandit Maragoto by the Lay-Brother Fray Pedro de Zaldivia on June 10, 1806'. They are vivid motion studies recounting the hold-up of the good friar and its dramatic *dénouement* in circumstantial detail, and they curiously anticipate the film both in their technique of isolating successive phases of a rapid action and in their melodramatic theme.

Finally, we must note the fact, revealed by Goya's drawings, that in his private thoughts he never ceased to be preoccupied with the condition of the people. The trend of ideas set in motion by the Caprichos was not exhausted by them. From the first years of the century date a large number of drawings, most of which bear slogan-like captions and are numbered like the Caprichos. All, except nine grotesque visions illustrating Goya's dreams during a single night, are realistic in style. They are a gallery of 'unfortunates': invalids, beggars, peasant women, courting couples. And their spirit is illustrated by the words which Goya wrote under a drawing showing an old cripple on crutches: 'Thus do the useful end their days' (fig. 42).

Chapter 3

'THE DISASTERS OF THE WAR'

THE WAR

In the night from 16 March to 17 March 1808, a great crowd of Madrileños, who had marched from the capital and had been reinforced by many peasants of the neighbourhood, besieged the royal palace at Aranjuez clamouring for the dismissal of Godoy. They sacked the house of the all-powerful minister. But the 'Chorizero'[1] was nowhere to be found. Two days later he was dragged, half suffocated, from a rolled-up carpet in an attic of his palace. Trembling for the life of his consort's lover, Charles IV then resigned, and Ferdinand, whom Maria Luisa's intrigues had made the hope of all the opposition parties, was proclaimed King of Spain. Thus began the great cycle of revolutions which links the Spain of Goya with the Spain of to-day.

So far the events of 16-19 March 1808 seemed in no way to differ from many similar occasions in the earlier history of Spain when the people wreaked their vengeance for the misdeeds of a favourite. Yet the Aranjuez rising had occurred under profoundly changed circumstances. The people might be eager to display their traditional loyalty to the established dynasty, but the fate of Spain was no longer in the hands of the Bourbons. During the preceding months the north of Spain with its key fortresses of Pamplona, Montjuich, San Sebastian, and Figueras had been occupied by Napoleon's troops, and Murat's army was approaching the gates of Madrid.

The French had entered Spain ostensibly to fulfil the provisions of the secret Franco-Spanish Treaty of Fontainebleau (October 1807) for the partitioning of Portugal. So far they had met with no resistance. In many places the people had, in fact, greeted them as liberators, for they believed—and the clergy encouraged them in that belief—

[1] 'The sausage-man', Godoy's nickname from his native province of Estremadura which was famous for its pig industry.

that Napoleon had come to free Spain from the yoke of the hated favourite and to establish Ferdinand, 'the Adored', on the throne of his ancestors.

But Murat's behaviour after his entry into Madrid on the day before Ferdinand was received in the capital amidst scenes of delirious rejoicing (24 March) gave rise to the gravest suspicions. He refused to recognise the new king and treated the deposed monarchs, who already regretted their hasty decision, with every mark of respect. Napoleon despised the cringing servility of the son as much as he suspected the treacherous opportunism of the mother, and he had now finally made up his mind to remove the Bourbons from his Spanish dependency. He concealed his intentions, however, until he had lured both Ferdinand and his parents with brilliant promises to Bayonne. Once in his power, the Bourbons submitted with shameful eagerness to the inevitable. Ferdinand resigned in favour of the father, whom he had dethroned a few weeks earlier, and Charles bartered the crown of Spain for a pension of 30 million reals (10 May).[1]

In rapid succession Napoleon then proclaimed his brother Joseph King of Spain, convened an assembly of Spanish notables at Bayonne, and granted a ready-made constitution to the country. But although the monarchs, the grandees, the higher clergy, and the bureaucracy treacherously submitted to the usurper, although the best units of the Spanish army had deliberately been removed far from the scene of these events to the distant North Sea island of Fühnen, the Spanish people refused to sacrifice their independence. On Sunday, 2 May 1808—the 'Dos de Mayo' glorious in the annals of Spain,—the unarmed citizens of Madrid, determined to prevent the forcible removal of the last royal princes, rose in revolt against the invader. With knives and sticks they hurled themselves for hours against the artillery and the Mamelukes of Murat. But they were taught the lesson of their impotence by the salvos of the execution squads which shattered the stillness of the night and continued their bloody work far into the following morning.

The news of these events and of the treachery of Bayonne

---

[1] Ferdinand capped his infamy by asking Napoleon for the hand of one of his nieces. The Emperor instructed Talleyrand to keep him from mischief by sending some actresses to Valençay, his seat of banishment.

kindled the flame of revolt in all parts of Spain. During the last week in May town after town, province after province, rose in a spontaneous outburst of national fervour, deposed or massacred the established authorities, and prepared themselves for the defence of their liberty. The signal was given on 25 May, when the province of Asturias, a region of 348,000 inhabitants, declared war on Napoleon, the master of the world. In Saragossa 'Uncle George', 'a man from the suburbs', rallied the people, dismissed the Captain-General, and compelled his successor to convene a junta. In Cadiz the people killed the Captain-General of Andalusia, who had questioned the advisability of an immediate attack on the French fleet anchored in the port, established a revolutionary junta, and actually compelled the warships of the enemy to surrender about a fortnight later. In city after city such scenes were repeated during this glorious week, when the people of Spain arose from three centuries of stupor and sent a thrill of hope through all the countries of Europe.

During the first months of the war the rising of the nation bade fair to drive the invading armies from the Spanish soil. Moncey encountered defeat when he attempted to occupy Valencia in June, and on 20 July, the very day on which Joseph entered his new capital, Dupont, whose army had committed frightful outrages in Cordova and whose wounded and rearguard had suffered an even more barbarous retaliation from the infuriated peasants near Andujar, was compelled by the Spaniards under Castaños to surrender with his entire force at Bailen. On the following day a similar fate was inflicted by the British on the French army under Junot in Portugal. Thus Joseph was compelled to leave Madrid in headlong flight only eleven days after his arrival. The furious siege which the citizens of Saragossa had resisted for three weeks was raised, and by the middle of August the invaders had retreated behind the line of the Ebro.

But for reasons which we shall presently discuss the Spaniards were unable to complete the task of liberation, or even to consolidate their gains. The renewal of large-scale hostilities in the late autumn of 1808 marks the turning point of the national revolution. The Spaniards had been greatly encouraged by the arrival, on 9 October, of 9,000 regular troops under Romana, who had escaped from Fühnen, and by the disembarkation of a British auxiliary force under Moore a few weeks later. But their armies lacked even the most elementary equipment for the task that awaited them, and their most reliable generals had been replaced by worthless intriguers on the eve of the new campaign. They were faced by 250,000 picked troops under the personal command of Napoleon. The Emperor arrived in Vitoria on 5 November. On 10 and 23 November three separate Spanish armies were routed near Espinosa, Burgos, and Tudela, and already on 5 December the French reoccupied Madrid.

The ignominious collapse of the Spanish armies in little more than a fortnight caused a terrible revulsion of feeling among the people, who had been led to cherish extravagant hopes of victory. When the enemy was approaching the gates of the capital their fury abandoned all restraint. Suspecting treason, they stormed the house of the regidor, the Marquis of Perales, killed him, and dragged his body through the streets. Similar scenes occurred in other parts of the country after the fall of Madrid. But their victims were often innocent patriots, while the real traitors escaped.

Having driven Moore's force out of Spain and settled his plan of campaign for the following spring, Napoleon left for France in the middle of January 1809. After his brilliant successes he had every reason to expect the complete subjection of the Peninsula in a short period of time. But he had reckoned without the Spanish people. Their regular armies might be dispersed, but every defeat only increased the number and determination of the guerrilleros. Ceaselessly harassed by an invisible enemy, who cut off their supplies and destroyed their communications, surrounded by an ominous atmosphere of sullen hatred, but without any tangible objective to strike at, the French armies were likened by a contemporary observer to a lion tortured to death by the stings of mosquitoes. Demoralisation spread in all ranks. Once Napoleon had turned his back on Spain, his generals refused to respect the authority of Joseph. Their mutual jealousy made collaboration between them impossible. Republican and royalist conspiracies were rife in the lower ranks. Soult, who had occupied Portugal in accordance with Napoleon's plan, at one time toyed with the notion of establishing himself as independent monarch of that country. Moreover, the challenge thrown out to the Emperor by the Spanish people began to be taken up by the other nations groaning under his yoke. Napoleon himself suffered his first serious set-back at Aspern during his Austrian campaign (May 1809). The revolt of the Tyrolean peasants, the exploits of Schill, Dörnberg, and Braunschweig, were ominous signs of the rising tide of European nationalism destined in the end to engulf the empire.

Thus almost a year went by without any decisive change in the relative positions of the contending forces in Spain. But in November the Spanish government, which had retired from Madrid to Seville, decided, against the advice of Wellington, to challenge the French in a decisive battle. The rout of the last regular Spanish army at Ocaña on 19 November 1809, and the subsequent retreat of the British troops into Portugal, left southern Spain at the mercy of the enemy. Early in January the combined French armies invaded Andalusia. The cities of Cordoba, Granada, Seville were occupied in rapid succession, and by 5 February 1810 the small island of Cadiz had become the last refuge of Spanish independence in the South.

The answer of the Spanish people to this challenge was a renewed outburst of guerrilla warfare on a scale never before experienced. It was this which determined the character of the fighting until Wellington was able again to resume the offensive with the help of the guerrilleros in 1812. In this war the primitive nature of the means employed was more than compensated by the barbarous cruelty which both sides inflicted on their victims. Hunted day and night like wild beasts and thrown onto their own resources, the guerrilleros assumed the reckless ferocity and independence of marauding adventurers. To defeat this menace which grew like an avalanche after every apparent success of the invaders, the French resorted to desperate measures of retaliation. Whole villages were burnt to the ground and their inhabitants massacred in a vain attempt to stamp out the resistance in the rear. But every act of terrorism only engendered a fiercer determination for revenge in the neighbourhood on which it was inflicted. And to this burning hatred was added the scourge of hunger, for under the conditions of such warfare any regular cultivation of the soil became impossible. Faced with the prospect of starvation, the peasants were driven to fight the foraging parties of the enemy for their very subsistence.

After his unsuccessful attempt to clear Castile of the partisans, General Kellermann wrote to Berthier in 1810: "This stubborn people is destroying our armies. It is of no avail to cut off the heads of the Hydra in one place, if they grow in another. Without a revolution in the spirit of the people you will not, for a long time, succeed in subjecting this great peninsula; it will devour the population and the wealth of France. We require more men. . . . In the meantime, however, the necessary supplies are running low, agriculture is ruined, money is vanishing; no one knows how to ensure the pay and maintenance of the troops, to supply the needs of the hospitals and the infinite requirements of an army short of everything. Misery and want breed sickness and perpetually weaken the army, while the partisan bands are spreading on all sides."[1] After two years of occupation Madrid lost 20,000 of its inhabitants from sheer starvation during the famine which lasted from September 1811 until the following August.

The fury of rural warfare was matched by the horrors endured by the citizens in barbarous sieges. For eight months Gerona withstood the onslaughts of the French before it was forced to capitulate in December 1809. Relieved from its first siege in the summer of 1808, Saragossa was again invested in the following December. In the interval the whole town had been converted into an armed camp, every house into a fortress, while its population of 50,000 had been doubled by a military garrison and thousands of peasants. With the help of the guerrilleros, who ceaselessly attacked the besieging army from the rear, Saragossa resisted the French for sixty-four days. After its defences had been razed to the ground it took fourteen days of terrible house-to-house fighting before the French could occupy two or three streets. Lannes, the French commander, a seasoned campaigner of fifteen years' experience in the most varied theatres of war, wrote to Napoleon: "Never before, Sire, have I witnessed such stubborn resistance as that put up by our enemies in defence of this town. I have seen women allowing themselves to be killed in front of a breach. We have to lay siege to every house."

An eyewitness has described the conflagration of the Saragossa Hospital as follows: "The evacuation of the hospital offered a frightful spectacle. . . . To escape the flames the

[1] Baumgarten, quoting Thiers.

sick flung themselves from the windows on to the bayonets of the soldiers; wounded wrapped in trailing, blood-stained blankets dragged their mutilated limbs after them with terrible effort; in the midst of these horrible scenes the madmen, whose cells had been opened, sang, laughed, and declaimed with a loud voice. . . ."[1]

The citizens of Saragossa were beaten, not by the mines and the bombs of the French or the conflagration which laid a third of their town in ruins, not by the horrors of battle or the pangs of starvation, but by the plague. When the city surrendered on 20 February 1809, 54,000 people had died of wounds, of hunger, or disease. Thousands of bodies lay rotting amidst the smoking ruins, and the city resembled a vast plague hospital. Of its surviving defenders only a third were still able to bear arms.

The French consolidated their gains with the capture of Valencia and the remaining Catalan fortresses towards the end of 1811 and in the following January. But in the spring of 1812 the tide of the war turned in favour of Wellington and the Spanish guerrilleros. Having captured Badajoz and Ciudad Rodrigo, the British general defeated the French in the battle of Arapiles, near Salamanca, on 22 July, and he entered Madrid at the side of the famous guerrillero 'El Empecinado' on 12 August 1812. Less than a fortnight later the siege of Cadiz was at last raised. But at the end of the year Joseph again succeeded in occupying Madrid, where he remained until the following May. The disastrous Russian campaign of 1812 and the gathering storm of the war of European liberation in the following year, however, made the position of the French in Spain untenable, and in the summer of 1813 their fate was decided by Wellington's last great success at Vitoria (21 June) which led to the expulsion of the invaders.

THE SOCIAL REVOLUTION

It is impossible to understand this terrible war of an unarmed people against the mightiest military machine the world had ever known, if it is regarded merely as a war of national independence. It was also the first attempt of the Spanish people to shake off the fetters which had been fastened to their limbs during three centuries of enslave-

---

[1] Don Manuel Caballero, *Défense de Saragossa*, 1815.

ment. The social revolution was a condition of successful resistance to the invader, since every step required for the needs of defence was at the same time a revolutionary step. Deserted by their government, the people had to elect new leaders. Without an army, they had to arm themselves. Without resources, they had to attack the property of the dead hand to purchase their equipment. The tasks of national and social emancipation were identical.

After twenty years of humiliation Spain seemed but a rotting corpse without power, without resources, without a will of its own. A sleight of hand, such as the farce of Bayonne, seemed sufficient to dispose of the carcase. Neither Napoleon nor anyone else in Europe could have foreseen in the spring of 1808 that, by removing the figure-head and the whole creaking machinery of Spanish ab-solutism, he would remove the incubus which had paralysed the vital energies of Spain for three centuries. It seemed impossible that the Spaniards themselves would ever achieve the social emancipation of their country. Napoleon believed that they might welcome the previous gift of liberty brought to them by a foreign king who was heir to the French Re-volution. The Constitution he proclaimed at Bayonne was an immeasurable advance on the repressive system of Bour-bon absolutism, and even before the second occupation of Madrid the Emperor and his brother had swept aside with a stroke of the pen all the most formidable obstacles to the emergence of a modern, bourgeois Spain. They abolished the Inquisition, the economic privileges of the Church, two-thirds of the monasteries, all feudal dues, the Council of Castile, and the fantastic tangle of internal customs barriers

These and other measures which Joseph encouraged whenever the military situation allowed, drew many pro-gressive Spaniards into his camp. By no means all of these were opportunists or traitors, like the deputy Morla who deserted to the enemy after having been entrusted with the defence of Madrid. For a time the graft and incompetence of the national leadership and the benighted fanaticism which the friars stirred up in the Spanish people made the Josefino solution appear the only one consistent with a progressive development of Spain. But if ever history has shown that social emancipation and imperialism are incom-patible, it was in the Spanish experience of 1808–14. For Napoleon was not merely the strong executive who completed the economic revolution in France, he was also the usurper who built his throne on the ruins of the republic. The progressive elements of his outlook were increasingly overshadowed and ultimately destroyed by his imperialism. From the first the liberal reforms of Joseph were rendered worthless by the despotic actions of the French generals. And the more Napoleon's hopes of rapid success were disappointed, the more completely did he abandon the liberal intentions with which he had embarked on the campaign. When, after the conquest of Andalusia, practically the whole of Spain was in his power and there might have been a chance of winning the nation by a progressive and conciliatory policy, the Emperor unmasked his real designs. He deprived Joseph of all authority, except in the immediate vicinity of Madrid, and divided the rest of Spain into a series of military provinces under the ultimate control of the imperial government.[1] Thus he challenged all the Spaniards' instincts of national self-preservation. By sacrificing the social and economic emancipation of Spain to his imperial ambitions he sacrificed both Spain and, ultimately, his empire.

The clash between the forces working for social progress and the defenders of reaction was even more fierce in the national camp. It was also more tragic. For although national liberty was achieved only through the victory of the social revolution, the expulsion of the invaders led to a crushing defeat of that revolution.

In the glorious week in May 1808 when all the provinces of Spain declared their determination to resist the usurper, the people everywhere revived the long-forgotten traditions of Spanish medieval democracy. They elected juntas, councils of local citizens, to take control of the situation. These councils immediately prepared for the defence of their respective regions. In those areas where the democratic tradition was still most strongly entrenched, notably in Asturias and Valencia, they did not hesitate to take all steps required for this purpose. They raised funds by the sale of church domains and they armed the people. But in most districts the dead-weight of a century-old servility prevented the people from taking the leadership of their

[1] With a few exceptions the French generals instituted a régime of shameless graft and repression in their new territories. They regarded the resources of Spain as their private loot. Soult, in particular, organised a thriving smuggling trade with stolen works of art from Seville.

movement into their own hands. Accustomed, as they were, to regard the ruling classes as their natural superiors, they turned to them even in the hour of their awakening and compelled them to take control of a rising from which they had hitherto remained aloof. In Seville, for example, "it was the first thought of the people that the parochial clergy and the heads of the convents should assemble to choose the members of a Junta". Almost everywhere the juntas thus elected were recruited from the old ruling classes who hated any kind of popular movement and had no dearer wish than to follow the example of the royal family and the bureaucracy in capitulating to the enemy. Even more equivocal was the attitude of the clergy. At first they had welcomed the invaders, and even after the Dos de Mayo the highest dignitaries of the Spanish Church had officially sanctioned the repressive measures of Murat.[1] But as soon as the constitution of Bayonne led the Spanish clergy to believe that they might share the fate of the Church in France, they threw their whole weight behind the national movement. They did their best to deflect that movement into the channels of reaction. Fanatical monks stirred up the peasants to a holy war against the French Anti-Christ, and they concealed the revolting features of the traitor Ferdinand under a halo of patriotic devotion. Thus the inspiring cause of the Spanish people was sullied from the first by the base self-interest of a leadership whose only aim was to prevent the national rising from becoming at the same time a movement for social emancipation. And the progressive Spaniards who remained loyal to the cause of their country had to fight for its independence in alliance with the blackest reactionaries, using the slogans of 'loyalty to the absolute king' and 'defence of the Church' to rouse the masses for the struggle.

These contradictions exerted their baneful influence even in the first glorious months of the rising. The movement which should have been above all a national revival saw the resurgence of all the worst features of Spanish regionalism. For more than three months Spain lacked a

[1] The Holy Office saw fit to issue a circular on 6 May fulminating against "the scandalous rebellion of the mob" and "the revolutionary excesses which disrupt the ties of loyalty and obedience under the mask of patriotism and love for the King". It enjoined the clergy to remind the people of their duty to the government. During the following days the secular authorities of Madrid swore allegiance to Murat as vice-regent, and in all parts of Spain the officials did what they could to check the revolutionary indignation of the people.

central government. The old Council of Castile which claimed this title had discredited itself by its cringing submission to the enemy, while the local and regional juntas who conducted the war were rent by disgraceful intrigues. It was not until the end of September that a Central Junta, composed of thirty-five delegates from the local councils, could assemble at Aranjuez. In this unwieldy executive committee the reactionaries formed the majority. Its president was the eighty-year-old Count Floridablanca, the former minister of Charles III, who had sacrificed his enlightenment without hesitation, as soon as it clashed with his loyalty to the absolutist cause. The progressive minority in the Central Junta was headed by the leader of the eighteenth-century reform movement, Don Melchor Gaspar Jovellanos. But he too was by now an old man, for his vitality had been sapped by the long years of rigorous imprisonment which he had suffered from the hands of Godoy. A thinker and educationist, rather than a man of action, he was quite unable to cope with the pressing emergencies of the situation which now confronted him.

When at last the Central Junta assembled, only the most urgent and drastic steps could have saved the gains of the preceding months. But that body saw fit to waste valuable weeks in devising pompous titles,[1] ceremonies, and uniforms for its own members. Instead of preparing the country for the decisive encounter with Napoleon, it did everything in its power to crush the patriotic ardour of the people. It re-established a rigorous censorship of the Press and appointed a new Grand Inquisitor. It blocked the only source from which the nation could supply its needs for the coming struggle by prohibiting the further sale of Church and other entailed property, and it even threatened to tear up the contracts which had been made in the preceding months of emergency. By their counter-revolutionary actions the delegates whom the Central Junta sent to the provinces discouraged and often demoralised areas which, like Asturias or Valencia, had most resolutely resisted the enemy. Worst of all, the Central Junta immediately undermined its own authority and created an official platform for the counter-revolutionary plotters by twice reviving that ancient bulwark of bureaucratic obscurantism, the Council

[1] The Central Junta as a body, for example, assumed the title of 'Majesty'.

of Castile.[1] The wisest councils of Jovellanos and his friends, the fervent manifestoes of its patriotic secretary, the poet Quintana, could not prevail against the pernicious actions of the Central Junta which, called upon to complete the revolutionary liberation of the country, only succeeded in crushing the exalted enthusiasm of the people.

Under revolutionary, still more than under ordinary circumstances [wrote Marx[2]], the destinies of the armies reflect the true nature of the civil government. The Central Junta, charged with the expulsion of the invaders from the Spanish soil, was driven by the success of the hostile arms from Madrid to Seville, and from Seville to Cadiz, there to expire ignominiously. Its reign was marked by a disgraceful succession of defeats, by the annihilation of the Spanish armies, and lastly by the dissolution of regular warfare into guerilla exploits.

The disasters of the last two months of 1808 and the incompetence[3] of the Central Junta in the following period, brought out the full opposition between the two factions in the national camp. With its policy of compromise in which progressive declarations were contradicted by reactionary deeds, the Central Junta could satisfy neither party. The middle classes and the youth of Spain were becoming more and more consciously radical. Only a democratic assembly, they argued, could accomplish the task of national liberation for which the people were sacrificing their lives, and they therefore demanded the convocation of a Cortes. But the reactionaries were no less successful in exploiting the hatred of the masses for the Central Junta. They pressed for the replacement of that body by a Regency Council. Both demands were supported by the British Ambassador, the Marquess of Wellesley, brother of Wellington. The reactionaries won the first round when the Central Junta resuscitated the Consejo Reunido which speedily declared the body to which it owed its revival illegal. But at the same time the pressure from the left was intensified, and in October 1809 the Central Junta consented to the convocation of the Cortes five months hence. Simultaneously,

---

[1] When it was resuscitated a second time it was called Consejo Reunido.
[2] *Revolution in Spain*, New York Daily *Tribune*, 20 October 1854.
[3] The Junta, who had neglected to spend the English subsidies and the funds collected from the people for the equipment of the Spanish troops, had even allowed this money to fall into the hands of the French together with the entire State archives.

however, it deprived this concession of all significance by adjourning indefinitely and handing over the government to an executive committee which was composed almost without exception of the staunchest reactionaries. It was this body which was responsible for the disaster of Ocaña and the resulting flight of the government to Cadiz (20 January 1810).

By that flight the Central Junta forfeited the last remnant of its authority. After appointing a reactionary regency, it resigned on the last day of January. But Cadiz, the centre of the Spanish-American trade, was the most radical city in Spain. Reinforced by thousands of progressively-minded refugees from all parts of the country, the people of Cadiz had elected a democratic junta of their own on the day before the regency was appointed, and this junta rapidly became the only effective authority in the island city. Thus the two parties representing the irreconcilable conflict between a free and modern Spain and a Spain hugging the fetters of absolutism stood face to face on the last few acres of free Spanish soil. In these desperate circumstances the issue between them was decided by the treachery of Ferdinand, the figure-head of Spanish absolutism. British government agents had made an unsuccessful attempt to engineer his escape. Fearing the Emperor's displeasure, Ferdinand wrote him a letter on 4 April 1810 in which he protested his loyal devotion to his master, stating that he had no more fervent desire than to be adopted by him. This letter was published in the *Moniteur*, and Ferdinand went out of his way to confirm his infamy, for he repeated his request on 3 May, at the same time expressing his satisfaction that the world at large had been informed of his attitude, and he again asked for the hand of an imperial princess.

The Spanish people refused to regard these letters as anything but impudent forgeries. But the members of the regency and the Consejo Reunido knew better. They were faced with a serious dilemma. Napoleon could have adopted no better plan than to accede to the request of the traitor. Had he married Ferdinand to a daughter of Joseph and acknowledged him as the latter's successor, the whole basis of the Spanish cause would have collapsed. For both the regency and the progressives claimed the allegiance of the masses solely in their capacity as the representatives of the captive king. Thus the Spanish government hastened to convene the Cortes, many members of which had already been elected under the earlier decree of the Central Junta.

The circumstances under which this first assembly, freely elected by the Spanish people in three hundred years, met in the small town of Isla de León outside Cadiz on 24 September 1810 "are without parallel in history. While no legislative body had ever before gathered its members from such varied parts of the globe, or pretended to control such immense territories in Europe, America and Asia, such a diversity of races and such a complexity of interests,—nearly the whole of Spain was occupied by the French, and the Congress itself, actually cut off from Spain by hostile armies and relegated to a small neck of land, had to legislate within sight of a surrounding and besieging army. From the remote angle of the Isla Gaditana they undertook to lay the foundations of a new Spain, as their forefathers had done from the mountains of Covadonga and Sobrarbe."[1]

The Constitution hammered into shape under the guns of the enemy by this assembly during the long months of 1811, and finally proclaimed on 19 March 1812, was a true product of the Spanish genius. It embodied what was best in the reform programme of the later eighteenth century, as steeled by the experiences of the revolution. At the same time all its essential elements were derived from the tradition of the medieval fueros, from the tradition of Spanish liberty which had been driven underground since the defeat of the comuneros. The Constitution of 1812 proclaimed the sovereignty of the nation. The people alone were entitled to enact the fundamental law of the country. Their representative organ was the Cortes, elected every two years by universal manhood suffrage, without any property qualification, and meeting for at least three months every year. The Cortes legislate jointly with the King, the King alone appoints the executive, the courts administer the law without any interference either from the King or the Cortes. The King may twice veto acts passed by the Cortes, but if they are voted during a third session he must assent to them. The annual determination of the budget, taxation, treaties, regulations concerning the armed forces, the appointment or dismissal of public and judicial officers, the interpretation of the law of succession and the nomination

[1] Marx *op. cit.*, article of 24 November 1854.

of a regency—in short all major actions of State are subject to the approval of the Cortes. During parliamentary
vacations a permanent committee of the Cortes safeguards
the Constitution against infringements on the part of the
executive. The King may neither marry nor leave the
country without the Cortes' approval. Deputies may neither
accept offices, pensions, nor titles from the King, and they
may be re-elected only two years after the prorogation of
the Cortes of which they were members. The King may
neither convene nor prorogue the Cortes. Ministers, who
are appointed by the Crown, report to the Cortes and take
part in their discussions, when requested to do so, but they
have no vote. Special sections of the Code enact a democratic form of local government and a progressive system of
universal education.[1]

The Constitution of 1812, which made the democratic
representatives of the people the only effective power in the
State, was the bugbear of the Holy Alliance during the
first half of the nineteenth century. Re-enacted in 1820
and again in 1836, it was the culminating achievement of
Spanish democracy until our own days.

The constituent Cortes, which remained in session until
20 September 1813, completed their task of uprooting
Spanish absolutism and preparing the soil for a modern
Spain, by enacting a number of important additional laws.
They completed the agrarian revolution by abolishing the
old seignorial privileges (providing for compensation only
if they had been acquired as a reward for some definite service); they decided to sell or distribute to army veterans
and poor peasants the vast royal and communal domains,
most of which had long been monopolised by small
cliques of privileged persons; they sanctioned enclosures
and abolished all feudal restrictions on the use of the land.
At the same time, they replaced the tangle of the existing
taxation system by a steeply graded income tax. They
even attacked the most powerful bulwark of reaction. For
although the Constitution had made the inevitable concession to Spanish fanaticism of proclaiming the Catholic
religion the only legitimate one in Spain, the Cortes
abolished the Inquisition and the oppressive ecclesiastical

---

[1] It is instructive to remember that in England, for example, the principle of universal
education was not made law until 1870. For a detailed analysis of the 1812 Constitution cf. Marx *op. cit.* and, from a conservatively liberal point of view, Baumgarten
op. cit.

taxes, and they took steps to dissolve the majority of the monasteries and other clerical sinecures and to confiscate their property.

Owing to the unprecedented circumstances under which they were elected, the first Spanish Cortes contained a greater number of progressive delegates than they would have done in ordinary times. But the *Liberales*[1] were by no means in the majority. The supporters of tradition, who gloried in the name of 'serviles', greatly outnumbered them. Nevertheless it is important to remember that the most radical restrictions on the power of the crown which mark the Constitution of 1812 were sanctioned by the re-actionary deputies. In some cases the liberal leaders even advocated a more moderate solution, but were outvoted by their opponents.[2] The Cortes had only been convened, in the first place, owing to the treachery of Ferdinand, and as long as he remained in Napoleon's power, the authority of the Spanish government, however reactionary, could only be safeguarded by placing the King under the strict control of the national assembly. But the very fact that the demo-cratic Constitution of 1812 was the offspring of a dire emergency which compelled even the servile majority to rally to its cause, implied the gravest danger for its future. As soon as the threat of foreign subjection had become less acute, the reactionaries strained every nerve to discredit the Constitution with the masses. And they redoubled their efforts when in the later sessions the Cortes attacked the privileges of the ruling classes. The reforms affecting the power of the Church and the property rights of the aristocracy were only accepted because the American dele-gates voted with the liberals against the serviles.

The success of the serviles in appealing to the people's loyalty to the absolute King and the Catholic Church was apparent in the elections for the first ordinary Cortes which took place in the late summer of 1813, after the French had been driven from Spain. But although the serviles re-turned with a greatly increased majority, the liberals were able to maintain their position, even after the Cortes had transferred their sessions to Madrid early in January 1814. For Ferdinand continued to play his role as the main support of democracy until the very end. Even after Napoleon

---

[1] The Spanish liberals were the first party to assume that name.
[2] For detailed evidence cf. Baumgarten *op. cit.*

had been defeated by the European powers in France, Ferdinand signed the Treaty of Valençay (11 December 1813), which, had it been accepted by the Cortes, would have delivered Spain bound hand and foot to the Emperor. It is not difficult to understand the collapse of the revolution when at last Ferdinand, 'the Adored', returned to his people some three months later. "Exclusively under the reign of the Central Junta, it was possible to blend with the actualities and exigencies of national defence the transformation of Spanish Society and the emancipation of the native spirit without which any political constitution must dissolve like a phantom at the slightest combat with real life. The Cortes were placed in quite opposite circumstances—they themselves driven back to an insulated spot of the Peninsula, cut off from the main body of the monarchy during two years by a besieging French army, and representing ideal Spain, while real Spain was conquered or fighting. At the time of the Cortes Spain was divided into two parts. At the Isla de León, ideas without action—in the rest of Spain, action without ideas."[1] When, after five years of ceaseless fighting, the Cortes were at last able to place their ideal Spain before the people, the nation was utterly exhausted. Spain's economy lay in ruins, and the best constitution could not for many years have realised even a fraction of the people's hopes for a better life.

Yet the suddenness of the collapse and the crushing defeat suffered by the democracy must remain incomprehensible, unless the equivocal position of the liberals during the national struggle is fully understood. We have already discussed the fundamental contradiction which compelled the liberals to enter the fight for the emancipation of Spain under the slogans of reaction. Their difficulties were further increased by their relations with the only two allies who could have assisted them in their revolutionary task: Great Britain and the Spanish colonies. The relations of the liberals with the Americans, in particular, illustrate the peculiar position of the Spanish middle class. For the middle class, no less than the absolute régime, was dependent upon the monopolistic exploitation of the colonies, and this was especially true of Cadiz, which lived on the American trade. The demand for emancipation was already

[1] Marx *op. cit.*, article of 27 October 1854.

strong in the Spanish colonies before the war began. Yet they rallied to the support of the mother country when it was threatened by the invader. The subsidies sent from America had been the main revenue of the Central Junta, and both the Junta and the Cortes acknowledged their indebtedness by the grant of political equality and representation to the colonies. But they could not accede to the colonial demand for independence, with its corollary of free trade, without destroying the foundations of what little bourgeois development existed in Spain. By 1812, however, the independence of the main American colonies was no longer an aspiration. It had for all practical purposes been accomplished during the two preceding years. Since the Cortes could not sanction this situation, the American delegates did all they could to weaken the power of the Spanish government. Although they supported the measures of social reform put forward by the liberals, they voted with the serviles on all political issues. Thus the governments elected during the constitutional period through this coalition between the Americans and the serviles were invariably composed of reactionaries who had no more fervent desire than to render the liberal intentions of the assembly inoperative.

In these circumstances only the support of the British government and of the British auxiliary force, the last remaining regular army in Spain, could have enabled the liberals to consolidate their régime. But the Spanish and the British middle classes were antagonised by the same economic conflict which caused the split between the Spanish liberals and the revolutionary colonies. The attempt of the British government to extort the privilege of free trade in America at a time when Spain was in dire distress caused an indignant protest even from Wellington. But there was another equally disastrous cause for friction. Britain was at that time in the throes of reaction. Although Spanish absolutism had once been the arch-enemy of protestant Britain, and although a Bourbon restoration would inevitably weaken the new Anglo-Spanish alliance, the personal sympathies of Britain's diplomatic and military representatives in Spain tied them more and more exclusively to the old ruling classes bent on that restoration. Ignoring the evidence of all British military observers, who contrasted the corruption of the Spanish upper classes with the heroic devotion of the people,[1] Wellington attributed the monstrous inefficiencies and blunders of the reactionary ministers and generals to the liberals, whom he hated with all the prejudice of his insular toryism.

At first, however, both Wellington and his brother, the ambassador, refrained from any interference in the conflict of the Spanish parties. By proclaiming the Constitution after his triumphal entry into Madrid in August 1812, the British general even strengthened the liberal régime (and he was appointed commander-in-chief of the combined Anglo-Spanish forces in recognition of that service). But in the subsequent period of the social legislation of the Cortes Wellington and Wellesley were increasingly disposed to give rein to their own class sympathies by supporting the machinations of the serviles against the 'Jacobin' Constitution. They insisted on a revision of the Constitution on British lines by the provision of an Upper Chamber equivalent to the House of Lords. But in a situation in which the mere suggestion of a revision would have implied surrender to the forces of reaction, such councils were worse than futile. In the spring of 1813, when Wellington was beginning to drive the French from the Spanish soil, the breach between him and the Cortes could no longer be remedied. Writing to his brother in April, he accused that assembly of working systematically towards the establishment of a republic. But the true reasons for his attitude are disclosed in another letter which he addressed on 21 April to the British Secretary for War, Earl Bathurst:

> I am very much annoyed by the conduct of the Cortes, who appear to follow the example of the Assemblies in France . . . [he wrote]. It is impossible to calculate upon the plans of such an assembly. They have no check whatever and they are guided and governed by the most ignorant and licentious of all licentious presses, the press of Cadiz. I believe that they mean

[1] Cf., for example, the evidence of Sir John Moore, who had every reason to complain of his treatment by the Spaniards: "The apathy of the people proved the inactivity of their rulers; for, on such an occasion, there should not only have been numerous armies on foot, but every man in Spain should have been armed, and ready to act when required. Nor did this appear to be impracticable. For the supineness was not owing to disaffection among the people: the peasantry and lower orders were all well disposed; but in ascending to the higher ranks, the spirit of independence evaporated" (James Moore, *A Narrative of the Campaign of the British Army in Spain commanded by . . . Sir John Moore*, London, 1809, pp. 27-8. Cf. also Sir John Moore's letter to his brother dated 26 November 1808, and reprinted on pp. 44-6 of the *Narrative*).

to attack the Royal and feudal tenths, and the tithes of the Church, under the pretext of encouraging agriculture; and I am sadly afraid that, finding the contributions not so productive as they imagined they would be, *they will seize the rents of the estates of my friends the Grandees*.[1]

After this remarkable passage Wellington continued:

If I am tolerably successful early in the campaign I intend to try and prevail upon them (*i.e.* the Cortes) to quit Cadiz, which I know the liberales consider their stronghold; and the other parties and my brother are of the opinion that the only chance of salvation is to remove the Government from thence.

On 5 September 1813 Wellington at last put the direct question to Bathurst:

I wish you would let me know whether, if I should find a fair opportunity of striking at the democracy, the Government would approve of my doing it.[2]

And Bathurst replied from "Downing Street, 25th September 1813":

You may be assured that if you can strike a blow at the democracy in Spain, your conduct will be much approved here.[3]

It would be difficult to find a document which more strikingly demonstrates the reactionary character of the British Tory government of that time than this letter of Bathurst. After the sentence quoted he proceeds to discuss the plan, of which Wellington strongly disapproved, to make the Princess of Brazil Regent of Spain. He states that Wellington's arguments against this project have not convinced him that it should be abandoned, and continues:

Now I am inclined to think that it is best for the monarchy that the person who is the heir apparent or presumptive should be Regent, without requiring the additional qualification of best capacity. I think so, not only because the heir is more likely to have an immediate interest in upholding the monarchy, but also because by so doing you approach nearer to the

---

[1] *Dispatches of the Duke of Wellington*, London, 1834–9, vol. x, pp. 310-12 (my emphasis).   [2] *Ibid.* vol. ix, pp. 88-91.
[3] *Supplementary Dispatches, etc., of Field-Marshal Arthur Duke of Wellington*, London, 1861, vol. viii, p. 275.

principle of hereditary monarchy, which excludes all idea of selection.

At the end of the letter he reverts to his opening theme. The British, he says, have hitherto avoided forming a party of their own in the Cortes, but in the present situation the wisdom of this policy seems open to doubt:

> Can we for example strike a blow at the democracy without connecting ourselves with those who feel the same inclination? Your Lordship, with the influence of public opinion in your favour, and with the opinion of strength which a military commander always possesses, although he may not intend to exercise it, may do much if a fair opportunity presents itself, and I heartily hope one will. Otherwise we must sit by and see the mischief done, without being able to prevent it, but not without the reproach of having permitted it.

Wellington and his brother, however, favoured a more circumspect policy. They preferred to strengthen the serviles in every possible way by their influence, until they should be strong enough to abolish the Constitution, by 'legal' means or even violently, but without the open intervention of the British.

> It is quite impossible that such a system should last [he wrote in the dispatch of 5 September, just quoted]. What I regret is, that I am the person that maintains it. If I was out of the way, there are plenty of Generals who would overturn it. Ballesteros positively intended it; and I am much mistaken if O'Donnell, and even Castaños, and probably others, are not equally ready. If the King should return, he will also overturn the whole fabric, if he has any spirit; but they have gone so far, and the gentlemen at Cadiz are so completely masters of their trade of managing the assembly, that I am afraid there must be another convulsion: and I earnestly recommend to the British government to keep themselves clear of the democracy, and to interfere in nothing while the government is in their hands, except in carrying on the war, and keeping out the foreign enemy.

Thus Wellington never committed himself openly to the cause of the serviles until the reactionary coup had actually been accomplished. But the true nature of his 'non-intervention' policy is revealed by the fact that he, who owed his position as commander of the Spanish forces to the Constitutional Cortes, did not prevent the British general Whittingham from occupying Madrid with reactionary troops and thus disarming the legal government on the eve of the coup (30 April 1814). Even before that event Wellington prevented a demonstration of loyalty to the Constitution among the Spanish troops near Toulon, and when Ferdinand had abolished the democratic régime he dissuaded the Spanish generals Freyre and the Prince of Anglona, on the grounds of military discipline, from declaring in favour of the Constitution.[1]

Having given a final proof of his treachery by signing the Treaty of Valençay, Ferdinand 'the Adored' returned to his country on 24 March 1814. Instead of following the route prescribed for him by the Cortes, he went in triumphal procession to Saragossa, where he spent Holy Week amid delirious scenes of loyal and religious fervour. Thence he proceeded to Valencia, where he received a document secretly signed by sixty-nine deputies of the Cortes, known as the 'Persians',[2] who denounced the Constitution and begged for the return of the old order. At the same time he was assured of the support of the army by the reactionary general Elio. On 4 May he issued a secret decree overthrowing the Constitution and promising a benevolent régime, but at the same time he appointed the most fanatical reactionaries to all key positions. In the night between 10 and 11 May, thirty of the most prominent liberals in Madrid were arrested in their beds. Next morning the streets of the capital and the other main cities were filled with howling mobs clamouring for the blood of the men who had led the country to victory. Headed by zealous monks carrying the banner of the Inquisition, they celebrated their return to slavery by smashing all the visible symbols of liberty and making bonfires of the Constitution code and all the liberal publications they could lay hands on.

On the ruins of Spanish freedom Ferdinand, who entered his capital on 13 May, established a régime of oppression rivalling the darkest days of Hapsburg absolutism. But the spirit in which the people resumed their

---

[1] *Dispatches*, vol. xii, p. 17. The policy of Wellington and Wellesley in their relations with the Cortes is fully analysed in vols. i and ii of Baumgarten *op. cit.*

[2] From the opening passage of this document: "It was the custom of the ancient Persians to spend five days in anarchy after the death of a king. . . ."

chains is characterised, more graphically perhaps than by many other documents, by the following passage from a widely distributed pamphlet of which numerous editions were printed by the serviles from the end of 1813 onwards in order to prepare the masses for the return of the King. Describing the life led by Ferdinand during his captivity, this account commences:[1]

The king rose at eight o'clock, heard mass, breakfasted, made afterwards a party of billiards, entered his closet to read his letters or a portion of the Holy Writ, embroidered at the tambour till two o'clock, at which time he took a short airing in his carriage—he dined on his return—made a short prayer, received his brothers, or those who were admitted to pay their court to him, supped, and before going to bed recited with all his household the litanies, which he toned himself.

An agent of Napoleon, whose impious presence he was forced to endure, employed all means of seduction to draw the infant from his holy occupations. He brought a troop of female dancers from Paris, and even his own wife, to endeavour to charm the king; but I perceived by certain signs that the breasts of these women, indecently exposed, were beginning to have a dangerous effect on the prince, who was ready to fall into the seventh deadly sin. I admonished him in time, and, like the slave of Potiphar, Don Ferdinand escaped these new sirens.

The king was above all things incensed at the poverty of the chief altar of the parish of Valençay, and at there being in the Château a playhouse, while there was neither a chapel nor an oratory—while the people were luxurious in their furniture and feasts, and miserable in the decoration of their temples. The king embroidered, himself, a beautiful robe of white silk, with gold pallets and gold fringe, for the Virgin. He had raised a superb altar, gilt, and he sometimes served, himself, the mass at the feet of the Queen of the angels. The Queen of the angels was most sensible to these royal attentions, and manifested to him her content by many signs. It happened in particular, that

[1] The passage is quoted in Hansard, *Parliamentary Debates*, vol. xxix, p. 1163, from '*Sermón pronunciado en la gran función que se celebró en Cadiz por Don Blaz de Ostaloza, capellan mayor de S.M.C. y su Confesor*. Ed. 7, en Burgos, de la imprenta de la Inquisición, 1814.' It was referred to by Whitbread in his speech on 1 March 1815, on the motion censuring the governor of Gibraltar for delivering into the hands of the reactionary police of Ferdinand four Spanish liberals who had taken refuge in the colony.

one night an ecclesiastic of the district being overcome by sleep in the church, the Virgin appeared to
him as coming out of the altar,—she advanced towards
the ecclesiastic, made several turns round him, to
display the elegance of her toilette, and said to him,
sighing, that her son received the vows of the king in
recompense of the fine robe that he had given her;
that the Spanish princes would not remain long without being delivered; and that they must form an order
of the Holy Sacrament, with which all the chevaliers
should be armed for his defence.

The priest, much touched by this speech, awakened,
and came to me to reveal the miraculous vision; but
I answered by assuring him that the Holy Virgin had
already said as much to the king himself—who in
thanking her had promised that on his return to Spain
he would make her worship flourish over all the provinces subjected to his dominion.

The author of this sermon was the Peruvian priest Don
Blas Ostaloza, a favourite of Ferdinand during his brief
period of power in 1808, who had accompanied him to Valençay, where he acted for a time as his confessor. Later he
led the intrigues of the serviles in the Cortes of Cadiz and
Madrid. After Ferdinand's return he was for a period one of
the most influential members of the camarilla and largely
instrumental in re-establishing the Inquisition. After his
removal from court in October 1815, he was appointed
inspector of an orphanage in Cartagena, but he exploited
the innocence of his wards with such shameless depravity
that he had to be removed to a monastery in April 1818.
Even there, however, he retained his pension of 10,000 reals.[1]

GOYA'S CONDUCT DURING THE WAR

These were the events which Goya depicted in the
series of etchings known as 'The Disasters of the War', the
crowning achievement of his documentary realism. But
before we discuss that work we must examine his personal
experiences during this period.

At the outbreak of the war Goya was sixty-two and
isolated by deafness from his fellow men. Many of his most
intimate friends joined the ranks of the Josefinos. Among
them were the poets Melendez Valdés and Moratin, the en-

[1] Baumgarten *op. cit.*, quoting the report of the Prussian ambassador, 12 April 1818.

lightened Canon Llorente, and the former minister Urquijo, who had tried in vain to dissuade Ferdinand from walking into the trap of Bayonne. The loyalty to the national cause displayed by Jovellanos or the old historian Capmany were the exception rather than the rule in the circle of the old eighteenth-century reformers. Most of the intellectuals, who, like the poet Quintana, devoted all their energies to the tasks of national and social emancipation, belonged to a younger generation. Yet Goya can justly claim a place of honour in their midst, for he alone among all the artists and writers of this time created an enduring monument to the heroism of the Spanish people.

Goya's name is linked with the first event in the long history of the Spanish Revolution, for immediately upon receiving the news of the Aranjuez abdication, the Academy of San Fernando commissioned him to paint an equestrian portrait of the new king. Ferdinand actually granted two brief sittings to the artist and, according to Sánchez Cantón,[1] the slightly idealised features of the picture (completed in October), which lack the caricature-like brutality of later portraits, seem to reflect the general feeling of hope and elation he then inspired, but later so grossly betrayed.

Goya was in Madrid during the terrible events of the 'Dos de Mayo', and the tradition, according to which he witnessed both the fighting[2] and the executions of the following night, is supported by the character of the two monumental paintings in which he later immortalised the heroism of his fellow citizens. After the liberation of the capital, Goya was called to Saragossa by General Palafóx to inspect the ruins left by the first siege of the town, where he had spent his youth, and to depict the glorious deeds of its inhabitants. According to Lady Holland,[3] a number of drawings by Goya of the ruins and of Agustina de Aragón, the heroine of the first siege, were later destroyed by the French, when they entered the room of Palafox after the capture of the town. Sánchez Cantón has shown that the equestrian portrait of Palafóx (Prado), previously ascribed to this visit, was actually painted in 1814, but a study and a three-quarter length of the general may well have been pro-

---

[1] *Op. cit.*
[2] Goya was at that time actually living in the Puerta del Sol, the scene of the fiercest street fighting.
[3] *The Spanish Journal of Elizabeth Lady Holland*, edited by the Earl of Ilchester, London, 1910.

duced at this time. If further proof is needed of Goya's patriotism during this period, there is a passage in one of his letters, dated 8 October 1808, in which he says: "I cannot spare myself because of the great interest I take in the glory of my fatherland".

Goya appears to have remained in Saragossa until shortly before the second attack of the French, when he took refuge in his native village of Fuendetodos. He did not return to Madrid until long after its renewed occupation by the enemy, probably in the late spring of 1809. He was still absent when the members of the Academy swore the oath of fealty to Joseph Bonaparte. If, as is likely, he remained in Fuendetodos, he was in the centre of active guerrilla warfare during the second siege of Saragossa, a supposition which is supported by many plates of the 'Disasters'. Two of them representing villagers in flight even bear the captions: 'I saw this myself' and 'This also'.

After his return to Madrid Goya resumed his official duties. He was selected with two other academicians on 20 December for the painful task of choosing fifty pictures from the palaces and churches of Spain for the Musée Napoléon in Paris. After ten months' delay the three artists deliberately chose canvases of little merit. In March 1811 Goya was awarded Joseph's decoration, the Order of Spain, but he later affirmed that he had never worn it. His portraits painted during the period of occupation include those of certain prominent Josefinos, such as the Minister of the Interior, Manuel Romero, and the two French generals Quéralt and Guye (whose nephew he also painted). Outstanding among them in its monumental simplicity and psychological penetration is the full-length portrait of Canon Juan Antonio Llorente. It was probably under the influence of this former secretary of the Holy Office, who was then writing his well-known indictment of that institution, that Goya began his series of historical drawings depicting famous prisoners of the Inquisition. The other portraits of this period are bourgeois portraits (the Goicoechea couple, whose daughter was married to Goya's son—both pictures are dated 1810) or intimate studies of children (including one of Goya's grandson).

Unique among Goya's works, and a puzzle to all who approach them in a spirit of pure aesthetics, is the 'Allegory of the City of Madrid' painted in 1810. It was commissioned by the city authorities as an act of homage to Joseph. Its style and atmosphere are wholly baroque. Emblematic female figures are holding a plaque, which originally bore a portrait of the French king, and the bourgeois upstart is thus legitimised with all the trappings of traditional symbolism. When the French left Madrid the portrait was erased and replaced by the word 'Constitución' (a compromise which is not quite so startling, if it is remembered that the Central Junta had assumed the title of 'Majesty' and that even the liberals in the Cortes retained their deference for ceremonial forms). After the fall of the constitutional régime this dangerous description was obliterated by a portrait of Ferdinand VII (painted by Vincente López), which in turn was replaced, in the mid-nineteenth century, by the present caption: 'Dos de Mayo'.[1]

There can be no greater contrast than that between this baroque picture and the 'private' works which Goya was painting at the same time, for it is in these that he revealed his true feelings. Three of the etchings in the series of the 'Disasters' bear the date 1810, and it is probable that most of the first sixty designs were completed—at any rate as drawings—during the period of the French occupation or shortly afterwards. But Goya suffered deeply from his equivocal position, and he gave vent to his agony in a number of wildly expressionist paintings. Most of them show assaults, rapes, and murders. A plague hospital, a flagellation scene, and a macabre 'Visit of a Monk' are also included in this series. Even Velazquez' 'Hilanderas' he transposed into an expressionist, rather than a realistic factory picture. But the famine of 1811–12 again turned Goya's mind to the sufferings of the people, which he depicted in the second main sequence of the 'Disasters'.

Even before the French were driven from the capital Goya must have succeeded in crossing the enemy lines. For according to a deposition of his son he made his first portrait sketch of Wellington immediately after the battle of Arapiles,[2] in Alba de Tormes on 23 July 1812.[3]

---

[1] Carderera stated that Vincente López had painted the portrait of Ferdinand VII on the medallion in a manner "que desarmoniza mucho el cuadro". Cf. the reproduction of Carderera's notes on Goya's paintings in *Archivo Español de Arte y Arqueología*, vii, 1931, 174.

[2] In English histories this is always called the battle of Salamanca: in Spanish, the battle of Los Arapiles.

[3] "A drawing made in Alba de Tormes after the Battle of Arapiles of the Duke of Wellington for whom the portrait was made" is the translation of the relevant

The equestrian and half-length portraits were painted after Wellington's entry into Madrid.

A series of small paintings of subjects similar to those of the 'Disasters' must have been produced either in the few months following the relief of Madrid in August 1812, or more probably after the final evacuation of the capital by the French in the following May. This group includes a sketch of the battle of Arapiles and two exciting scenes showing the manufacture of gunpowder and bullets by the guerrilleros on the open Sierra (figs. 45, 46).

On 24 February 1814, one month before Ferdinand's return to Spain and almost three months before his entry into the capital, Goya addressed a remarkable letter to the government. Expressing his "ardent desire to perpetuate by means of painting the most remarkable and heroic actions and scenes of our glorious insurrection against the tyrant of Europe", he asked for assistance to execute this plan. He obtained a grant on 9 March, and there is no doubt that the two monumental canvases now in the Prado were painted as part of this scheme (if he planned additional ones, as is probable, he did not execute them under the changed circumstances of the following period). The two existing paintings depict the heroic struggle of the citizens of Madrid on the Puerta del Sol on 2 May 1808, and the executions of the following night. Like David in the picture of the 'Oath in the Tennis House', planned under the immediate impression of the revolution, Goya now cast off the convention which regarded contemporary history as an unworthy subject for major works of art. With supreme economy Goya focussed the dramatic fervour of the action. The tension is heightened by the contrast between the wild movements of the citizens throwing themselves with knives and sticks on to Murat's Mamelukes, and the terribly static quality of the execution scene. The latter with its sombre colouring, illuminated only by the lantern on the ground, with its agonised victims and statuesque soldiers, is the culmination of Goya's monumental realism. Nothing remains of the eighteenth-century tradition. Out of the spontaneous observation of an actual event,

passage in the letter signed by Goya's son which accompanies the drawing. Both were acquired by the British Museum from Goya's son through Colnaghi's. Wellington was in fact near Alba de Tormes on 23 July 1812 (the day after the battle), for one of his letters to Lt.-General Sir R. Hill was written on that day "on the heights near Alba de Tormes" (*Dispatches*, vol. ix, p. 300).

surpassing the wildest fantasy in its dramatic appeal and inspired by a profound social feeling, Goya created a new style (figs. 43, 44).[1]

What was the significance of these paintings conceived at a moment of acute political tension? The Cortes had closed their final session at Cadiz in December 1813. The Regency had entered the capital on 5 January, and the liberals had to face a greatly increased servile majority in the new Madrid Cortes. Yet they were so strikingly superior to their adversaries in intelligence, skill, and enthusiasm that, instead of suffering a severe setback, they actually improved their position during the last months before the coup of 10 May. They strained every nerve to win the people for the Constitution. To the debates in the Cortes they added the fervent appeals of the radical Press, the political clubs, and the stage.

The ambassador Wellesley wrote to his brother the Commander-in-Chief from Madrid on 27 January 1814: "I cannot say, however, that I like the appearance of things. The Jacobin speeches in the Cortes and their daily publications have certainly made an impression upon the people. *They act Jacobin plays almost every night at the theatre and sing coplas against the Serviles, which are more applauded than I ever recollect them to have been at Cadiz.*"[2]

To appreciate this remark one must know that during the first decade of the nineteenth century the stage had again become a living force in the artistic life of Spain. The revival initiated by Ramón de la Cruz in the subsidiary sphere of the *entr'acte* sainete had gradually been extended to the major plays. The reappearance of good dramatists, like Moratin and Quintana (whose 'Pelayo' of 1805 had a strongly political flavour), was of first-rate importance for this development. But the revival was mainly the achievement of a romantic actor of genius, Isidoro Maiquez[3] (1768–1820), as important in the history of

---

[1] In painting major pictures of contemporary historical events Goya had been anticipated not only by David and Gros, but also by the American artists West, Copley, and Trumbull shortly before and during the American Revolution (cf. Edgar Wind, "The Revolution of History Painting", *Journal of the Warburg Institute*, vol. ii, London, 1938–9). But whereas most of these artists merely painted classical compositions in modern dress, Goya was the first to create a new form adequate to this new content. His achievement was paralleled, in the same year, 1814, by Géricault with his 'Cuirassier blessé' (Paris. Louvre).

[2] *Supplementary Dispatches*, vol. viii (my emphasis).

[3] The following particulars are taken from D. Emilio Cotarelo y Mori, *Isidoro Maiquez y el teatro de su tiempo*, Madrid, 1902. Goya painted a splendid portrait of Maiquez

the Spanish stage as Garrick was for the English. His repertoire included not only contemporary works, both Spanish and foreign, and French and Italian classical plays, but also some of the best Spanish seventeenth-century works (including Lope de Vega and Calderón) and Shakespeare (Othello was one of his most celebrated and oft-repeated roles).

There can be no better proof of the new vitality of the Spanish theatre than the fact that it was capable of an immediate response when the people rose to free their country from the invader. No less than nine new patriotic plays were produced in the two theatres of Madrid alone between the end of September and the beginning of December 1808. On 14 August, the day after Castaños entered Madrid, one of the theatres was already staging a show entitled 'Aragón restored by the Valour of her Sons'. It is interesting to note, as a parallel to Goya's activity in Saragossa immediately after the first siege, that the first full-length play of the patriotic series dealt with the siege of that town. It was a piece in three acts by D. Gaspar de Zavala y Zamora[1] entitled 'The Patriots of Aragón' and was performed for the first time on 24 September. The chief character is a woman, María, who joins with the soldiers and citizens in fighting the enemy, a fact whose significance will be apparent when we discuss Goya's 'Disasters of the War' in detail. A sequel to this play by the same author, 'The Bombardment of Saragossa', was performed on 22 November. Among the other plays of this series were 'The Defence of Valencia' and 'The Defence of Gerona'; a sainete-like playlet, 'The Judgment of the Provinces', in which popular characters discuss the merits of the different regions of Spain in the fight with Napoleon; a 'Gerundiesque' satire by D. Félix E. Castrillo: the 'Fruitless Sermon of Joseph Botella in Logroño', based on an actual speech by Joseph after the defeat of Bailen; and two very interesting additional works by D. G. de Zavala y Zamora. The first is an allegorical play on the alliance

in 1807. In March 1815 an etching of this picture by Esteve was issued by public subscription as a tribute to the actor.

[1] D. Gaspar Zavala y Zamora was born during the latter half of the eighteenth century and died in Madrid in 1813. He was what we should now call a competent script-writer for the Madrid stage. Of his numerous plays, which were very successful with the public, some twenty-six were published. He is mentioned as a popular hack in the standard literary histories, but does not seem to have been considered worthy of further comment.

between Spain and Britain. Just as in the old 'autos sacramentales' or in the court masques—and also of course in Goya's 'Allegory on the City of Madrid'—the characters are all symbolic figures, such as 'Spain', 'Abundance', 'Commerce', 'Navigation'. The other Zamora play called 'Shades of Pelayo, or the Happy Day of Spain', is a dramatisation of the Aranjuez revolt and the fall of Godoy.

In 1809 Maiquez, who had been a prisoner in France since shortly after the 'Dos de Mayo', was allowed to return to Madrid, where, like Goya and Moratin, he accepted employment under the invader. In collaboration with Moratin he produced many bourgeois comedies (including some of Molière's works) and classical plays (including those of Corneille and Racine) during the period 1809–12. A parallel to the Goya Allegory is the classico-allegorical 'loa' on Joseph entitled 'La Clemencia de Tito' by the same Zavala y Zamora. But that the conflict of a divided allegiance tormented all the artists, whether they were painters, writers, or actors, is evident from the prominence of macabre plays such as 'Macbeth', and, above all, Arnault's 'Oscar', in Maiquez' repertoire. To judge by contemporary accounts, Maiquez' interpretation of 'Oscar' must have been as profoundly disturbing as Goya's most wildly expressionist pictures of robbery, rape, and murder.

The interval between the second and third French occupations of Madrid was too short to allow of any real revival of the patriotic theatre. Improvised monologues with choral accompaniment, a few revivals from the earlier series and of plays first performed in Cadiz, and a full-dress performance in English for the benefit of the British officers, had to suffice. But after the French had finally abandoned Madrid on 27 May 1813, a wave of radical patriotism swept over the stages of the capital. In a little over nine months, from July onwards, more than thirty political plays, most of them new, were performed in the 'Principe' and 'Cruz' theatres in addition to their ordinary non-political repertoire.[1]

---

[1] The following programmes were shown at the 'Principe' during January 1814:

Jan. 1   'Dupont rendido' and the sainete 'Los locos'.
  „   2 & 3 'El pastelero de Madrigal'; the tonadilla 'El marido impertinente'; and the sainete 'Los estudiantes hambrientos'.
  „   5 to 8 'La gran batalla de los Arapiles'; operetta 'El quid pro quo'; sainete 'Los tres huespedes burlados'; Illumination in honour of the entry of the Regency into Madrid.

By far the most significant, from our point of view, is the play with which Maiquez opened this patriotic season at the 'Principe'. It is a three-act tragedy by D. Francisco de Paula Martí[1] entitled 'El día Dos de Mayo de 1808 en Madrid'. We are told that this play was staged with new decorations which represented the four main centres of the street fighting on 2 May: the Buenavista, Puerta del Sol, Parque de Artilleria, and El Pardo. The characters include certain famous historical personalities, in particular the two artillery officers Daoiz and Velarde who died fighting side by side with the people, but are mainly drawn from the middle and working classes. One of the chief parts is that of Doña Antonia, wife of Don Luis, who avenges the death of her husband by killing the French commander. Maiquez himself played the part of the hero of the people, named Sebastian. The fact that the 'Dos de Mayo' had a run of ten consecutive days when it was first performed (9-18 July 1808), whereas the Madrid theatres normally changed their programmes daily, and that it was twice revived within six months (once in September and a second time for three days in January 1814) is evidence of its outstanding success. The spirit in which it was received is revealed by the notice announcing its last revival in the *Diario de Madrid*:

The actors of this theatre have resolved to revive a spectacle full of grief and horror, a spectacle which the audience greeted with expressions of fury and pain when it was first presented. But since those tears can only increase our hatred for the abhorred tyrant, it has

Jan. 9 to 11 'El dia Dos de Mayo'; tonadilla 'Doña Toribia'; sainete 'En tocando a decasar acude todo el lugar'.
  „ 12   'El alcalde de Zalamea'; sainete 'El payo de continela'.
  „ 14-19   'El chasco de los afrancesados'; sainete 'El chasco de los cesteros' (de magia).
  „ 20   'La escuela de los maridos'; sainete 'Los zapatos'.
  „ 21   'El celoso confundido'; sainete 'El quid pro quo'.
  „ 22   'El astrólogo fingido'; opereta de ayer.
  „ 23   'La caida de Godoy'; tonadilla 'El tripili'; sainete 'La Constitución'.
  „ 24   'La huerfanita', sinfonía oriental; sainete 'Los parvulitos'.
  „ 26   'Los dos hermanos, disipador y egoista'; sainete 'La casa de vinos'.
  „ 27 & 28 'Gayo Graco'; sainete 'La embarazada ridícula'.
  „ 29   'El Tartufo'; sainete 'Tragabalas'.
  „ 30   'La muerte de Abel'; sainete 'El castigo de la miseria'.
  „ 31   'El Fenelón'; sainete de ayer.

[1] Francisco de Paula Marti (1762–1827), principally known as the adapter of shorthand writing to the Spanish language and as the first teacher of that art in Madrid, was also a professional engraver and writer. Apart from the plays mentioned in the text, he wrote another political piece during the 1820–23 revolution, entitled 'La entrada de Riego en Sevilla', and several non-political plays.

been decided to refresh our memory of a calamity which was undoubtedly cruel, but from which there arose the liberty, the glory and the happiness of our common mother, valorous Spain.

The final performance of this play took place less than three weeks before Wellesley wrote the letter from which we must infer that, in the eyes of the serviles and their British friends, patriotism was synonymous with 'Jacobinism'. For it is a striking fact that, with a few exceptions, these plays stress the patriotic fervour rather than the radical convictions of their authors. A few titles may serve to illustrate this point: 'La gran batalla de los Arapiles' (also the title of Goya's one specific battle picture), by D. F. G. Gonzalez, dedicated to Wellington (who was played by Maiquez); 'Dupont rendido en los campos de Bailen', dedicated to Castaños; 'Mina en Arlabán' ("a few inhabitants of a village in Navarre, among them two women, alone resist an attack of the French, and perceiving the hopelessness of their cause, the men die in the plaza, while the women blow up their house with barrels of gunpowder the moment the enemy comes in"); 'El triunfo mayor de España en los campos de Vitoria' (battle scenes ending with the apotheosis of Wellington); 'El valiente Empecinado en los campos de Alcalá'; 'Fernando VII, Rey de España, o la catástrofe de Bayona' (re-enacting the entire Bayonne incident with Napoleon, Ferdinand, Charles IV, Maria Luisa, and other living historical characters), etc. Wholly overshadowed by such patriotic full-length plays were a few sainetes or songs of a more definitely radical character, among them Francisco de Paula Martí's 'La Constitución vindicada' and a play by D. G. de Zavala y Zamora called 'La palabra Constitución y su sentido'. The latter must have been an interesting essay in political propaganda, for the entire action consists in discussions between the alcalde and some other citizens of a town who explain the 'glorious Constitution' to one another. 'La instalación de las Cortes' was a 'solo' sung by La Molina.[1]

In addition to documentary plays on contemporary

[1] Francisco de Paula Martinez de la Rosa (1787–1862), a Cortes member in 1813–14 and, as leader of the 'moderado' liberals, Prime Minister in 1834–5, also wrote one of the radical plays performed during this season. It was entitled 'La viuda de Padilla' (*i.e.* the heroic widow of the leader of the comuneros of 1520–21) and was performed at the 'Cruz' on 28 October 1813.

events the liberals also staged certain old Spanish or classical Italian and French pieces with an obvious political appeal, and also Schiller's 'Kabale und Liebe'. Among the old Spanish plays were a piece, dating from 1664, which bears the significant title 'Las vísperas sicilianas', and Calderón's 'Alcalde de Zalamea'. The French pieces included J. Chénier's 'Gayo Graco', which was first performed in Paris in 1792, and, above all, Alfieri's 'Bruto primo, o sea Roma Libre' of 1785.[1] This play had achieved a sensational success on the eve of the French Revolution. It had also inspired David's painting (exhibited in 1789) of the founder of the republic, who condemned his own sons to death when they betrayed the cause of liberty. The father of Roman liberty had been for centuries a symbol of the bourgeois revolution—as opposed to the Caesar-cult of the renaissance 'tyrants' and the absolute princes—and the appeal of his name was so much the more powerful, since it was another Brutus who slew the usurper. Alfieri's Brutus was played in Cadiz to celebrate the proclamation of the Constitution of 1812; it was one of the plays performed in Madrid during the interval between the second and last French occupations, and it was finally staged by Maiquez in March 1814 as one of the last radical gala shows with a seven-day run.

We have already noted that the classicism of the David school was the style adopted by the younger generation of Spanish 'history' painters during the first decades of the nineteenth century. It had also affected the Madrid stage even before the outbreak of the war. It is not, therefore, surprising that, following the lead of the French revolutionary theatre, it was now also adopted for the purposes of patriotic and liberal propaganda. But compared with the documentary presentation of topical reality which is the outstanding and most characteristic achievement of the Spanish revolutionary stage, classicism played a subordinate role as a propaganda medium. Goya's paintings and etchings of the war period correspond both in subject-matter and form to the realistic productions of this revolutionary theatre. Like these plays, his works expressed the outlook of a

---

[1] Marie-Joseph-Blaise Chénier (1764–1811) was intimately associated with the production of stage plays and public festivals during the French Revolution. Victor Comte de Alfieri (1749–1803) wrote a number of radical plays with classical themes. He played an important role in the preparatory and early phases of the French Revolution, but left Paris in 1792.

vanguard fighting for social, no less than for national freedom.

After the overthrow of the Constitution Goya was cited before a commission of judges appointed to investigate the conduct of all members of the royal service during the French occupation. In spite of the ruthless purge of all known or suspected Josefinos during those months, Goya passed the test (21 May 1814). He was present at the meeting of the Academy on 8 July, which was visited by Ferdinand, and he resumed his official duties. We can therefore conclude that Goya followed the same line of conduct during the revolutionary period as during the reactionary Godoy régime. While complying with his official duties, he expressed his true feelings in the works which remained concealed in the privacy of his studio; but whenever the situation allowed he came into the open and placed his art at the service of the revolution.

'THE DISASTERS OF THE WAR'

'The Disasters of the War' were first published by the Academy of San Fernando in 1863. A set of proofs was given by Goya to his friend Cean Bermúdez, who edited the captions and entitled the work: *Fatales consecuencias de la sangrienta guerra en España con Buonaparte y otros caprichos enfáticos en 85 estampas inventadas, dibujadas y grabadas por el pintor original D. Francisco de Goya y Lucientes.* This set included the two final plates, which were omitted from the Academy edition of 1863, when the work received its present title, and three additional etchings of prisoners.

'The Disasters of the War' are divided into three parts dealing with separate themes, while the last sequence also differs in style from the first two. If we ignore the first plate, which resembles the final sequence both in spirit and style, the first part, comprising plates 2 to 47, consists of fighting and guerrilla war scenes. Most of these designs were produced during the actual period of the war. The second sequence, Nos. 48 to 64, depicts the agony of the Madrileños during the famine of 1811–12, and it was also, in all probability, conceived under the immediate impression of that disaster. The last 18 plates are those which Bermúdez called 'caprichos enfáticos'. They are symbolical fantasies treated in a broader manner than the earlier designs, and they were certainly not etched before the return of Ferdinand, some probably not before the second liberal revolution of 1820, when the whole set was completed. Only the first two parts of the 'Disasters' concern us in this chapter.

The work begins with a plate (dating from the post-war period) which foreshadows its underlying mood. 'Sad presentiments of things to come' is Goya's caption. A man dressed in rags is kneeling with outstretched arms in the foreground. His upward gaze expresses deep sorrow. In the gloom of the background the head of an immense monster (which recurs on two other plates of the cycle) is barely discernible (fig. 94).

In the following sequence of 47 plates we are plunged into the horrors of the guerrilla war. In staccato rhythm its cruelty and chaos are unfolded before our eyes. 'With reason or without it' and 'The same' are the captions of the first two plates showing fierce encounters between peasants armed with knives, pikes, and axes, and French soldiers. 'Women give courage', 'And they are like wild beasts' is written on the following two designs in which women take the place of men in hand-to-hand fighting. Women recur in nine out of the first eighteen plates of this sequence, fighting, firing a cannon, outraged within sight of their children or their men folk, or mourning the dead. They strike the predominant note in this opening movement of the guerrilla war sequence (figs. 47-53).

After the wild crescendo with which this part begins, there is a sudden pause: action is interrupted by its antithesis—death. French soldiers surround a dying officer, the ebb and flow of battle continues as a dim accompaniment in the background.

Framed by this scene of death and by a plate which shows a fallen horse and rider in the foreground of a wild cavalry charge, is a design which is both deeply moving and exhilarating (plate 7). It is the only plate in the 'Disasters' in which the horrors of war are ennobled by a sense of heroic elation, the only plate, also, in which Goya deliberately depicted one specific event in the struggle. Significantly enough, it celebrates the valour of a woman. The scene is a breach in the ramparts of Saragossa. The ground is strewn with bodies, killed before they could fire the gun which would stay the enemy's assault. Towering above the dead, the lithe figure of a young girl stands facing the foe. She has torn the match from her dying lover's grasp and is firing the gun. Thus the heroic Maid of Saragossa saved the breach and forced the enemy to retreat 'foil'd by a woman's hand, before a battered wall' (fig. 51).[1]

Women assaulted, struggling violently on the ground, and outraged in a gloomy vault facing a church steeple, are the themes of the next three plates—'They are unwilling', 'These also', and 'Not for these' are their descriptions. And after another interlude: the frightful pile of the dead with a single figure collapsing in agony and spitting blood—'For that you were born'—the theme is continued in plate 13: a rape in a cellar witnessed by the handcuffed husband: 'It is bitter to be present' (figs. 49, 50).

Plates 14 and 15 foreshadow the *leit-motif* of the last part of the sequence: martial law and barbarous executions. The first of the two is a grim hanging scene directed by a priest, but not including soldiers. It is generally interpreted as an allusion to the massacre of the French residents in Valencia during the first week of the rising, but it could also apply to any execution of traitors in the Spanish ranks: 'Hard is the step!' is its caption. 'And there is no remedy' is that of the second design, one of the most stirring in the set, which shows patriots tied to stakes facing the firing squad (fig. 52).

Two of the next four designs take up the theme of the following movement: death and the agony of the wounded. In plate 16 soldiers are looting the dead—'They provision themselves'; in plate 18 an old couple are grieving over a heap of nude corpses—'Bury and be silent'. The intervening plate ('They cannot agree') shows officers on horseback arguing in face of the enemy—an allusion to the rivalry of the French generals.

The first movement concludes with a final, wildly exciting repetition of its main theme: soldiers assaulting women and about to sabre a man are interrupted by an officer who rushes to the scene, shouting, "There is no time for that now" (plate 19, fig. 53).

The fury of the opening sequence is exhausted in this

[1] The three stanzas in which Byron sings the praises of the 'Maid of Spain', Agustina de Aragón ('Childe Harold's Pilgrimage', Canto I, stanzas liv-lvi), were written some eighteen months after this heroic deed. The poet actually saw her during his visit to Seville in July 1809, where, as he explains in a footnote, "she walked daily on the Prado, decorated with medals and orders, by command of the Junta".

last tempestuous throb. Then comes the sombre but passive agony of the second brief movement of eight plates: field hospitals and deserted battle-fields strewn with dead bodies. 'Heal them and on with the job', 'It comes to the same thing' (dead are carried away, a woman is crying), 'The same and worse', 'The same elsewhere', 'They can still be patched up for service', 'These too' (plates 20-26). Then a sudden, though muted, flash-back to the opening theme: 'One cannot bear to see this'—men and women hiding in a cave are discovered by their pursuers, whose presence is indicated only by the menacing bayonets of their muskets (fig. 55). The movement ends with the plate entitled 'Charity': nude bodies flung into a pit by peasants hardened to their task (fig. 56).

A staccato interlude of three plates introduces the renewed horrors of the third movement. Two of them show furious mobs dragging a half-naked body through the streets. The first is usually identified as the massacre of the Marquis de Perales immediately before the capitulation of Madrid, but we have noted how frequent such occurrences were during the early phases of the war. We also noted that their victims were as often honest patriots as traitors, and Goya emphasised this in his captions: 'Mob' is that of the first, 'He deserved it' that of the second plate. In the third design of this group Goya's art reaches another climax. 'Ravages of war' is the title of the plate which shows the cellar of a bomb-shattered house, strewn with broken beams, furniture, and the tangled bodies of men, women, and children (fig. 54).

The next and most ghastly sequence of this work reveals the utter bestiality of this endless stalemate warfare. Sadistic hangings, the barbarous mutilation of the dead,[1] men strangled by the garotte, men lashed to a tree and shot in the back, pass in uninterrupted succession on plates 31-9. 'That is an outrage!', 'For what', 'Is there anything more one can do to him?', 'For a knife', 'No one knows for what', 'Nor here', 'That is worse', 'Barbarians!', and 'Great valour—with the dead!' are the captions of these terrible designs (fig. 57).

[1] The documentary character of these terrible designs is underlined by Goya's note on a proof of plate 37: 'El de Chinchón'. Chinchón is a village near Madrid, where Goya's brother was at that time parish priest. Goya evidently saw the mutilated body depicted in this print himself, or else his brother told him about the outrage, *v.* fig. 57.

Having reached the limits of the endurable in the plate with the chopped-off limbs and mutilated bodies suspended like butchers' meat from a tree, Goya grants us a brief moment of respite. Plate 40 is a symbolic design, dating from the post-war period; it shows a man struggling with the beast of war.

The last movement of this first part of the 'Disasters' is composed of seven variations on the themes of flight and destruction. The first of these is the lugubrious 'Flight through flames', reminiscent of the description of the con-flagration in the Saragossa hospital, already quoted. Plates 42 and 43 show terrified monks and nuns running for their lives ('Everything is upset'). These are followed by two moving prints of villagers escaping from their homes, with women and children in the foreground, which Goya in-scribed 'I saw it myself' (fig. 58), 'And this also'. And the whole guerrilla sequence ends on a note of tension: the massacre of a priest ('This is bad') and the looting of a church, whose priest has collapsed at the altar-rail: 'Thus it happened' (No. 47).

In the second main part of his work Goya turns from the horrors of the guerrillero war to the sufferings of the 'pacified' population in the conquered capital, to the agony of the 'año del hambre', 1811–12, when 20,000 people in Madrid died of starvation:

> Men, women, and children lay dying in the streets, they cried out for a morsel of grass, a potato, a miser-able bowl of soup, however watery. It was a spectacle of despair and anguish: to see countless human beings struggling in the agony of death on the open street in broad daylight, to hear the moans of the women, the pitiful cries of the children beside their suffering fathers and brothers. Twice daily the carts of the parishes came to remove the corpses. The ceaseless wailing, the groans of so many unfortunate people in their last agony, filled the few, who dared to venture on to the streets and were themselves racked with hunger, with insurmountable fear and gave them too a cadaverous appearance. The atmosphere was filled with poisonous exhalations and seemed to spread a vast shroud over the whole city. . . .

Such is the account of this disaster quoted by Beruete[1]

---

[1] *Goya Grabador*, Madrid, 1918.

from Mesonero Romanos' *Memoirs of a Septuagenarian*.
Goya visualised these scenes with an intensity which is
accentuated by the sombre monotony of accumulated
misery. 'Cruel misery', 'Charity of a woman', 'Unhappy
mother', 'Thanks for the broth', 'They come too late',
'He died without assistance', 'Vain cries', 'To beg is the
worst', 'To the cemetery', 'The sound and the sick', 'Cries
are of no avail', 'What is the use of one cup?', 'No one
can help them', 'If they are of different descent', 'Beds of
Death', 'Piled corpses', 'Cartloads to the cemetery'—such
are the captions of this procession of wretchedness (plates
48-64). Three variations on the theme of death are its
macabre conclusion. They are the 'Beds of Death' (No.
63), one of the most moving designs of the set, which shows
an old, deeply shrouded woman standing alone in the gloom
of the morgue; the gruesome 'Store of bodies' flung onto a
pile with some coffins (63); and the carrion-cart with its
horrifying contrast between the beauty and the limp life-
lessness of a young woman, dragged from the truck by
her shoulders and ankles to be flung into the vault of the
dead (64) (figs. 59-64).

Goya's 'Disasters of the War' are documents of a great
social movement. Together with the drawings and paintings
of his last years they are the culmination of his realism. But
they do more than merely mirror reality: they interpret and
call to action.

Goya's method of disclosing the truth is documentary,
but not photographic. He shows the actual, but only in so
far as it is significant. Where he alters its image, it is for the
purpose of enhancing its truth. Nothing could characterise
this war between the largest and best-disciplined army of
the world and a 'rabble' of peasants more strikingly than his
device of giving to the French soldiers—all the soldiers in
the 'Disasters' are French—a statuesque immobility even
in the wildest action scene, while the Spaniards are full of
vital movement. Nor could anything more clearly indicate
on which side Goya's sympathies lay. And that he did not
forget the social in the midst of the national struggle is
shown by the plate in the famine sequence (62) which he
entitled 'If they are of different descent'. For in this plate
Goya opposes the starving poor to the well-dressed bourgeois, separating the two by a policeman. All the scenes he
depicts occurred, but they occurred a hundred times, and,

what is most important, they are typical of this war. Even the Agustina plate derives its stirring appeal, not from its anecdotal quality, but from the fact that war is not a respecter of age or sex, or of the sanctity of the home, that in a revolution women, no less than men, are called upon to play their part in the struggle for freedom.

In the 'Caprichos' Goya had shown the world as a stage on which men play their parts controlled by forces, whose identity is concealed from them by the power of an illusion. There is little or no spatial depth in the designs. The figures move detached and imposing in the lime-light of the proscenium. The geometrically simple designs still show a trace of classical formalism.

The 'Disasters' show the people in action. Every figure, every movement is intelligible only as part of a wider social process whether present or past. Isolated figures and large-scale foreground compositions are rare. The groups, usually placed in the middle distance, are intimately related to the landscape in which their actions take place. The brutal reality depicted no longer admits the poise and tonal harmony of the 'Caprichos', it demands violent contrasts of light and shade and the chaos of struggle. Where calm reigns, it is the calm of death. The rhythmic sequence of the 'Disasters' differs in a similar way from that of the 'Caprichos'. The exquisite balance and variation of the latter is replaced by a violent alteration of action clashing with immobility. The sequences of passive agony are overwhelming precisely because of the monotonous repetition of a single theme—just as the 'año del hambre' was monotonous with its succession of death-groans, corpses, and carrion-carts.

In short, it is impossible to compare the two great cycles of Goya's etchings on abstract aesthetic grounds. Judged by its own standards each is supreme. But their standards differ, because each expresses a different phase in the history of the revolution.

In the rising of the Spanish people reality had discarded its fantastic mask. The social struggle revealed itself naked and undisguised. That is why Goya no longer had to search for strange shapes "which have never existed in nature". The reality before him was stranger than the wildest fancy; above all, it was more significant and compelling. Therefore realistic observation reigns supreme in the style of the 'Disasters'. But fantasy and invention have not been discarded. In comparing the 'Disasters' with earlier illustrations of war, especially Jacques Callot's 'Misères de la Guerre' (1633), Dvořák[1] defined what was really new in Goya's approach to that theme. In all periods artists have been called upon to glorify war or to extol the personal and communal virtues through which victories are won. Other artists have turned to battle scenes, primarily, because they enabled them to work out technical problems that interested them, problems of perspective, for example in the case of Ucello, or problems of anatomy, movement or composition. Callot was the first artist who studied war objectively, in the same spirit of detachment in which the great scientists of the seventeenth century studied natural events, and he was therefore the first to depict the horrors and miseries of war. But it was Goya who first drew, not only the objective experiences of war, but rather those experiences reinforced by the emotions and passions they aroused within himself as a feeling and suffering human being and a Spanish patriot. Thus the new element in the 'Disasters' is the artist's interest in his own, personal, relationship to his theme, the same element which Wordsworth described about this time when he defined poetry as "emotion recollected in tranquillity".[2] It was this active preoccupation with the problems of their time, and the urge to express the emotions those problems aroused in them, that made the great romantics the spokesmen of their people's national and social awakening. As Dvořák puts it, the 'Disasters' paraphrase the shattering impact of warfare on a sensitive soul, his passionate protests and ardent wishes for a better world.

Hence it is wrong to regard the 'Disasters' merely as a fierce condemnation of the criminal futility of war in general. The whole character of the work precludes abstract generalisation. In every plate, in every caption, Goya referred to this particular war and to the actions of his people in that war. He did not do so, it is true, in a spirit of mystical exaltation or benighted fanaticism. He did not conceal the horrors of the war, nor did he cherish any illusions concerning the ghastly futility of its immediate results.

But in spite of all its horrors and disasters Goya recognised the positive significance of the struggle: the heroic

---

[1] *Op. cit.*   [2] In the preface of 1802 to the *Lyrical Ballads*.

awakening of his people after centuries of dumb enslavement. By their deeds the people, however immature and ensnared in the nets of reaction, had given substance to what, until then, was but the wish-dream of a small group of intellectuals. For, however cruel the immediate outcome, however bitter the experience of howling delirium drowning the voice of liberty and acclaiming the Inquisition—the foundations of feudal repression had been shaken by the great revolution of the Spanish people. And the seeds had been sown for a new and happier society cherishing the sacred heritage of freedom.

Thus in spite of their sombre anguish, in spite of the sadistic bestiality and the horrors which make the 'Disasters' the most eloquent condemnation of war and of the social conditions which breed war, they are pervaded by a note of elation. Their theme, throughout, is the people in action, the common people, workers and peasants. And in the final plate of the work Goya[1] asserted his conviction that their privations, their anguish, and their heroism had not been in vain.

[1] Cf. next chapter, p. 197.

Chapter 4

MONSTERS OF OPPRESSION

REACTION

IN his manifesto of 4 May Ferdinand had promised to inaugurate a régime of benevolent moderation. His conception of moderation is revealed by the series of decrees culminating in the re-establishment of the Inquisition on 21 July 1814. Following the restoration of the old despotic system of local government (4 May), of the monasteries and convents (20 and 23 May), of the Council of Castile with its fantastic agglomeration of bureaucratic and juridical functions (27 May), of the grotesque tangle of feudal taxes and monopolies (23 June), and the liberation of the clergy from all taxation (24 June), the edict reviving the Inquisition demonstratively completed the resurrection of Spanish despotism.[1] It was in a real sense a triumph of the most fanatical section of friars and confessors in the camarilla. Only two days before its publication the Prime Minister San Carlos had given his word to Wellesley that nothing of the sort was contemplated. When the ambassador complained after the event, San Carlos excused himself by stating—probably quite truthfully—that neither he himself nor the Minister of Justice had known of the edict until they had read it in the newspaper.

The manner in which this enactment was engineered, evidently against considerable opposition, illustrates perhaps better than the decree itself the atmosphere then prevailing in Spain. Early in July the officers second in command in Cadiz, Seville, and Valencia received orders signed by the Minister of War for the immediate arrest of their superiors, the Captains-General of those provinces. After these arrests they were to open a second letter with further instructions which were to be carried out instantly. Strange as these orders were, the surprise of the officers to whom

[1] The preamble of this law, so symbolical in its bombastic, uncouth phrasing of the spirit in which it was conceived, will be found in note V of the Appendix, p. 219.

they were addressed was as nothing compared with the shock received by the only one of them who actually arrested his chief. For the second note contained the command to execute the Captain-General on the spot. Now even this officer considered it his duty to write to Madrid, as the others had done, for confirmation of so extraordinary a command. The three enquiries came as a bombshell to the minister Eguia, who disclaimed all knowledge of the proceedings, and on 12 July an official manifesto informed the public of the horrible plot which had been hatched against the Serene Majesty of the King. The clerical party were not slow in exploiting this sensational incident. Pulpit and press vied with each other to persuade the people how necessary for their protection was the strong arm of the Inquisition. A reward of 200,000 reals was offered for the discovery of the wretch who had misused the name of the King's minister. But, once the excitement had died down, the petty official, who was implicitly convicted of the forgery, was not only released, but remunerated with a liberal pension.

The country was now at the mercy of the camarilla. "The committee reigns supreme", wrote the new Prussian ambassador von Werther; "It issues decrees and orders the arrest of all whose opinions it suspects. The countless victims, who are jailed indiscriminately with robbers and murderers, include many men distinguished both for their talents and for their services to the nation. This despotism is so much the more revolting because it is exercised by fanatical, avaricious, and revengeful priests, equally lacking in ability and in moral sentiment. The finances are in a state of hopeless confusion. Yet the King gives everything that comes into the exchequer to the friars." [1]

The exultation of the clerical party in those days is expressed in a refrain which they had the effrontery to spread among the masses:

Vivan las cadenas,	(Long live our chains,
Viva la opresión;	Long live oppression;
Viva el rey Fernando,	Long live King Ferdinand,
Muera la Nación!	Death to the nation!)[2]

It would serve no purpose to follow the ceaseless intrigues and the abrupt changes of personnel in the cama-

---

[1] Dispatch of 25 August 1814; cf. Baumgarten *op. cit.* The moral indignation expressed by the representatives of all the great powers little accords with their actions, which were dictated by a strict policy of 'non-intervention'.   [2] Baumgarten *op. cit.*

rilla or to describe the squalid details of its misrule. For although Ferdinand gave his creatures full licence to exploit his subjects in the most shameless manner, he took good care to remind them that he alone was the ruler of Spain. Abruptly and without any apparent reason he debased all whom he had raised from the gutter. After a brief spell of power ministers, lackeys, confessors, and police spies (whose duty it was to amuse the King with the unsavoury details of the Madrid *chronique scandaleuse*) would suddenly find themselves in some remote jail or monastery, with ample leisure to meditate on the blessings of arbitrary despotism.

Under such conditions only a past-master of intrigue could maintain his position for any length of time. A virtuoso of this stamp arrived in Madrid in September 1814 in the person of the Russian ambassador Tatischeff, who quickly succeeded in making himself leader of the camarilla. Skilfully exploiting Ferdinand's aversion to the British, Tatischeff brought about a complete reversal of Spain's foreign policy. The British Tories could have retained the dubious allegiance of their protégé only if they had granted the lavish subsidies which Ferdinand's ever-penurious court was clamouring for. But although Wellesley opened his purse to meet some of that court's most pressing needs, the price demanded in the long run greatly exceeded the value of any proffered return. When no more money was forthcoming from that quarter, Ferdinand turned in disgust from the heretical English and flew into the arms of their most feared opponent:

> the coxcomb Czar,
> The autocrat of waltzes and of war!
> As eager for a plaudit as a realm,
> And just as fit for flirting as the helm; . . .
> Now half-dissolving to a liberal thaw,
> But harden'd back whene'er the morning's raw;
> With no objection to true liberty,
> Except that it would make the nations free.[1]

Alexander's Spanish policy fully bears out Byron's charge. Until 1820 the Russian influence at the court of Ferdinand reflected the Czar's flirtation with 'enlightened ideas'. But as soon as the Spanish liberals succeeded in overthrowing the despotic régime and restoring the Constitution of 1812, Russian absolutism was untiring in its efforts to drive the Holy Alliance to armed intervention.

[1] Byron, 'The Age of Bronze', 1823.

But Spain had ceased to count as a power in the European concert, once Ferdinand had resumed his throne in 1814. The nation which had given the signal for the wars of independence was treated with contempt at the Congress of Vienna. And Ferdinand's behaviour invited such treatment. When Napoleon made his final bid for power in March 1815, Ferdinand played for safety. In spite of the urgent entreaties of the allies he refused to act until the Emperor's cause was irredeemably lost. Only in August, when everything was settled, did a Spanish army under Castaños cross the frontier —for the opportunity of feeding the starving and discontented troops at the expense of the French, even if it were only for a few days, was too good to be missed.

In the internal history of Spain it is possible to distinguish three main phases during the six years of oppression which followed the six years of the war. The first phase lasted until November 1816 and reduced the country to a state of chaos. This was the period when the military tribunals, established in October 1814 to deal with political cases, vied with the Inquisition and the secret police in making indiscriminate night arrests;[1] when the stream of high officers and public servants coming to Madrid to petition for the payment of salary arrears overdue by as much as fifteen months assumed such proportions that a decree was issued prohibiting any Spaniard from coming to the capital without the express permission of the President of the Council of Castile (October 1814); when naval officers whose pay was not forthcoming were advised to make a living as fishermen (February 1815); when all newspapers, except the official *Gazeta* and the *Diario de Madrid*, were suppressed (final decree, April 1815); and when the Jesuits, who had been expelled in 1766, were not only recalled, but reinstated in the possession of most of their former property (May 1815).

> Two years had passed since Ferdinand had resumed absolute power [wrote M. de Martignac, who acted as Commissioner for the French government during the war of intervention in 1823], and still the proscriptions continued, instigated by a camarilla recruited from the dregs of mankind. The whole machinery of the state was turned upside down. Dis-

---

[1] Those condemned to perpetual banishment as Josefinos alone numbered 12,000.

order, stupidity, confusion reigned everywhere. The taxes were most unevenly distributed, the state of the finances was deplorable, there was no credit for loans and no possibility of providing for the most urgent requirements of the state. The army remained without pay and the magistrates indemnified themselves by taking bribes. The corrupt and rotten administration was incapable of introducing improvements or even of maintaining the existing state of affairs. Hence the universal discontent of the people.[1]

The second phase of Spain's agony began in December 1816, with the appointment of Don Martin Garay to the Ministry of Finance. Garay had been a disciple of Jovellanos and minister of the Central Junta, but he had not taken any part in the work of the Cortes. Supported by the influence of Tatischeff and the new queen,[2] he attempted to introduce the administrative and financial reforms which a junta appointed in November to enquire into the causes of the existing anarchy had reported indispensable. Even the Vatican now recognised the need for immediate action if the cause of Spanish absolutism were to be saved. It recalled the nuncio Gravina, one of the most bigoted members of the camarilla, and temporarily relaxed its ban on the taxation of the clergy. During the first months of 1817 Garay worked out his scheme of reform, which was based on a partial replacement of the old consumption dues by direct property and income taxes for all classes, including the nobility and clergy. He also insisted on strict budgetary control of each ministry's expenditure. In spite of strong opposition, and to everyone's surprise, Garay's scheme

[1] Martignac, *Essai historique sur les révolutions d'Espagne et l'intervention française de 1823*, Paris, 1832. The passage is quoted by Marx *op. cit.*, article of 2 December 1854.
[2] Maria Isabel Francisca, Princess of Portugal, Ferdinand's second wife, arrived in Madrid in September 1816. For a time she exerted a moderating influence over the King. (It was also due to her that Ferdinand allowed the paintings scattered in neglected corners of the royal palaces to be exhibited in the Natural History Museum, now the Prado, which was opened in 1819.) Her influence did not, however, last for long. When she discovered the King in the arms of a mistress just before her second confinement, she collapsed and died shortly afterwards, on 26 December 1818. Less than four weeks later Ferdinand sent an envoy to the European courts to find him a third wife (21 January). In October 1819 he married the timid and bigoted Saxon princess Maria Josefa Amalia, who died in May 1829. Seven months later Ferdinand married a fourth time. His last wife was Maria Cristina of Bourbon, the Cristina of the Carlist War, who turned the tables on her royal spouse, for soon after his death she secretly married a sergeant of the guards with whom she raised a numerous family. Of the morals of Ferdinand's only surviving child and successor, the "virtuous Isabel" of the Marx-Engels correspondence, the less said the better.

received the royal assent, but all attempts to put it into operation during the next two years only served to increase the existing confusion. The reforms which might have introduced some measure of control into the administration were systematically sabotaged by Garay's reactionary colleagues in the cabinet and by the bureaucracy. At the same time the sudden replacement of indirect taxation by direct payments placed an intolerable burden on the bankrupt farms and business enterprises of the country. Instead of netting a steady revenue, the authorities found themselves inundated with unsaleable household goods and tools seized by the tax collectors from the impoverished peasants, while the wealthy found means of evading their obligations. Under such conditions all efforts at reform had to be abandoned. After carrying on with an impossible task for almost two years, Garay was at last dismissed in September 1818, and the country fell into a state of anarchy exceeding all previous records.

Life in Spain during 1819, the last phase of the period we are now reviewing, is described in the following terms by Baumgarten:

> To judge by the conditions then prevailing in Spain one might have thought that the state had been expressly invented to *organise* the "war of all against all". The servants of the state waged war on the peasants and citizens, whom they plagued with the law and hounded with tax collectors, policemen, and inquisitors. Their victims retaliated with conspiracies, wholesale smuggling, theft, and robbery. Not for centuries had banditry flourished as it did then. Every province had its famous bandit leader, whose brave deeds were universally acclaimed. And how easy for these robbers to be more just, humane, and noble than such a king and such captains-general! In every town and village families, coteries, and individuals fought bitter feuds by intrigue and murder unhampered, nay encouraged, in their fanaticism by the authorities. There was no trace of law or order superior to the arbitrary greed of the individual. The whole country was riddled with secret societies, whose revolutionary aims appeared to offer the only possible salvation from such disgraceful conditions. But worse than the chaos in any wild mountain region was the clash of unbridled passions raging in Madrid. . . .

The battle of intrigues in the capital which split the camarilla into two bitterly hostile camps of bishops, confessors, lackeys, and cabinet ministers was now an open struggle for the spoils of corruption. The prize was the rake-off from the supplies for the great expedition gathering at Cadiz to restore the allegiance of the insurrectionary colonies. English merchants had offered to provide the ships and equipment for this campaign—in spite of the British support for the colonial independence movements—but, in the words of the Prussian ambassador, the Spanish government "preferred to ruin its cause with its own hands". The final outcome was a plot hatched by Tatischeff to complete the alienation of Ferdinand from the British, and to bind him even more closely to his master, the Czar. Alexander sold eight Russian warships to Spain for the fantastic sum of 54,400,000 reals (over £2,000,000 at the rates of exchange then prevailing). According to Altamira,[1] the graft from this deal was shared by Ferdinand, Tatischeff, the ex-lackey Ugarte, whom the people called Antonio I, Emperor of Spain, and the war minister Eguia. Moreover, Ferdinand had the satisfaction of making the British pay part of the price, for just at that time he exacted £400,000 compensation for at last agreeing to suppress the slave trade at a date sufficiently in advance not to disturb him. When the ships arrived after much delay, they had none of the necessary equipment for transatlantic navigation. Their condition was such that no captain was willing to sail them. When one of them was about to be loaded with armaments, its bottom fell out. When the ship of the line *Emperor Alexander* put to sea, in spite of warnings, it was unable to withstand the waves of the Atlantic and had to return immediately.

The corruption and incompetence in the army equalled, if it did not exceed, that in the navy. The war minister scarcely ever put in an appearance at his office and indignantly refused to be troubled with official business at home (he was known as the 'plumber-killer' because he had run his sword through a plumber who had 'insulted' his wife). In his dispatch of 12 June 1818 the Prussian ambassador reports that Ferdinand had complained about the incompetence of his officers. But he had desisted when told "the distinguished officers recommended by the

Supreme War Council are all liberals; the creatures are at least loyal subjects".

Towards the end of 1819 the government was compelled publicly to confess its impotence. The confusion created by the plots of the rival cabals had been systematically exploited and even accentuated by the members of the secret societies with whom every department of state was riddled. They had turned the table on their oppressors by a grand-scale repetition of the trick which had led to the revival of the Holy Office. The whole country had been thrown into a state of panic by a mass issue of faked government instructions calling the militia to arms, advancing or reducing the rank of countless officers, and ordering the removal of whole regiments to different garrisons. Countermanding orders only increased the chaos, for no one in the provinces could be sure any longer whether a particular government instruction was genuine or forged. Panic-stricken, the King now destroyed the last remnant of his authority. He gave a detailed account of the forgeries in a decree dated 18 December 1819, at the same time appealing to his loyal subjects to restore order in his administration.

"King Ferdinand had filled the cup of his iniquity to overflowing", writes Baumgarten; "things had come to such a pass, that the maltreated people no longer had any choice but to take the reins from his hands."

The voice of liberty had not been silent in these long years of terror and oppression (though Ferdinand had sought to legislate it out of existence by prohibiting the use of the terms 'liberales' and 'serviles' in his decree of 26 January 1816). All attempts to obtain a legal conviction against the liberal leaders arrested in the razzia of 10 May 1814 had failed, and Ferdinand, who had threatened them with summary execution in September 1815, was at last compelled, two and a half years after their arrest, to condemn them on his own authority to indefinite terms of imprisonment or banishment (preferably in notorious African jails). Even more important is the ever-recurring evidence of active opposition. In September 1814 the guerrillero Mina raised the flag of revolt in Navarre and attempted to occupy Pamplona. But he mistrusted his followers and escaped to France. A year later Porlier, a no less famous general, proclaimed the Constitution in Corunna. He was defeated and executed. In February 1816 the lawyer Richard plotted to kidnap the King in Madrid. He was hanged. In April 1817 another hero of the war of independence, General Lacy, proclaimed the Constitution near Barcelona. But he was no more successful than his predecessors. Fearing demonstrations of the people in the Catalan capital, the authorities secretly conveyed their prisoner to Majorca where he was shot in the following July. During the same year a similar fate befell the advocate Navarro and four of his comrades in Valencia. There the captain-general Elio had illegally reintroduced torture and executed some 300 political prisoners. A group of army officers and citizens planned to kidnap him in the theatre on 1 January 1819. But the theatres were closed owing to the death of the Queen, and the conspirators had to postpone their plot. They were betrayed and thirteen patriots lost their lives in the cause of liberty.

The despised régime finally foundered on the very scheme which had provided the happiest hunting-ground for its corruptions: the expedition of Cadiz. The graft and favouritism which had vitiated this enterprise, the terrors of ocean transport in coffin ships with rotten food supplies, and the ferocity of colonial warfare for a hated cause, combined to make this campaign appear a punitive expedition against the Spanish troops, rather than the insurgent colonies. Ever since the preparations had started in 1816, a spirit bordering on revolt had been rife in the regiments condemned to participate. The freemasons and other secret societies of Cadiz had established contact with the officers' corps, and in July 1819 a mutiny of seven battalions was only averted by the last-minute treachery of the commander-in-chief, Count La Bisbal.[1] The spirit of rebellion was not, however, crushed. On 1 January 1820 Rafael de Riego, commander of the second Asturian battalion, began the coup which led to his heroic march with 1,500 men through Andalusia (27 January to 11 March). Surrounded by hostile, but on the whole inactive armies, Riego and his men proclaimed the Constitution of 1812 wherever they went. When the last of the faithful band were finally compelled by fatigue and lack of supplies to disperse and their cause

---

[1] Henry O'Donnel, Count La Bisbal, was an experienced trimmer. When Ferdinand returned to Spain, La Bisbal sent a confidential messenger to him with two separate letters. One lauded the Constitution to the skies, the other damned it as a work of infamy. The messenger was to deliver whichever conformed to the policy of the King. In later years La Bisbal found repeated opportunities for further treachery.

seemed lost, the flame of revolt had spread to the north and thence through the rest of the country. Two days before Riego abandoned his attempt the King had been forced by the citizens of Madrid to swear the oath of loyalty to the Constitution (9 March 1820).

During the years of despondency the Constitution of 1812 had been the flaming symbol of liberty to all progressive Spaniards. Completed at a time "when there were no territories in which to proclaim it",[1] it had been invested with the mystic spell of a talisman to freedom. "For the majority of Spaniards it was like the Unknown God worshipped by the Athenians."[1] Now it was proclaimed. The prison gates were thrown open to release the victims of reaction. A wave of jubilant exaltation swept the country. To the Spanish people, crushed by six years of barbarism, it seemed the dawn of the millennium.

> England had to suffer fifty years of turbulence with a sacrifice of half a million lives; France had to endure twenty-five years of misery and war; but Spain achieved the greatest good by "six years of patience, one day of declaration and two of rejoicing".

Thus the Junta of Madrid addressed the citizens at the 'Dos de Mayo' celebrations of 1820.[2] We, who are separated[2] by more than a century from these events, can still recapture the echo of the Spanish people's exultation. Indelibly engraved in the tradition of revolutionary Spain, it lives in the triumphant beat of the 'Hymn of Riego'.

'EL SORDO'

Persecution and censorship cast their shadow over the cultural life of Spain during the six black years of reaction. Most of the leading intellectuals were exiled or imprisoned. Those who had escaped that fate were careful to avoid suspicion. But beneath a surface of apparent calm there burrowed the 'old mole', the revolution. Spies and conspirators measured their wits in a tangled skein of plots and counter-plots. Secrets guarded by terrible oaths and the constant fear of treachery shrouded Spain in a heavy cloak of mystery.

Against this sombre background a solitary figure stands

---

[1] Marx *op. cit.* article of 2 December 1854.   [2] Baumgarten *op. cit.*

out as a symbol of courage and enlightenment. The actor Maiquez, too, had been arrested as a liberal during the razzia of 10-11 May. But he was allowed to return to the stage after a short imprisonment. He revived many of his most famous productions during the following three seasons: 'Othello', 'Orestes', 'Numancia', 'Oscar', and even such plays tainted with the virus of Jacobinism as 'Pelayo' and the 'Horacios y Curiacios'. Ceaselessly harassed by police and inquisitors, his courage made him the idol of the people of Madrid. Equally significant: his performances were pointedly avoided by the King. In 1817 the authorities at last succeeded in hounding Maiquez from the stage of the capital. He returned in the following season, but was finally exiled in June 1819. Wrecked physically and mentally by the persecution he had endured, his powers of resistance were undermined by the conditions of his banishment in a remote provincial town. He lost his reason and died on 17 March 1820, a few days after the triumph of the cause he had so valiantly supported.

Although he retained his rank of court painter, Goya now disappeared from the public scene. He had retired, even before the return of Ferdinand, to a small country seat he owned on the opposite bank of the Manzanares, and he buried his grief behind the walls of the cottage which the people called the 'Quinta del Sordo' (the deaf man's house). Except a few intimate friends, none of his contemporaries ever saw the works which we cherish to-day (with the Caprichos) as the finest fruits of his genius: the 'Disasters of the War', the 'Disparates', the 'pinturas negras', and the treasures of his sketch-books. To the rising generation of Spanish artists, versed in the polished classicism of the David school, he had already become a legend.

Most of the people Goya portrayed during these years were friends or members of his family, among them his grandson Mariano, his pupil Ascensio Julia, the engraver Rafael Esteve, the composer Quijano, the architect Cuervo, the secretary of the Academy Munarriz, and a few liberal-minded clerics, like the writer Fernandez de Rojas. His most celebrated self-portrait dates from 1815. A brilliant portrait of an unknown soldier holding a letter with the legend 'Auctibus Reipublicae Expulsus' is traditionally identified with the guerrillero Mina; a portrait of El Empeci-nado is of doubtful authenticity.

The few official portraits Goya still painted date from 1814 to 1815. They are confined to some ceremonial effigies of the King (but he painted no other member of the royal household) and one or two portraits of ministers (*e.g.* the Duke of San Carlos and D. Ignacio Omulryan y Rourera). Society portraits of this period are even rarer, those of the young Duke of Osuna (the son of Goya's former patron) and the Duchess of Abrantes being notable exceptions. Yet Goya, like Rembrandt, concluded his public activity with an official composition which is a milestone in the history of art. Curiously enough this picture, too, was painted for a body of citizens, not for the court. It represents a meeting of the Philippine Company, the great monopoly of the Spanish colonial merchants (Castres Museum). More than three-quarters of a canvas, measuring 4·20 by 4·50 metres, is filled with the bare walls and boldly patterned floor of a vast and gloomy chamber. A cold patch of sunlight falling through a deep window recess in the right-hand wall on to the centre of the floor is the sole illumination. In the distant background the King is seated behind a raised table, the centre in a row of doll-like portrait busts framed by the oval backs of their chairs. Ranged along the walls of the room on the extreme right and left of the canvas, the members of the company are sitting in closely packed ranks. Vividly individualised in type, attitude, and expression, they present a striking contrast to the ceremonial stiffness of the high table. Collectively they are the upper middle class incarnate.

How faithfully the musty brown, which pervades this monumental anticipation of Daumier's 'Ventre Législatif', reflects what must have been the mental atmosphere of that assembly! Ferdinand regarded the worthy merchants of his capital as a juicy orange to be squeezed dry by ever-repeated requests for compulsory advances to his bankrupt treasury. As time went on their relations degenerated into a state of open warfare. In October 1818 a forced loan of 20 million reals was imposed upon the Madrid merchants. Protests were answered with the threat to imprison the directors of the Bank of San Carlos and the leaders of the five major guilds, unless the money were supplied without delay. Shortly afterwards the Philippine Company refused the demand for a new contribution of 8 million reals on the grounds that they had already advanced a total of 145 millions to the royal treasury. Early in 1820 Ferdinand ordered an inspection of the Company's books and the confiscation of all its assets. At this period the merchant companies and bank could protect what resources were left to them only by distributing the money they received from day to day immediately among their shareholders. In view of these facts it is impossible to assume, as has recently been advocated,[1] that Goya's picture was painted 'about 1820'. It must have been commissioned in the first flush of loyal enthusiasm, or at any rate during the first phase of the régime, while the merchants were still on speaking terms with their sovereign.

About the same time Goya also made his last public appearance as an engraver. Apart from the 'Caprichos', the 'Tauromachia' is the only one of his great series of etchings that was published during his lifetime. It was issued in the autumn of 1816 in an edition of 33 plates to which 11 further ones were added by later editors. In this work Goya was not concerned, like the author of *Pan y Toros*, to condemn bull-fights as inhuman. He must rather have regarded them, much like Picasso a century later, as a symbol of the fierce contradictions that tormented the Spanish people. In the savage ritual of the bull-ring, as Goya depicted it, blind fury is matched with valour, brute force with agile skill; but there are also scenes of dreadful carnage, in which men are impaled on the horns or trampled under the hoofs of the bull, scenes of terror and panic. Everything is subordinated to action in these designs. The bulls are disproportionately small, but fierce and mobile (as Sánchez Cantón puts it, they could not be less exact or more true). Again, as in the 'Caprichos', the backgrounds are closing backcloths rather than beckoning vistas. Occasionally the rising tiers of the amphitheatre are visible, crowded and deeply shaded. But more often the brightly lit stockade around the arena sets off the dark group of struggling men and animals. Or the action takes place on a burning patch of sunlit sand encircled by shade; or it is moved (as later in Degas' paintings of race-horses) right to the edge of the design, leaving

[1] By Georges Grappe, *Goya*, Paris, 1937—a useful reminder how dangerous it is to date Goya on purely aesthetic grounds. Incidentally, Ferdinand dealt in a similar way with the Mesta. In 1815 he presided at one of its meetings, also of course in order to cajole a 'loan' from this ancient guild of the graziers, whom he afterwards presented with a full-length portrait of himself in commemoration of the event. *v.* Klein *op. cit.*

more than half the plate empty. The 'Tauromaquia' is, in fact, the most impressionist of all Goya's works,[1] and although he presented the series in the popular form of famous incidents from the history of bull-fighting, it was not a success (of the French artists only Géricault and Gautier seem to have known it).

MONSTERS

To appreciate the terrible conflict which tormented Goya in this period one must turn to the 'private works' which he created without regard for the market. Foremost among these nightmare visions are the 'pinturas negras'—the black paintings—of the Quinta del Sordo. These paintings, now in the Prado, originally covered the walls of the two main rooms in Goya's country retreat. In the ground-floor dining-room Goya painted a 'Manola', a bearded old man with a monster shouting into his ear, a visionary 'Pilgrimage to San Isidro', a 'Witches Sabbath,' 'Judith and Holofernes', and the terrifying figure of 'Saturn devouring one of his Children'. A haunting landscape with the head of a dog, the 'Fates' suspended in mid-air, two men fighting with clubs as they sink into a bog, grinning women, men mocking a reading figure, two old people eating soup, the miraculous 'Font of San Isidro', and a fantastic vision of soldiers shooting at figures who float in the air of a gloomy landscape filled the room on the upper storey (figs. 66, 69, 108, 109).[2]

Ghost-like apparitions of towering dimensions, massed faces distorted by terror, or bodies without gravity, emerge from spaceless gloom or float in sombre landscapes with huge rocks in this gruesome nightmare. For the most part only half life-size, they give the impression of a superhuman scale. The same breadth distinguishes their treatment: all superfluous details are eliminated, and the colouring is reduced to a macabre harmony of black, brown, and white.

Equally macabre are twenty-two monumental etchings, eighteen of which were first published in 1864 by the Madrid Academy under the title 'Proverbios'. Although they may not have been etched until 1820, they were certainly con-

---

[1] Goya's style of painting also changed at this period. His larger works were becoming more and more monochrome, but there are also occasionally surprising experiments with vivid primary colours, not seen in painting since Greco, nor repeated until the twentieth century. Sánchez Cantón speaks of a complete renovation of technique, a 'fourth youth' of the septuagenarian. [2] Mayer *op. cit.*

ceived in the same period as the 'pinturas negras', *i.e.* some time between 1814 and 1819. The title 'Proverbs' chosen by the Academy is a travesty of Goya's intention. He himself called these enigmatic fantasies 'Disparates' (his original captions, 'Disparate feminino', 'Disparate de miedo', 'Disparate furioso', 'Disparate pobre', etc., were discovered on contemporary proofs of a number of the plates). The term 'disparate' means 'folly', 'vagary', 'something without rhyme or reason'; its significance is thus similar to that of 'capricho'. But what makes its adoption by Goya especially significant is the fact that it is the term generally used by the older Spanish writers to describe the works of Hieronymus Bosch:

> Bosch, the Flemish artist celebrated for the "disparates" of his painting. . . . [Argote de Molina, *Libro de la monteria*, Seville, 1582.]
>
> Although people generally call his pictures the "disparates" of H. Bosch, he cannot be accused of heresy. [Fray José de Sigüenza, *Historia de la Orden de San Gerónimo*, Madrid, 1605.]
>
> He painted themes and objects which are extremely unusual and were never seen before, so that it has become the custom to call Bosch "el disparate". [J. Martinez, *Discursos practicables del nobilisimo arte de la pintura*, mid-seventeenth century.][1]

This use of the word persisted in Goya's time. In his article on El Bosco in the *Diccionario* of 1800 Cean Bermúdez paraphrased Sigüenza's critique, but he retained the term 'disparate'.[2]

Additional evidence that Goya consciously chose the title 'disparate' to indicate the affinity of his visions (the ghost-like quality of which must not blind us to their deep moral intent) with the dreams of Bosch may be found in a curious drawing of the Prado collection. It also shows in a striking manner in what sense one may speak of 'influences' in Goya's imaginative work. One of the paintings by Bosch in the Prado, which was undoubtedly known to Goya, is the 'Cure of Folly'. A pompous-looking doctor is cutting a stone out of the forehead of a man who is seated at a table; two other figures watch the operation. The satirical impression produced by this scene is heightened by

---

[1] *v.* Tolnay *op. cit.*

[2] Two other favourite terms of Goya occasionally applied to Bosch are 'sueño' (*e.g.* by Quevedo) and 'capricho' (by Ponz).

the large funnel which is incongruously placed on the doctor's head, instead of a hat. Goya's drawing, which he significantly entitled 'Gran disparate', shows a decapitated man spoon-feeding his own head placed on the table at which he is sitting. A man behind him is pouring a liquid out of a jug into the funnel, which has been inserted into the severed trunk, in place of the head. A third figure watches these strange proceedings. *Formally* Goya's freak is a completely new invention. But in view of his title it is not unreasonable to assume that Goya was struck by the incongruous use of the funnel in El Bosco's 'Folly' and that it was this *detail* which inspired the invention of his own 'Disparate'. By retaining the detail of the funnel, Goya stuck closer than would appear at first sight to the hidden *motif* of Bosch's painting. In Bosch's days the funnel was widely used in popular satire as a symbol for the lifeless, purely mechanical learning of the scholastics. The 'Nürnberger Trichter', for example, is a miraculous device through which the indolent student has knowledge poured into him without any effort on his part. In Goya's drawing knowledge, *i.e.* the official view of things, is poured straight into the trunk of the man, who does not even need his head to absorb the dope. Nor is this all; Goya has reinforced the 'funnel' symbol with the synonymous one of 'spoon-feeding' —the trunk spoon-feeds its own head and thus passes on the dope it has absorbed—and it was this latter symbol which he had used some twenty years earlier in the 'Chinchilla' plate of the 'Caprichos'. Thus Goya's 'Gran Disparate', like the disparates of Bosch, conceals a profound meaning under a mask of folly, and the same is true of all the fantastic images we are now considering (figs. 67, 68).

The twenty-two plates of the 'Disparates' are not, therefore, morbid essays in 'satanism' for its own sake. But they are the most dream-like of all Goya's etchings,[1] and their symbols are consequently more personal and elaborate than those of the earlier prints. Nevertheless, some of them can be traced back to the Caprichos and even to the tapestry cartoons. Indeed, two cartoons reappear entirely, the 'Pelele' and the 'Game of blind-man's-buff'. To appreciate the road Goya had travelled one should compare the original

---

[1] This applies even more to the preliminary drawings, not all of which were engraved. Blamire Young, *The Proverbs of Goya*, London, 1923, is an unconventional attempt to interpret the 'Disparates'.

conceptions of 1791 with the nightmare visions into which he transferred them a quarter of a century later. Other details of the 'Disparates', such as the repeated introduction of figures on stilts or the plate of the sack-race, strengthen the impression that the series as a whole is in some respects a sardonic revival of Goya's main theme in the cartoons: the portrayal, 'in pleasing style, of the manners, customs and games of his country' (figs. 70, 75).

One of the most striking of the Capricho symbols revived in the 'Disparates' is that of the double-faced woman who represents the Duchess of Alba in the suppressed plate known as the 'Dream of Lying and Faithlessness'. In the eleventh plate of the 'Disparates' a similar young woman with two separate heads is running away from the shadowy figure of an adoring lover towards a dark gateway in which four other women are waiting for her. Three are lined and crippled with age, the fourth, somewhat younger than her companions, looks up in despair. With one of her heads she looks back tenderly towards her lover and she beckons to him with her raised hand. The other head is bent low towards the human wreckage in the gateway; its face is deeply shaded and rigidly set, with the blank stare of a person obsessed. Beneath it appears a second, more sharply defined image of the lover, now reduced to the state of a raging madman, with dishevelled hair and gaping eyes and mouth (fig. 72, cf. also fig. 22). Even more horrifying is the way in which the Capricho symbol of the married couple (fig. 36) has been intensified in the 'Disparates'. The man and woman tied together have been fused into a single monstrous being, a gigantic nightmare image of Plato's primordial man-woman, before the separation of the sexes (fig. 74).

Personal feelings and experiences thus play a crucial part in the 'Disparates', and there are repeated examples of sexual symbolism, as in the plate with the stallion who has seized a woman with his teeth and is raising her from the ground, or in the various illustrations of flying (figs. 76, 77). But all these allusions to the 'vices and follies of private life', or even to Goya's own personal experiences, are again, as in the Caprichos, linked with meditations on the 'frauds of public life'. Once again Goya was attempting to show, in an even profounder way, how both spheres transfuse and distort each other (figs. 70-77, 110, 111).

The Quinta paintings and the 'Disparates' are the

supreme embodiment of Goya's 'satanic' expressionism. They are Caprichos on a gigantic scale. "Black-wingéd demon forms"—

> Like animated frenzies, dimly moved
> Shadows, and skeletons, and fiendly shapes,
> Thronging round human graves, and o'er the dead
> Sculpturing records for each memory
> In verse, such as malignant gods pronounce,
> Blasting the hopes of men, when heaven and hell
> Confounded burst in ruin o'er the world:
> And they did build vast trophies, instruments
> Of murder, human bones, barbaric gold,
> Skins torn from living men, and towers of skulls
> With sightless holes gazing on blinder heaven,
> Mitres, and crowns, and brazen chariots stained
> With blood, and scrolls of mystic wickedness,
> The sanguine codes of venerable crime.[1]

> The Fiend whose name was Legion: Death, Decay,
> Earthquake and Blight, and Want, and Madness pale,
> Wingéd and wan diseases, an array
> Numerous as leaves that strew the autumnal gale;
> .   .   .   .   .   .
> Fear, Hatred, Faith, and Tyranny, who spread
> Those subtle nets which snare the living and the dead.[2]

There is no more striking resemblance than that between the visualised anguish of the lonely old artist, who retained his faith in the cause of liberty even at a time of catastrophic defeat, and the imagery of the young poet, whose very being breathed revolt. Both had discovered the cause of their agony in the concrete social evils of their day. Like Goya in the donkey sequence of the 'Caprichos', Shelley even went to the length of identifying the demonic visions of his dreams with living politicians:

> I met Murder on the way—
> He had a mask like Castlereagh—
> Very smooth he looked, yet grim;
> Seven blood-hounds followed him:

> All were fat; and well they might
> Be in admirable plight,
> For one by one, and two by two,
> He tossed them human hearts to chew
> Which from his wide cloak he drew.

> Next came Fraud, and he had on,
> Like Eldon, an ermined gown;
> His big tears, for he wept well,
> Turned to millstones as they fell.

[1] Shelley, 'The Daemon of the World', 1815.
[2] Shelley, 'The Revolt of Islam', 1817.

And the little children, who
Round his feet played to and fro,
Thinking every tear a gem,
Had their brains knocked out by them.

Clothed with the Bible, as with light,
And the shadows of the night,
Like Sidmouth, next, Hypocrisy
On a crocodile rode by.

And many more destructions played
In this ghastly masquerade,
All disguised, even to the eyes,
Like Bishops, lawyers, peers, or spies. . . .[1]

Shelley clearly understood the significance of the 'romantic agony' in Restoration art and literature:

Methinks, those who now live have survived an age of despair. . . . The revulsion occasioned by the atrocities of the demagogues, and the re-establishment of successive tyrannies in France, was terrible, and felt in the remotest corner of the civilised world. Could they listen to the plea of reason, who had groaned under the calamities of a social state, according to the provisions of which, one man riots in luxury, while another famishes for want of bread? Can he who the day before was a trampled slave, SUDDENLY become liberal-minded, forbearing, and independent? This is the consequence of the habits of a state of society to be produced by resolute perseverance and indefatigable hope, and long-suffering and long-believing courage, and the systematic efforts of generations of men of intellect and virtue. Such is the lesson which experience teaches now. But on the first reverses of hope in the progress of French liberty, the sanguine eagerness for good overleaped the solution of these questions, and for a time extinguished itself in the unexpectedness of their result. Thus many of the most ardent and tender-hearted of the worshippers of public good have been morally ruined, by what a partial glimpse of the events they deplored appeared to shew as the melancholy desolation of all their cherished hopes. Hence gloom and misanthropy have become the characteristics of the age in which we live, the solace of a disappointment that unconsciously finds relief only in the wilful exaggeration of its own despair. This influence has tainted the literature of the age with the hopeless-

---

[1] Shelley, 'The Masque of Anarchy' ('written on the occasion of the Massacre at Manchester'), 1819.

ness of the minds from which it flows. Metaphysics, and enquiries into moral and political science, have become little else than vain attempts to revive exploded superstitions, or sophisms like those of Mr. Malthus, calculated to lull the oppressors of mankind into a security of everlasting triumph. Our works of fiction and poetry have been overshadowed by the same infectious gloom. But mankind appear to me to be emerging from their trance. . . .[1]

Shelley, an ardent admirer of Spanish literature, especially Calderón, was deeply stirred by the events in Spain. His 'Ode to the Assertors of Liberty' ('Arise, arise, arise!— There is blood on the earth that denies ye bread . . .') was 'written October 1819, before the Spaniards had recovered their Liberty'. The Revolution of 1820 itself he glorified in his 'Ode to Liberty', and the revolutionary wave it inspired in other countries in the 'Ode to Naples' and the poem 'Liberty' (all 1820). The following passage from a letter to Leigh Hunt, dated Pisa, 5 April 1820, also reveals Shelley's attitude to the Spanish liberal movement:

> Much stress is laid upon a still more southern climate for my health, which has suffered dreadfully this winter, and if I could believe that Spain would be effectual, I might possibly be tempted to make a voyage thither, on account of the glorious events of which it is at this moment the theatre. You know my passion for a republic, or anything which approaches it.[2]

Both Goya and Shelley belonged to that band of inspired intellectuals whose art was the clarion call of militant democracy. But while Shelley deserted his class to join the ranks of the revolution, Goya rose from the people. Moreover, Goya, born in 1746, grew to manhood with the tide of bourgeois rationalism as it surged towards its revolutionary climax. Himself in the thick of the struggle, he saw his people in action. And although he shared their defeat, he never wavered in his militant materialism. Shelley, on the other hand, was born in 1792. He grew up in the backwash of the revolution, when the upper middle class, having attained its aims, had cast aside its democratic pretensions and a wide rift had appeared in the structure of hope built on the foundation of bourgeois

[1] Shelley, Preface to 'The Revolt of Islam', 1817–18.
[2] *The Letters of Percy Bysshe Shelley*, ed. by Roger Ingpen, London, 1914, vol. ii.

rationalism. Moreover, he died too young to experience anything but the first storm signals of the renewed rising of the people in the Reform Bill agitation. His brief span of life was confined to a single epoch of fierce repression in the history of his country, to a period when the people, as yet only dimly aware of their true aims, remained on the whole inactive, and fervent hope could be the only solace of 'the generous few'.

> The system of society as it exists at present [Shelley wrote to Hunt on 1 May 1820] must be over-thrown from the foundations with all its super-structure of maxims and forms before we shall find anything but disappointment in our intercourse with any but a few select spirits. This remedy does not seem to be one of the easiest. But the generous few are no less held to tend with all their efforts towards it. If faith is a virtue in any case it is so in politics rather than religion; as having a power of producing a belief in that which is at once a prophecy and a cause.[1]

Because Shelley's revolutionary fervour could find an outlet only in the imagery inspired by his faith, and not in action, he could never wholly master an inclination towards philosophical idealism. Although he confessed, in 1819, that he had "founded much of his persuasions regarding the imagined cause of the universe" on the principle that "mind cannot create, it can only perceive",[2] he was never-theless increasingly fascinated by Plato's metaphysical speculations.

Goya's sober materialism, on the other hand, is evident even in the 'Disparates'. He repeatedly went out of his way to prove how little he had succumbed to the satanic mysti-cism which seems to pervade that work. In one of the 'Caprichos' he had used a barren tree on which an empty cowl is spread to symbolise the material roots of established religion. He employed a similar device in two plates of the 'Disparates'. In the 'Folly of Fear' (No. 2: 'Disparate de Miedo') a gigantic phantom faces a group of soldiers. Some have fallen, terror-stricken; another is running away. In the middle distance their comrades are preparing for a desperate night action. They are training a gun at the enemy, who is

[1] *Op. cit.*
[2] *Op. cit.* Letter to Hunt, Livorno, 27 September 1819. *v.* also the selection from the Shelley–Hunt correspondence and from Hunt's *Examiner* articles edited by R. Brimley Johnson, *Shelley—Leigh Hunt*, London, 1928.

rendered invisible by the dark range of hills in the background. But on closer inspection the 'ghost' turns out to be a commonplace contraption of sticks and winding-sheets, from one of the sleeves of which there leers the revolting face of an impostor: by playing on the superstitions of the people, the 'fifth column' of reaction attempts to demoralise the rear of the army which is fighting for the real values of life[1] (fig. 73).

Plate 19, 'Disparate conocido' ('Folly exposed'), reveals a more truculent mood. A crowd is facing two similar contraptions of wood and cloth, one of which is flourishing a sword. A respectably dressed figure on the left of the group still exhibits signs of fear, but the leader of the crowd, a man of the people, drastically reveals his contempt for the sabre-rattling scare-crows of despotism (fig. 75).

The 'pinturas negras' and the 'Disparates' are moving manifestations of Goya's struggle to preserve his faith in a moment of deep despondency. Hence the difficulty of tracing their *specific* inspiration. In the last eighteen plates of the 'Disasters of the War,' on the other hand, Goya was far more open in his social criticism (these plates, too, were produced at various dates between 1814 and 1820). If we neglect the somewhat enigmatic plate 65 (weeping women running from a table at which an officer is sitting: 'Why all this clamour?'), the sequence opens with two quite unambiguous comments on the benighted fanaticism which still blinded the Spanish people: plate 66, 'Strange devotion', shows a donkey bearing a glass coffin with a mummified saint past a devout multitude; in plate 67 ('This is no less so') statues of saints are carried on the backs of men. 'What madness!' is the caption of the next design, which shows a grotesque monk sprawling among piles of masks, puppets, and other symbols of superstition.

The plate (69) which is the climax of this introductory sequence was described in the following terms by Théophile Gautier in 1845:

> Parmi ces dessins qui s'expliquent aisément, il y en a un terrifiant et mystérieux, et dont le sens, vaguement entrevu, est plein de frissons et d'épouvantements. C'est un mort à moitié enfoui dans la terre, qui se soulève sur le coude, et, de sa main osseuse, écrit

---

[1] *v.* also Young *op. cit.*

sans regarder, sur un papier posé à côté de lui, un mot qui vaut bien les plus noirs du Dante: *Nada* (néant). Autour de sa tête, qui a gardé juste assez de chair pour être plus horrible qu'un crâne dépouillé, tourbillonnent, à peine visibles dans l'épaisseur de la nuit, de mons-trueux cauchemars illuminés çà et là de livides éclairs. Une main fatidique soutient une balance dont les plateaux se renversent. Connaissez-vous quelque chose de plus sinistre et de plus désolant? [*Voyage en Espagne*] (fig. 84).

Of the following nine plates one shows a procession of men, including clerics, tied to one another with ropes and groping their way in single file through a desolate land-scape ('They do not know the way')—most likely an allusion to the incompetence of the camarilla; another a plucked 'carnivorous vulture' of gigantic size chased from the scene by a man armed with a pitch-fork (a reference to the defeat of the French); and a third a cleric (identified as the *Pope* in the preliminary drawing) precariously balancing on a tight-rope which is frayed to breaking-point ('May the rope tear'). Two plates (72 and 78) refer to the Spanish people: in the former they are represented by a prostrate man beset by vampires ('The result'), in the latter by a horse fighting with wolves and hounds ('He defends himself well'). The remaining designs are 'caprichos enfáticos' exposing the misdeeds of clerical reaction: 'Against the common-weal', 'Feline pantomime', 'Comedy of charlatans'. "Mísera huma-nidad, la culpa es tuya" is the legend which a fox, aided by a priest, is writing on a large scroll in the etching entitled 'That is the worst of it!' The background is filled with a crowd of dejected-looking people, among them the gaunt figure of a handcuffed madman (74). Of the last four designs of the 'Disasters' only one concerns us in the present context. It shows a monster devouring his victims (81) (figs. 82-5, 90).

Goya's link with Bosch reveals the antecedents of his use of fantastic symbolism in the people's cause. Shelley's poems are a literary parallel. But there are also pictorial parallels in contemporary English caricature. Most sig-nificant in this respect are the illustrations drawn by George Cruikshank (1792–1878) for William Hone's famous pam-phlets of 1819–21.[1] 'The Political Showman' of 1821 closely

[1] The most important of these, including 'The Political House that Jack built', 'The Man in the Moon', etc., are collected in *Facetiae and Miscellanies* by W. Hone,

resembles Shelley's 'Mask of Anarchy' in its imagery. In it the members of the British cabinet are presented in the guise of 'vermin' and monsters. There is Eldon, the crocodile whose tears turn to millstones;[1] Wellington appears as a scorpion, and Castlereagh's bloodhound buries his teeth in prostrate Liberty's throat. The final print shows the Holy Alliance as a monstrous vampire devouring the people, while the following verse by Moore serves as its caption:

> Those Lords of pray'r and prey—that *band* of Kings,
> That Royal, rav'ning BEAST, whose vampire wings
> O'er sleeping Europe treacherously brood,
> And fan her into dreams of *promis'd* good,
> Of Hope, of Freedom—but to drain her blood!

The use of symbolic animals, including the ass and the monkey, so important in Goya's Caprichos, was, indeed, an established tradition among English caricaturists. It is frequently found during that significant phase of English politics which anticipated the democratic movements of the nineteenth century, the phase, during the 1760's and 1770's, when John Wilkes and 'Junius' fought for the people's rights against parliamentary corruption and the reactionary tendencies of the 'King's Friends'. Two examples will suffice to show how closely the English satirists anticipated Goya's imagery. The first is a cartoon called 'The Evacuations' published in December 1762 from Mary Darly's well-known print-shop in Leicester Fields, and directed against the negotiations which led to the Peace of Paris in the following year. Standing on a mountebank's stage, Lord Bute, the elder Fox, and Smollett, the author, are acting as quack doctors to Britannia, whom they are compelling to vomit various places conquered during the Seven Years' War into a basin held by a monkey representing France. Bute has the head of an ass and blows bubbles to the people in the background; Fox, who is holding a huge clyster-pipe, has the head of a fox; they are trampling on the shield of the City of London and the spear and cap of Liberty (fig. 79).

While the print just described resembles the Godoy-donkey sequence of the 'Caprichos', the other example has a close affinity to the 'satanic' designs not only of the 'Caprichos' but also of the 'Disparates' and the 'Disasters'.

London, 1827. Cruikshank, it will be noted, was born in the same year as Shelley; he was sixteen years older than Daumier, who survived him by one year.

[1] The pamphlet quotes Shakespeare: "Trust not the cunning waters of his eyes:—His eyes drop mill-stones".

The political situation, as viewed by the opposition, was, indeed, strikingly similar in the England of the 1760's and in the Spain of the 'Capricho' period. The role attributed by the Spanish reformers to Maria Luisa and Godoy was attributed thirty years earlier in England by the opposition to the Dowager Princess of Wales (the mother of George III) and Lord Bute. These two personalities appear in our second example, the print 'Multum in parvo' of 1763, as a booted goat riding on a she-goat with the head of a woman. They are the centre group in a procession of satanic monsters—including a wolf in sheep's clothing, a bespectacled and horned owl, a giant drummer, etc.— moving towards the gaping mouth of hell. This print was republished in a collection of cartoons called *The British Antidote to Caledonian Poison*, where it is accompanied by the following goyaesque 'explanation':

A Group of drol Caricatures going to receive the Reward due to their Merit; but who they are, or where they are going, or for what they are going, we don't think so convenient to explain at present, as we have no great Inclination to pop our Heads through a certain wooden Machine, invented by a Set of arbitrary Men, to punish all those who are so unfortunate as to be wiser than themselves[1] (fig. 80).

Examples of English caricatures with symbolic monsters or animals could be multiplied indefinitely. Even Hogarth used them in some of his early prints, the most fantastic of which is entitled *Royalty, Episcopacy and Law*, 'Some of the Principal Inhabitants of ye Moon, as they were Perfectly Discover'd by a Telescope brought to ye Greatest Perfection since ye last Eclipse; Exactly Engraved from the Objects, whereby ye Curious may Guess at their Religion, Manners, &c.' (1724) (fig. 78). Hogarth also engraved a burlesque view of the *Beggar's Opera* where the actors on the stage have human bodies and animal heads (1728). The imagery of such caricatures is derived from two main sources. Ever since early Christian times religious and political antagonists

[1] Catalogue of Prints and Drawings in the British Museum, Division I, *Political and Personal Satires*, vol. iv, by F. G. Stephens, London, 1883. The prints described are catalogued as Nos. 3917 and 4078. They were republished in a reduced form in vols. i and ii of *The British Antidote to Caledonian Poison: containing fifty-three Anti-ministerial, Political, Satirical and Comic Prints, for those remarkable years 1762 and 1763*. Seventh edition. Printed for J. Pridden, at the Feathers in Fleet Street, London, n.d. They are plates 44 and 4 respectively.

were apt to identify their enemies with the monsters of the *Apocalypse*, a method which was still very popular in Goya's time, when Napoleon was widely regarded as the Antichrist. In an English print by W. O'Keefe, entitled 'A Vision' and published in 1796, Pitt plays a similar role, while Fox looks out from behind the clouds as the moon (fig. 81).

The second source was the animal fable, a favourite theme of popular art in all countries since the earliest times. Illustrations of the ass playing a harp and of other animals carrying trays of food or otherwise imitating the ways of men occur among the Sumerian finds of Ur which date from *c.* 3000 B.C. In medieval Europe animal imagery abounded in the illuminated manuscripts and in decorative sculpture. Moreover, its transformation from the truly satanic, obsessional terror images of the early and high middle ages into the liberating satires of gothic art can here be followed step by step. With Bosch and Brueghel the broad humour of the gothic designers reached the highest plane of philosophical and social symbolism. But the ancient imagery entered on what was probably the most active phase of its whole development with the birth of political caricature in the sixteenth century. In the shape of the political lampoon it was intimately linked with the daily affairs of men during the religious wars in Germany, France, and the Netherlands, then in seventeenth-century Holland, eighteenth-century Britain and revolutionary France, and finally throughout Europe during the Napoleonic period.

In employing monsters and symbolic animals Goya was actually therefore using a language that was universally understood by the common people. Nevertheless, there is an immense difference between his unforgettable designs and the crude forms in which the same symbols were currently expressed. Only a great artist can probe the full meaning of the profoundest, because simplest and most universal popular symbols. In wrestling with their meaning he recreates them in their most perfect and expressive form.

THE PRISONER'S CHALLENGE

The spirit of Goya's Quinta paintings, the 'Disparates', and the later 'Disasters' is reflected in many of his contemporary drawings. Some are preliminary sketches of those works,[1] others are additional manifestations of Goya's agony. In the words of Felix Boix,[2] they are a new set of Caprichos, but more tendentious and bitter than the earlier series. Apart from the 'daemonic' fantasies, two groups are particularly important. The first consists of variations of the 'prisoner' theme. As we have noted, this theme already appeared in the 'Caprichos' and it was revived by Goya in the historical form of 'famous prisoners of the Inquisition' during the Josefino period. Since the restoration of that tribunal by Ferdinand made the latter theme even more horribly topical after 1814, it is probable that Goya continued the series in the years of reaction. But he also returned to the wider theme of imprisonment as such, and the majority of the drawings of this period are not directly related to the Holy Office. Some are dungeon scenes in which the victim's hopeless anguish is smothered in darkness. More often they show single figures, whose brutal shackles brand the fiendishness of a prison system inherited from the days of the torture chamber: 'The fetters are as barbarous as the crime'; 'One need not torture a prisoner to secure him'; 'If he is guilty, let him die quickly'; 'What cruelty!' 'Because their ancestors were Jews'; 'They gagged her, because she spoke, and beat her face with sticks. This I saw near Orioso Morena in Saragossa.' Nor are the victims of political persecution forgotten in this gallery of unfortunates: the drawing of a woman chained by her neck to a pillory, her feet secured in a heavy block, bears the caption: 'Por Liberal' (figs. 86-9).

Goya made etchings of three of these designs, and the importance he attached to their theme is shown by the fact that he added them to the proof set of the 'Disasters' which he asked Cean Bermúdez to edit in 1820. Countless are the haunting folk-songs inspired since immemorial times in Spain and elsewhere by the prisoner's anguish.[3] When, as in the Restoration period, a dying system seeks to perpetuate its rule by mass arrests and terrorism, the inarticulate cry of the oppressed becomes a challenge. Like the 'prisoners' chorus' in Beethoven's 'Fidelio' (first performed 1805, final

---

[1] Most of these are reproduced in P. d' Acchiardi's monumental work, *Les Dessins de F. Goya au musée du Prado*, Rome, 1908.

[2] *Los Dibujos de Goya*, Madrid, 1922; cf. also F. Boix and F. J. Sánchez Cantón, *Goya: Cien dibujos inéditos*, Museo del Prado, Madrid, 1928.

[3] For modern prisoners' drawings v. Hans Prinzhorn, *Bildnerei der Gefangenen*, Berlin, 1926.

version 1814), Goya's drawings voice the challenge of this age-old folk-theme in the 'universal idiom' of grand art.

The second outstanding group among Goya's drawings of 1814–20 are scathing attacks on the clergy (especially the monastic clergy) and thus related to many of the later plates of the 'Disasters'. Their significance must be considered in relation to certain contemporary paintings with religious themes which we must now examine.

CHRIST IN HIS AGONY

Ferdinand's policy of enriching the clergy enabled the Church to celebrate its victory with lavish building schemes, despite the poverty of a country ravaged by war and economic chaos. In Madrid alone more than twenty churches and monasteries were built or refitted during the 1814–19 period. Goya, too, was given certain ecclesiastical commissions. The first, which came from Seville, appears to have been an extensive project, for a number of sketches dealing with the legends of various saints associated with that city have survived. Only one of these was executed, the life-size altar-piece of Saints Justa and Rufina of 1817 (Seville Cathedral). Its derivation from Murillo's version of this theme (Seville Museum) has been pointed out by Sánchez Cantón and other authorities. But Goya's indebtedness to a seventeenth-century model appears to have been closer than this. The Witt Library contains a reproduction of another version attributed to P. de Moya (1610–66; Coll. Sánchez del Campo, Aznalcazar). Whether this attribution can be accepted or not, the painting undoubtedly dates from the seventeenth century, and it is of great interest that its composition is much more similar to that of Goya than to that of Murillo. Both the 'Moya' and Goya versions are more baroque and melodramatic in feeling than the Murillo. In the latter the Saints are standing before a neutral landscape background and holding a model of Seville's Cathedral Tower between them. Their connection with that city is thus indicated in the traditional form of the attribute. But in the other two paintings, the local tie is emphasised more directly and realistically, for the figures are placed in front of a picturesque view of Seville with the Cathedral as the most prominent feature. Goya's main innovation, compared with the 'Moya', was to place the tower, not between, but to the right of the saints, whom he could thus move closer together. It is of course impossible to tell whether Goya saw this particular specimen of what is, after all, a typical baroque solution of the theme, but it is difficult to escape the conclusion that he took his composition almost literally from a seventeenth-century model.

Copying of this order was wholly foreign to Goya's conception of art, and the few similar examples we have had occasion to note were almost invariably early ecclesiastical paintings. One is probably justified, therefore, in regarding the fact that he did not take the trouble to invent a new composition for the Seville picture as proof that he approached the theme in the spirit of a conventional Church commission.

It is difficult to imagine a greater contrast than that between the Seville altar-piece and two pictures with religious themes which Goya painted two years later. 'The Communion of St. Joseph of Calasanz' and the 'Christ in the Garden' of 1819 are generally placed among the most significant of Goya's later works. Technically they have been compared with the styles of the late nineteenth, rather than of the seventeenth, century. Their genuine feeling is beyond dispute. It is this sincerity which has induced certain authorities to claim that in his old age Goya experienced a revival of religious feeling. Sánchez Cantón, for example, calls 1819 "l'heure religieuse" in Goya's life (figs. 95, 97).

Goya's attitude to religion has been hotly disputed for almost a century. Personal conviction, rather than a dispassionate historical approach, has distinguished many of the contributions to this controversy. Romantics, like Théophile Gautier or Matheron, interpreted the 'Nada' plates in the 'Disasters' and similar works as proofs of Goya's philosophical nihilism; while devout Catholics, like Zapater, sought to vindicate the artist's orthodoxy. Although recent writers have, on the whole, adopted a more cautious line, it has not been sufficiently emphasised that for Goya, as for most of the Spanish intellectuals of his generation, the problem of religion appeared in an entirely different light. To appreciate their attitude we must return, for a moment, to the pamphlet *Pan y Toros*.

The religious programme of the Spanish reformers, as defined in *Pan y Toros*, may be summarised briefly as follows. They demanded that "the plain simplicity of the word of God" be restored to the people and that the "eternal edifice of the Gospel" be cleansed of the "temporal and corruptible supports" added by those who have erected upon it "the idol of tyranny". They also demanded that the clergy should direct the people "by ways of peace, and not of legal process".

For Goya and his friends the problem of religion was not, therefore, primarily the abstract philosophical contest between Christianity and Theism or Atheism. They were mainly concerned with the more practical and immediate problem whether the Spanish Church should express the genuine feelings of the people and minister to their needs, or whether it should remain—what to a large extent it manifestly was—an instrument of oppression. Hence they bitterly attacked all those sections of the clergy and those institutions which embodied the flagrant elements of cor ruption in the Spanish Church. But they were equally zealous in supporting those forces within the Church who strove to make it an instrument for the enlightenment of the people. Their attitude could scarcely have been other- wise in a country which was still so completely under the influence of the clergy as was the Spain of Goya's time.

That this was also Goya's own attitude no one familiar with his work will deny. Virulent attacks on clerical cor- ruption occur, as we have seen, not only in the 'Caprichos', but also in the 'Disasters'. The finished plates do not, however, reveal the full length to which Goya was pre- pared to go. As already noted, the preliminary drawing for plate 77 of the 'Disasters' identifies the mountebank priest of that design as the Pope, and this is not the only example among Goya's contemporary drawings in which he ridicules the head of catholicism. In the last plates of the 'Disasters', which we shall presently discuss, and in a number of related drawings, priests are branded as the enemies of truth and justice. Most of the anti-clerical drawings of 1814–23 are, however, directed more particularly against the friars. Goya never wearied in depicting them as lazy scoundrels battening on the sweat of the people. His indignation is most graphically expressed, perhaps, in a drawing which shows a fat monk riding on the shoulder of a peasant who is tilling the soil (Prado). It is clear, moreover, that Goya did not simply regard the monks of his day as the corrupters of a noble ideal: he despised the whole conception of personal salvation through retirement from life. This is indeed a point in which Goya's outlook was radically opposed to that of Bosch and other popular artists of the late medieval period. The Prado collection contains at least one drawing of a hermit which might be interpreted as a direct parody of his predecessor's grand fantasies of St. Anthony in his desert retreat. Even in the calmer mood of the last Bordeaux years Goya's anti-clericalism is evident, as we shall see, from a number of drawings showing old people in various attitudes of devotion (figs. 90-93).

Quite distinct from the polemical aim of all these works is the genuine feeling not only in the two paintings of 1819, but also, significantly enough, in another scene from the Passion Cycle, the Toledo 'Capture of Christ' of 1798, which we have mentioned in an earlier chapter. Between these two extremes range Goya's Church commissions from the conventional baroque histories of his youth to the gay Caprichos of San Antonio de la Florida.

In spite of such concessions to the religious traditions of the people—which compelled even the constitution-makers of 1812 to proclaim Catholicism the only legal faith in Spain—Spanish liberalism of the Goya period was nevertheless a genuine offspring of eighteenth-century rationalism. Its programme was based on a belief in the inherent perfectibility of man, rather than on a plea of divine inspiration. Hence its zeal for education and the general enlightenment of the people.

Goya's religious pictures of 1819 were both painted for San Antón Abad, the church of the Madrid *Escuelas Pias*. The life-size altar-piece shows St. Joseph of Calasanz (1556–1648), the founder of the order which maintained that school and many similar establishments in Spain and other countries. Calasanz is one of the most remarkable figures in the history of education.[1] Although he was a Spanish nobleman by birth, his outlook was strikingly democratic. His legend abounds with visions similar to those of St. Francis of Assisi; according to one of them he was married to 'Poverty' by that saint. This did not, however, prevent him from regarding the poverty of the people as the ultimate

[1] The following details are taken from the articles 'Escuelas Pias' and 'José de Calasanz' in the *Encyclopedia Universal Ilustrada* (Barcelona, n.d.) and W. E. Hubert, 'Der Heilige Joseph Calasanz', *Lebensbilder katholischer Erzieher*, Mainz, 1886.

cause of their sins. The poor, he argued, have no time to educate their children, hence their degradation is the inevitable result of ignorance and neglect. Thus convinced, he devoted his life to the struggle for free and universal education.

The story of his struggle has the dramatic flavour common to all great reform enterprises. It is interesting that he did not, apparently, at first regard the direct participation of the Church as essential for the success of his scheme. He began by trying to persuade the *secular* teachers of Rome, where he was then living, to admit poor scholars free of charge to their classes. Only when his further plea that the Senate should subsidise free places in the schools had failed, did he turn to the religious orders famous for their educational work. Both the Jesuits and Dominicans, however, rejected his scheme. Undaunted by these refusals, St. Joseph at last decided to carry out his plan himself. With three devoted followers he founded the first 'pious school' in the autumn of 1597 in Rome. Hounded by ceaseless intrigues and even arraigned before the Inquisition, he fought for his aims and kept up the work of his school, until, twenty years later, he was able to consolidate his cause by founding the order of the *Escolapios*. After another two decades, in 1637, his organisation embraced 27 schools with 372 teachers, and before Calasanz died its work had been extended to his native Spain and other Catholic countries.

Judged by the standards of his age, Calasanz's educational principles were advanced. He divided his pupils into age grades, each with a separate class-room and teachers, and he prepared curricula for primary, secondary, and higher education, in which religious teaching was combined with secular and practical instruction. Above all, he insisted that a teacher "must not only know *what* he teaches, but also *how* to teach".

The work begun by this great man was continued by his followers even through the darkest periods of his country's degradation—during the later seventeenth century and also in the period of reaction after 1814. It is not difficult to understand why Goya should have felt deeply moved, when he paid tribute to one whose inspiration was so profoundly akin to his own. Nor is this all: Calasanz, like Goya, was a native of Aragón, and no one familiar with the latter's intense local pride—or indeed with the whole spirit of Spanish regionalism—will under-estimate the importance of this fact in the present context; finally, Goya himself had received his first tuition at the 'pious school' of Saragossa, founded in 1732. Tradition reports that he charged only a nominal fee for his altar-piece and that he made a present of the small 'Agony', which is an entirely separate work, to the good Fathers of the Escuelas Pias.

Goya chose as the subject for his altar-piece, not some conventional miracle, but the act of Communion, the solemn moment when the great teacher returned to the roots of his inspiration to draw from them the strength he needed to continue his battle. He is kneeling on the raised platform of the altar, facing the priest who is placing the wafer into his mouth. His limp body and half-closed eyes express that ultimate concentration in which the self is wholly abandoned to a greater cause. The nave below is filled with the boyish heads of his pupils and the apostolic figures of their teachers—a silver treble and solemn base accompanying the main theme of the saint's devotion. A ray of light, falling from above onto the head of the saint, barely penetrates the gloomy expanse of the vault (fig. 95).

Well might Goya ponder on the theme of moral courage at the time which Sánchez Cantón calls his "hour of religion". He received his commission from the Fathers of the Pious School[1] on the day before the fifth anniversary of that night of terror, 10-11 May 1814, when the leading liberals had been arrested in their beds and dragged off to the jails in which many of them were still languishing, that night which gave the signal for the restoration of oppression. 1819 was, as we have seen, the year in which the hideous corruption of the régime revealed itself in utter lawlessness and chaos; the moment when Garay's failure had made it clear for all that only a rising of the people could restore peace and order to Spain. 1819 also witnessed the last and most sensational of the many unsuccessful attempts at revolt. Before Goya delivered his altar-piece the Cadiz mutiny of July had been betrayed by La Bisbal.

In this lurid atmosphere of terror and treachery, rent by the distant flashes of the approaching storm, the theme of the great reformer seeking courage for his struggles

---

[1] The altar-piece was commissioned on 9 May 1819 and completed by 27 August, the festival of the saint, when the altar was consecrated.

assumed the force of a universal symbol in Goya's mind: "Father, if thou be willing, remove this cup from me: nevertheless, not my will, but thine, be done". The dark vault has become the desolate night on the Mount of Olives. The kneeling figure is Christ, spreading his arms in His agony and raising His eyes to the angel who is approaching with the cup in a beam of light (fig. 97).

Less than six months had elapsed since Goya delivered the altar-piece of St. Joseph and his minute gloss on its meaning (the 'Christ' measures no more than 47 × 35 cm.) to the good Fathers of the Pious School, when D. Rafael de Riego and his Asturians again unfurled the banner of revolt (1 January 1820). Their famous march through Southern Spain (27 January–11 March) gave the signal for the overthrow of despotism. On 9 March Ferdinand swore the oath of loyalty to the Constitution of 1812, and on 4 April Goya attended a meeting of the Academy convened for the same purpose.[1] He expressed his exultation in a number of drawings, one of which is of great significance in the present context. It is a literal translation of the 'Christ in the Garden' into a mood of ecstasy. The same broad beam of light traverses the scene, banishing all but the last traces of the preceding gloom. Leaning back to gaze with radiant joy into the light is the same kneeling figure. Halo and gown are replaced by the ordinary hat and great-coat of the period. On the ground before him are an inkstand with pens and paper, and below is written: 'Divina Libertad' (fig. 98).

If we now look back to the other works in which Goya expressed his grief in the days of darkness, we shall find yet a fourth version of the 'kneeling man' image. He is again, of course, a 'man of sorrow', and he may have been the first of the series to have taken shape in Goya's mind, although one is tempted to date him between the 'Christ' and the 'Divina Libertad' drawing. The kneeling figure now faces the spectator. He is emaciated and clothed in rags. The darkness of the rocky desert in which he kneels is haunted by dimly discernible monsters. His arms are half-raised in a gesture of helplessness, and his brow is clouded by the 'sad presentiments of things to come', for he represents the people of Spain in Goya's frontispiece to the 'Disasters of the War' (fig. 94).

[1] It was the last of the 81 meetings of that body which Goya attended. The first had been that of 14 July 1781, at which Jovellanos read his 'Elogio de las bellas artes'.

It is thus evident that even in his 'hour of religion' Goya did not abandon the theme which was the mainspring of all his imaginative creations: the hopes and struggles of his people. In the periods of oppression which cast their shadows over his later life the Spanish people no longer appeared to him in the gay disguise of the 'majo', symbol of confident youth and vitality, but in the image of the 'man of sorrow'. In a moment of supreme agony[1] and in the context of a religious commission for which Goya felt deep sympathy, that image fleetingly assumed the likeness of Christ. By expressing his credo of life and action through the symbol of Christ, Goya struck a chord to which his people had long been attuned. Because Goya's religious pictures do not, like so many later works, express the despair of an artist seeking to escape from his social isolation, because, on the contrary, they are profoundly 'popular' and democratic, Goya may justly be regarded as the last great religious painter. He was the final link of the tradition which ran from Cimabue to Rembrandt, its modulations ranging from Dürer's imagery of spiritual conflict to the grand moralities of Bosch and Grünewald. Nevertheless, the religious symbol was but a momentary choice for Goya. When, for a brief instant, the black night of reaction was dispelled by the dawn of freedom, he proudly proclaimed the social meaning of his image.

There is a beautiful drawing in the Prado which summarises Goya's attitude to the traditional faith of his people more succinctly, perhaps, than any of his other works. A monk is crouching on a stone, raising a crucifix in his right hand and pointing with his left to a skull on the ground. He is looking sternly at a peasant boy who is standing before him and raising his mattock in a defiant gesture. The opposition between the *vita contemplativa* and the *vita activa* is the theme of this design. And the symbolism chosen—on the one side agile youth raising the instrument of creative labour towards the sun, on the other the crouching monk pointing downwards to the symbol of death—can leave no doubt which of the two Goya, whose vitality

---

[1] It is interesting to note that in this period of social stress, as in the similar circumstances of 1792, Goya again experienced a physical breakdown. When he recovered, early in 1820, he painted a portrait of himself on the sick-bed together with his doctor Arrieta, whom he thanks, in the dedication, "for saving his life in the grave and dangerous illness he suffered at the end of 1819 in the seventy-third year of his life" (Coll. Lucas-Norman, Paris).

neither old age, nor deafness, nor disease could crush, had made his own (fig. 91).

Goya's attitude to religion is another proof how fundamentally his 'romanticism' differed from that of many of his contemporaries and also from the romanticism of the mid-nineteenth century. Two quotations, linked by a curious chain of circumstances, may illustrate this point. The first is from the *Vorschule der Aesthetik* (1804), by Jean-Paul Richter (1763–1825); the second from another 'Agony': the 'Mont des Oliviers' (1843; last stanza, 1862), by Alfred de Vigny (1797–1863).

In his chapter 'Über die romantische Poesie' (vol. i, pp. 109 *et seq.*) Richter defines romanticism as the antithesis of classic art with its joyous affirmation of sensory reality. Having destroyed the world of sense-perception "as in a Last Judgment", Christian art, which, for Richter, is synonymous with romantic art, replaced it by a new spirit world. Mythology was replaced by demonology, the affirmation of the present by the contemplation of the infinite. He writes:

> Das Christenthum vertilgte, wie ein jüngster Tag, die ganze Sinnenwelt mit allen ihren Reizen, es drückte sie zu einem Grabeshügel, zu einer Himmels-Staffel und Schwelle zusammen und setzte eine neue Geisterwelt an die Stelle. Die Dämonologie wurde die eigentliche Mythologie der Körperwelt und Teufel als Verführer zogen in Menschen- und Götterstatuen; alle Erdengegenwart war zu Himmels-Zukunft verflüchtigt. Was blieb nun nach diesem Einsturz der äusseren Welt noch übrig?—Die worin sie einstürzte, die *innere*. Der Geist stieg in sich und seine Nacht und sah Geister. Da aber die Endlichkeit nur an Körpern haftet und da in Geistern alles unendlich ist oder ungeendet: so blühte in der Poesie das Reich des Unendlichen über der Brandstätte der Endlichkeit auf. Engel, Teufel, Heilige, Seelige, und der Unendliche hatten keine Körperformen[1] und Götterleiber; dafür öffnete das Ungeheure und Unermessliche seine Tiefe; statt der griechischen heitern Freude erschien

---

[1] At this point Richter interpolates an extraordinarily suggestive footnote the theme of which is closely akin to the fundamental idea in Marx's aesthetic studies of 1842, the idea which was later crystallised in his conception of commodity fetishism. v. M. Lifshitz, *The Philosophy of Art of Karl Marx*, Critics Group, New York, 1938. Richter wrote: "Oder das Überirdische knüpfte sich un *unkünstlerische Verkörperungen*, an Reliquien, Kreuze, Kruzifixe, Hostien, Mönche, Glocken, Heiligen-Bilder, die alle mehr als Buchstaben und Zeichen denn als Körper sprachen. . . .''

entweder unendliche Sehnsucht oder die unausprech-
liche Seeligkeit—die zeit- und schrankenlose Ver-
dammniss—die Geisterfurcht, welche vor sich selber
schaudert—die schwärmerische beschauliche Liebe—
die gränzenlose Mönchs-Entsagung—die platonische
und neuplatonische Philosophie (pp. 121-3)

The "night of the infinite", Richter continues, arouses
fear rather than hope in the human soul. Hence the importance of fear and even of *superstition* in romantic art. Richter
devotes a whole section of his chapter to what he calls "die
Poesie des Aberglaubens". What is the true element in
superstition, he asks, and he answers:

> . . . das Gefühl, das früher der Lehrer der Erzie-
> hung sein musste, eh' es ihr Schüler werden konnte,
> und welches der romantische Dichter nur verklärter
> aufweckt, nämlich *das ungeheure, fast hülflose Gefühl,*
> *womit der stille Geist gleichsam in der wilden Riesen-*
> *mühle des Weltalls betäubt steht und einsam.* Unzählige
> unüberwindliche Welträder sieht er in der seltsamen
> Mühle hinter einander kreisen—und er hört das
> Brausen eines ewigen treibenden Stroms—um ihn her
> donnert es und der Boden zittert—bald hie, bald da
> fället ein kurzes Klingeln ein in den Sturm—hier wird
> zerknirscht, dort vorgetrieben und aufgesammelt—
> *und so steht er verlassen in der allgewaltigen blinden*
> *einsamen Maschine, welche um ihn mechanisch rauschet*
> *und doch ihn mit keinem geistigen Ton anredet*; aber
> sein Geist sieht sich furchtsam nach den Riesen um,
> welche die wunderbare Maschine eingerichtet und zu
> Zwecken bestimmt haben und welche er als die
> Geister eines solchen zusammengebauten Körpers noch
> weit grösser setzen muss als ihr Werk ist. *So wird die*
> *Furcht nicht sowohl der Schöpfer als das Geschöpf der*
> *Götter* . . . (pp. 128-9, my emphasis).

From this conception of the human soul, lonely and
terror-stricken in face of the immensity of the universe, it
was but a small step for the romantics to seek consolation
in the Christian faith, when their cherished hopes in the
progress of liberty had been shattered. Hence the success
in France of the fashionable revival of Catholicism, strongly
tinged with erotic and exotic elements, by opportunists
like Chateaubriand, "that manufacturer of belles lettres
who unites, in a most obnoxious manner, the polite scepticism and Voltairianism of the eighteenth century with the

polite sentimentalism and romanticism of the nineteenth".[1]

The rapid disintegration of the old society by the industrial revolution exposed the falsity of this compromise to many honest intellectuals in France. But with few exceptions they had lost touch with the people. Their passionate desire to play a part in re-shaping society was frustrated by their conviction of being an *élite*, that final offspring of romantic isolation. Nothing was left for them but the ultimate escape into philosophical nihilism. Strangely enough, it was Jean-Paul (who abhorred what he dimly perceived to be the logical outcome of his position) who gave them their clue.[2] Nothing could be further apart in spirit than the imaginative work of Goya and that of Jean-Paul. Yet the latter, too, is a specific combination of realism and fantasy. Introspective and sentimental in the manner of Sterne (but more pedantic), his novels are interminable records of petty domesticity interspersed with wild flashes of fantasy. Mme. de Staël, who disliked the provincialism of his sentimental vein, wrote that he truly mirrors the feelings of the heart, but as it beats in the small towns of Germany. Yet she admired the daring of his fantastic visions. Though shocked by its implications, as indeed Jean-Paul himself had been, she included one of the most curious of these as a specimen of Richter's style in her famous account of German thought and literature, *De l'Allemagne* (final version, 1813). It is the first 'flower-piece' from the novel *Blumen-, Frucht- und Dornenstücke: oder Ehestand, Tod und Hochzeit des Armenadvokaten Firmian Stanislaus Siebenkäs* (1796–7). Having stated that if ever he should lose his faith in God, he would re-read this flower-piece: it would shake him to the core and he would regain his faith— Jean-Paul gives a remarkable definition of the significance of atheism in the context of romantic 'loneliness':

> Niemand ist im All so allein wie der Gottesläugner —er trauert mit einem verwaisten Herzen, das den grössten Vater verloren, neben dem unermesslichen Leichnam der Natur, den kein Weltgeist regt und zusammenhält, und der im Grabe wächset; er trauert

---

[1] Marx's letter to Engels, 26 October 1854. Marx–Engels, *Historisch-kritische Gesamtausgabe*, Aut. III, vol. 2, p. 58, Moscow, 1927–35.

[2] For the following v. I. A. Henning, *L'Allemagne de Mme de Staël et la polémique romantique*, Paris, 1929; F. Baldensperger, *A. de Vigny*, Paris, 1912, especially the section 'Le Songe de Jean-Paul dans le romantisme français'; P. Flottes, *La Pensée politique et sociale d'A. de Vigny*, Strasbourg, 1927; and the critical edition of *Les Destinées* by E. Estève, Paris, 1924.

so lange, bis er sich selber abbröckelt von der Leiche.
Die ganze Welt ruht vor ihm, wie die grosse halb
im Sande liegende ägyptische Sphinx aus Stein; und
das All ist die kalte eiserne Maske der gestaltlosen
Ewigkeit.[1]

There follows the 'dream' which Mme. de Staël included
in her book: Midnight in a graveyard. The dead arise from
their tombs and flock into the church. High up in the vault
Christ appears in an aura of light. In vain He has roamed the
universe in search for God. He has now returned to tell the
dead that there is no God. Groaning in anguish they go
back to their graves. Then the little dead children arise.
Christ, tears in His eyes, tells them that they, and He, are
orphans, for there is no Heavenly Father.

This travesty of the Last Judgment profoundly stirred
the French romantics. It was reprinted and retranslated at
least three times between 1827 and 1843, not counting the
later editions of Mme. de Staël's book. Torn from its context by a stroke of genius, it made the gentle Jean-Paul a
figure of Byronic fascination for his French admirers, who
knew little or nothing of his other work. Its influence on de
Vigny is beyond dispute. Still under the impact of the July
Revolution, he wrote in his diary:

> Un doute m'a saisi—le Christ même ne fut-il pas
> sceptique?—Oui, il le fut, et d'un doute plein d'amour
> et de pitié pour l'humanité. . . . Pardonnez-leur, car
> ils ne savent ce qu'ils font ! C'est la doute même!
> (11 December 1830).[2]

In 1834 we find: "La terre est révoltée des injustices de
la création; elle dissimule par frayeur le mal et le mort . . ."
and in the following year the vision of a young suicide who
reproaches God for having made him miserable and for
having created "le mal de l'âme, le péché, et le mal du
corps, la souffrance". Finally the following outline for a
poem to be written:

> Le Jugement Dernier. Ce sera pour-là que Dieu
> viendra se *justifier* devant toutes les âmes et tout ce qui
> est vie. Il paraîtra et parlera, il dira clairement pourquoi
> la création et pourquoi la souffrance et la mort de

---

[1] *Siebenkäs*, vol. ii, p. 217, 2nd ed., 1818 (in the first edition the piece appeared at the beginning of vol. i).
[2] The passages from de Vigny's *Journal* are quoted from Estève, *op. cit.*

l'innocence, etc. En ce moment ce sera le genre humain ressuscité qui sera la juge, et l'Éternel, le créateur, sera jugé par les générations rendues à la vie.

All these ideas reappear, together with certain other motives, from 'Jean-Paul's dream', in the monologue of Christ in de Vigny's 'Mont des Oliviers' (1843). That he chose the image of the 'agony' as the final form in which he clothed a theme so alien in spirit to the old tradition of religious art and also to the meaning of Goya's 'Agony', was probably due to the fact that he saw Mantegna's painting of that subject during his London visit of 1839 in the house of Lady Blessington (now in the National Gallery). Towards the end of his life de Vigny studied a recent book on Buddhism. "Bouddah . . . dit: Soyez charitable, donnez tout et vous aurez enfin le repos dans le Nirvana. *Est-ce l'union à Dieu ou le néant? Là est la question*", he wrote in his diary in 1862. He gave his answer in the final stanza which he added in the same year to his poem:

LE SILENCE

S'il est vrai qu'au Jardin sacré des Écritures,
Le Fils de l'homme ait dit ce qu'on voit rapporté;
Muet, aveugle et sourd au cri des créatures,
Si le Ciel nous laissa comme un monde avorté,
Le juste opposera le dédain à l'absence
Et ne répondra plus que par un froid silence
Au silence éternel de la Divinité.

The romantic conception of Christ's Passion appears even more clearly as the antithesis of Goya's interpretation in Baudelaire's poem 'Le Reniement de saint Pierre' (*Les Fleurs du mal*, cxviii, the first in a group of three poems entitled 'Révolte': Charles Baudelaire lived 1821–67). While Goya recognised the Saviour's agony as the moment of supreme decision in a drama of action, Baudelaire, like de Vigny, viewed it as a symbol of renunciation and defeat. In the concluding lines of his poem he specifically dissociated action from the 'dream' of Christian resignation.

—Certes, je sortirai, quant à moi, satisfait
D'un monde où l'action n'est pas la sêur du rêve;
Puisse-je user du glaive et périr par le glaive!
Saint Pierre a renié Jésus . . . il a bien fait!

None of the romantics was more deeply influenced by Goya's art than Baudelaire. It is reported that a small book on Goya (it must have been Matheron's published in

1857) and the works of Edgar Allan Poe were constantly at his side.[1] As this combination shows, it was the 'satanic' element in Goya's style that fascinated the author of *Les Fleurs du mal*:

> Goya, cauchemar plein des choses inconnues,
> De fœtus qu'on fait cuire au milieu des sabbats,
> De vieilles au miroir et d'enfants toutes nues,
> Pour tenter les démons ajustant bien leur bas.[2]

Increasingly isolated, as they were, from the people, the mid-nineteenth-century romantics were fascinated by Goya's macabre imagery without perceiving that it is but the foil which offsets the radiant essence of his genius: his profound optimism, faith in reason, and heroic affirmation of human dignity and freedom. But it is highly significant that the attitude of those artists who remained in touch with the people, *i.e.* of the cartoonists, who carried on the struggle for the cause of democracy, was precisely the reverse. They retained the spirit, even when they abandoned the form of Goya's art. This is strikingly apparent in the present context. Realising the continued hold of religion over a section of the people, especially in the country districts, the French nineteenth-century cartoonists, like Goya, occasionally adapted themes from Christian iconography for their ends. In doing so they took up the thread, however, where Goya left it, not in the Mount of Olives painting, but in the 'Divina Libertad' drawing of 1820. That is to say, they showed not Christ, but a symbolic figure of Liberty or France suffering the agonies of the Passion. 'Parodies' of this kind modelled on the Mocking of Christ, Christ before Pilate, and similar images appear fairly frequently in *La Caricature* of 1830–35, and one of the most moving series of cartoons published during the Paris Commune of 1871 is entitled 'La Grande Crucifiée'.[3] It con-

---

[1] The authority for this statement is Troubat; *v.* Jean Adhémar's essay in the catalogue of the Bibliothèque Nationale Goya exhibition, Paris, 1935.

[2] *Les Fleurs du mal*, vi: 'Les Phares' (1st ed. 1857). The essay, 'Quelques caricaturistes étrangers', quoted in a previous chapter, also dates from 1857. The section devoted to Goya, or rather to the fantastic element in Goya's art, will be found *in extenso* in note VI of the Appendix.

[3] Britannia crucified is the subject of an English caricature of 1762 (B.M. Catalogue No. 3964). But this is not really an anticipation of the French prints here discussed, since the symbolism is anti-Scotch (*i.e.* anti-Bute) rather than religious, the cross being the St. Andrew's Cross. This is also true of one of the details in Paul Sandby's 'Satire on Lord Bute' of 1762 (B.M. No. 3910), where Bute is shown in the guise of the Angel (wearing a Scotch bonnet) appearing to the Shepherds (*i.e.* the Scotch place-hunters). Such instances are, however, exceptional. Where the English caricaturists of the 1760's used religious imagery at all (always excepting the Apocalyptic imagery, already mentioned), they generally took it from the Old Testament,

sists of nine naïve prints by E. Courtaux showing 'Liberty' or 'Paris' in various stages of the Passion. On the title-print she is crucified before a map of France (fig. 99), while another plate shows her on her own Mount of Olives—the Paris city wall—receiving the cup—a Prussian helmet—filled to the brim. An even more recent example of this type of symbolism is George Grosz' noble design of suffering humanity crucified, wearing a gas-mask and soldier's boots, with the famous caption 'Maul halten und weiter dienen!' This was the drawing for which Grosz was convicted of blasphemy by the same tribunal which later became notorious through the Reichstag Fire Trial of 1933.

THE DAWN OF FREEDOM

The transformation of Christ into a figure of Liberty, as it occurs in French nineteenth-century caricature, leads us to yet another image which occasionally occurs in Goya's work of 1814–20, as it does in Shelley's poetry, in English caricature and beyond it in the tradition of the miracle plays or the 'autos sacramentales'. The use of an allegorical female figure of Liberty, Justice, Hope, or Truth, placed in opposition to the monsters of oppression, may, indeed, have been suggested to Goya by a real experience which he recorded in a tragic drawing of the Prado collection. A man, whose closed eyes and gestures are those of a somnambulist, is standing on a ladder smashing a statue with a pick-axe. 'He does not know what he is doing' is Goya's caption. Fragments on the ground show that the statue was a classical female figure—a symbol of liberty smashed in an orgy of reaction (fig. 100).

Later the statue came to life in Goya's mind, for he used symbolical figures of 'Justice', 'Truth', or 'Reason' in a number of drawings and in several plates of the 'Disasters', including the 'Nada' design. But the seed which was most firmly planted in the creative subsoil of his imagination by the statue-smashing episode was the vision of the *death* of Truth (or Liberty or Justice). It is this conception which he finally chose for plates 79 and 80 of the 'Disasters'.[1]

as, *e.g.*, in the numerous prints representing Bute and the Princess of Wales as 'Gisbal and Bathseeba', or in certain cartoons (B.M. Nos. 4031, 4055), where Wilkes appears as Daniel in the Lion's Den.

[1] The Metropolitan Museum, New York, has a drawing in which Truth is still standing upright among the monsters who assail her (fig. 101).

'Truth has died' is the caption of the former. But instead of showing the blind tool which enacted the outrage, Goya now exposed its instigators. A bishop is standing over the prostrate figure, raising his hands in the gesture of benediction; behind him a crowd of friars are eagerly waiting with their spades and mattocks to bury Truth, at whose feet Justice sits weeping. Only the rays which emerge like a mandorla from Truth illumine the sinister scene (fig. 102).

Even more dramatic is the following plate: 'Will she rise again?' It is a stirring answer, both to the murderers of Truth and to the hopeless 'Nada' of plate 69. Like the dead man in that plate, Truth is lying half buried in the soil. Though she is still in a death-like trance, her noble features cast a brilliant radiance into the surrounding blackness. Hideous monsters are lurking in the gloom. The fear that Truth might arise from the dead has thrown them into a frenzy of terror. One lifts a book to exorcise the reawakening spirit, another, a monk, raises a club to stun her should she open her eyes (fig. 103).

It is interesting how closely also in this instance Goya's imagery resembles Shelley's:

> Let us follow the corpse of British Liberty slowly and reverently to its tomb; and if some glorious phantom should appear, and make its throne of broken swords and sceptors and royal crowns trampled in the dust, let us say that the Spirit of Liberty has risen from its grave, and left all that was gross and mortal there, and kneel down and worship it as our queen.[1]

And is not Goya's 'Truth' prostrate at the feet of reaction, yet triumphant over it, reminiscent of 'Hope' halting the march of Anarchy's 'ghastly masquerade' in Shelley's poem?

The Revolution of 1820 fulfilled the promise of Truth's awakening, and the 'death of Truth' image was as strikingly transformed in Goya's mind as was the 'man of sorrow' image. In both the radiant light of freedom dispels the haunting shadows of despair. It is borne in the hands of Truth, as she glides to earth greeted by an eager throng of people:

---

[1] 'An Address to the People on the Death of the Princess Charlotte, by the Hermit of Marlow' (motto: 'We pity the Plumage but forget the Dying Bird'), 1817. For this image, too, there is a precedent among the cartoons published during Wilkes' struggle with parliament in 1769. It is the print catalogued as No. 4288 among the *Political and Personal Satires* in the British Museum and entitled 'The Funeral of Freedom'—Britannia and Justice are mourning at an empty grave surmounted by a bust of Wilkes.

'Lux ex Tenebris'; or it emanates from the scales of Justice suspended in the sky like a sun in a similar drawing (both Prado; in the second all the people in the crowd below look up with joy, except the black priest in the foreground who runs away in terror). In yet a third design the figure of 'Reason', the scales of justice in her left, and a whip in her right, hand, drives away a flock of ravens:[1] 'Divine Reason—don't spare any of them' (Prado). Finally, the Fitzwilliam Museum, Cambridge, has a drawing which may be regarded as a combination of the 'kneeling man' and 'Truth–Justice' images; an apostolic old man kneels with raised hands, facing the spectator; he holds a pair of scales in which the pen is weightier than the sword[2] (figs. 96, 104-6).

Goya was not, content, however, with the mystical elation inspired by such abstract idealisations of Truth and Liberty. In the design which he chose for the last plate of the 'Disasters of the War' he descends to earth and defines what he regarded as the true essence of freedom. "What is Freedom?" Shelley asks in 'The Masque of Anarchy' (1819):

> Thou art not, as impostors say,
> A shadow soon to pass away,
> A superstition, and a name
> Echoing from the cave of Fame.
> For the labourer thou art bread,
> And a comely table spread
> From his daily labour come
> To a neat and happy home.
> Thou art clothes, and fire, and food
> For the trampled multitude—

And in the final plate of the 'Disasters' the figure of Freedom places her arm on the shoulder of an aged peasant, bent by toil, who approaches with his hoe in his hand; around them are spread the fruits of his labour: sheaves of corn, a sheep, a basketful of produce, a fruit-laden tree—'This is the Truth', wrote Goya (fig. 107).

---

[1] Goya used the raven as a symbol for evil thoughts or lies in a drawing entitled 'Bad dream' (Prado): a man is looking at a mirage of his own face, surrounded and pecked by ravens.

[2] There are two other Goya drawings in the same collection; both are fantastic visions of the 1814–19 period. One shows a double-headed being, half man, half woman, with the caption 'Segura unión natural'; the other a pile of heads reminiscent of the Quinta paintings.

Chapter 5

"The transient nature of ignorance and error,
And the eternity of genius and virtue."

THE REVOLUTION OF 1820–23
AND ITS AFTERMATH

"The new constitutional system was received with enthusiasm by the great towns, the commercial and industrial
classes, the liberal professions, the army and the proletariat.
It was resisted by the monks, and it baffled the country-
folk." So wrote M. de Martignac,[1] one of the foremost
agents of the intervention which smashed that system.
But intervention was not the only cause of the second
defeat of Spanish liberty: "One of the principal reasons for
the fall of our Constitution", wrote Evaristo San Miguel,[2]
companion of Riego on his heroic march and the head of the
most radical ministry during the liberal régime, "was the
fact that the French Revolution had previously taken place.
That great upheaval had been accompanied by so much
bloodshed, so much horror, so many dreadful crimes, that
its memory, still fresh in our minds, filled the best and most
devoted friends of our Constitution with anxiety. The fear
of following the same path, of precipitating ourselves into
so terrible an abyss, paralysed our spirits. Anything rather
than court the danger of imitating the French—that was
the general feeling."

The Revolution of 1820 occurred at a time when the
bourgeoisie, in spite of its far-reaching reforms, no longer
had the revolutionary energy and determination necessary
to consolidate its gains. On the other hand, the democratic
lower classes, though impatient for action, lacked con-
structive leadership. Hence the mystical quality of their
liberalism, their exaltation, which surrounded the abstract
concept of liberty, as symbolised by the 'Holy Codex' of
1812, with a nimbus of blind devotion. The Constitution of

[1] *Op. cit.*
[2] *Vida de D. Agustin Argüelles,* Madrid, 1851–2, vol. ii, quoted by Baumgarten *op. cit.*

1812 had now assumed the rigidity of an unalterable article of faith. Like the Creed, it was explained in numerous 'catechisms' published for the use of schools and churches: *Catecismo político arreglado á la Constitución de la monarquia española: para la ilustración del pueblo, instrucción de la juventud y uso de las escuelas de primeras letras* is the title of one of these publications issued in Valladolid. Yet this Constitution tied the cause of freedom to a king, the legal head of the executive, who betrayed it at every turn. It appointed a monarch, whose every thought was reaction, executive to the revolution. Compelled to accept as his ministers men whom he had persecuted for six years with implacable hatred, Ferdinand used every 'legal' pretext for obstruction. While fanning the embers of clerical and rural counter-revolution, he discredited the liberal leaders with their followers by his delaying tactics and thus succeeded in splitting the ranks of the progressive party.

It was then that Spanish liberalism was first divided into its 'moderado' and 'exaltado' factions. Aiming to establish the conditions necessary for the development of capitalism in Spain, but anxious at all cost to avoid the stigma of 'Jacobinism', the former moved more and more to the right. Recruited from the 'substantial' classes and including many of the famous liberals of 1812, the moderados were essentially conservative in outlook, despite their doctrinaire radicalism. They hoped to share power with the former ruling classes, and only the stubborn determination of the King to defend his absolute power frustrated their efforts:

> Just as it was the King who was mainly responsible for precipitating the country into the chaos of this revolution [writes Baumgarten], so it was he who frustrated every attempt to calm the extremists and to establish a government of reasonable moderation. He was and remained the evil genius of his people.

Although the moderados of 1820–23 were, on the whole, still sincere in their attack on the obsolete elements of feudalism, they took the first step which led the Spanish upper middle class away from the path of revolutionary opposition to the feudal powers. In the later history of the nineteenth century the name of moderado was to become a byword for cynical corruption and even in 1823 the treachery of the generals entrusted with the defence of the Constitution[1] clearly foreshadowed an inevitable development.

The exaltados, on the other hand, were the party of the urban lower middle classes,[2] and of the younger intellectuals and officers inspired by Riego's example: they made up for their lack of policy by their enthusiasm. Unable to formulate a consistent programme of action, they dramatised their fervent dreams by "strutting on the stage of history dressed up as characters of the past".[3] Padilla and the comuneros were their heroes. Terrible oaths and the trappings of a mysterious ceremonial shrouded their impotence in a cloak of romanticism. Again and again they fell victims to the *agents provocateurs* of clerical reaction and obstructed the government even, or rather invariably, when it was about to enforce really progressive measures. When at last the exaltados were called upon to take the helm into their own hands, they were as paralysed as the moderados had been, by the fear of losing their respectability should they strike at the real enemy. Even when the King had openly shown his hand by arresting the cabinet during a mutiny of the Madrid guards in the first week of July 1822, neither his life nor his constitutional authority was in any danger after the rebellion had been crushed by the citizens and loyal troops of the capital. In the last ignominious chapter of the liberal régime the exaltado government reduced the fiction of constitutional government to a farce. The Cortes had demoralised the liberal forces seven weeks before the French army of intervention had even crossed the frontier by deciding to desert Madrid. But when they were obliged by the rapid advance of the enemy to continue their flight from Seville to Cadiz, they were faced with the absolute refusal of the King to move a step further. They then declared him temporarily insane and thus unfit to exercise his royal prerogative, in order that they might compel him to leave without infringing the letter of their sacred constitution.

---

[1] Not all of them, however, were moderados. The exaltado Mina was the only one among them who did his duty by fighting against overwhelming odds to the very end. The exaltado Ballesteros fought one engagement after a prolonged retreat and then capitulated with his entire force. Morillo and La Bisbal, known reactionaries, betrayed their country without even the pretence of an engagement.

[2] Baumgarten stresses the importance of the non-commissioned officers in their ranks.

[3] Marx's classical analysis in the *Eighteenth Brumaire of Louis Bonaparte* applies with equal force to the Spanish situation.

Time after time in the course of the revolution the King
and his reactionary supporters exploited the violent quarrels
between the liberals in attempts to overthrow the constitutional régime. In the face of the common danger the
factions united to defend the constitution. But when each
successive attempt had failed—invariably through the
cowardice of the King—the newly established unity of the
progressives was always shattered by the government's
reluctance to take energetic steps for safeguarding the gains
of the revolution. As Baumgarten points out, it was the
tragedy of the revolutionary party that its moderate wing
could not be really moderate without betraying the revolution, while the 'revolutionary' faction, intoxicated with its
bombastic 'radicalism', lacked the energy and discipline
to translate its vague slogans into consistent, effectively
directed action.

Profiting by these ever more violent internal disagree-
ments and by the liberals' inability to make effective the
reforms they had enacted,[1] Ferdinand and his clerical
friends more and more openly supported the counter-
revolutionary movements in the backward rural areas.
By the end of 1821 the country was already overrun by
marauding 'bands of faith'—fanatical peasants, smugglers,
old guerrilleros often led by monks, such as the notorious
'Trappist',—and in spite of Mina's energetic and successful
measures in the north the government was unable to cope
with this menace. But, however feeble the forces of liberalism, however vicious the calumnies of the friars who spread
sedition through all the provinces, the reactionary bandits
would never have succeeded in restoring arbitrary despotism without the support of military intervention from
abroad.

From the first the attitude of the European powers had
been one of unconcealed hostility to the Spanish liberals.
That the Spanish Constitution was a dangerous canker in
the body politic of Europe was the unanimous view of the

[1] All the progressive legislation of the first constitutional period was re-enacted during
1820–23, and, in addition, even more far-reaching reforms were introduced in many
spheres, notably education, the military system, and in the offensive against feudal
privileges. Some of these measures were grave tactical blunders, however, the most
striking example being the 'revolutionary' step of 'arming the people' and sub-
ordinating the regular army to the militia. It was the regular army which had in
fact initiated the revolution of 1820, while to create a militia in the smaller towns
and country districts meant to arm the reactionary 'bands of faith'. In a similar
manner the hitherto predominantly liberal lower nobility was alienated by the
complete prohibition of entail.

British Tories[1] and the French government, no less than of
Metternich and Alexander. Opinions differed only as to the
means by which it was to be eradicated. Intervention, constantly and eagerly invited by the traitor King and advocated from the first by the Czar, had been actively pursued
by the French under the cloak of 'neutrality' ever since the
reactionaries had taken up arms in the north of Spain. It
was ultimately adopted as the common policy of the Holy
Alliance at the Verona Congress (October–December 1822).
On 7 April 1823 a French army under the Duke of Angou-
lême invaded Spain. On 23 May it occupied Madrid; and
on 1 October, Cadiz, again the last refuge of Spanish
liberty, surrendered, and Ferdinand was restored to power
as the arbitrary ruler of his people.

Under the pressure of the Holy Alliance the invading
army acted on a highly instructive principle of 'non-intervention'. Having driven out the legal authorities by force
of arms, the French military command steadfastly refused
to interfere in the internal affairs of Spain and left the
occupied territories at the mercy of the fanatical 'bands of
faith'. The secretary of the Prussian embassy, Jentzsch,
reported to his government on 5 June 1823, twelve days
after the occupation of Madrid by the French, that the
Spanish bandits of the 'army of faith' pillaged, robbed, and
murdered to their hearts' content. In Aranjuez they sacked
every house regardless of whether it was occupied by royalists
or liberals. "The lot of Madrid and countless other towns is
worse than that of a city taken by assault. For there order is
restored as soon as the soldiers' lust for plunder has been
satisfied; but here the inhabitants are day and night at the
mercy of a soldadesca who have no trace of military discipline
and no other thought but revenge, looting and thieving. . . .
In the small town of Palencia 120 of the most respected
citizens, who had never meddled in politics and were all
orderly, quiet people, were imprisoned simply because the
lowest scum, who had made themselves masters of the
town, coveted their property. . . ."[2]

The restoration of Ferdinand initiated a decade of
fierce oppression exceeding the worst excesses of the period
1814-19. Symptomatic of the new spirit which triumphed

---

[1] Castlereagh's 'protest' against the resolutions of the Troppau Congress of 1821 was
    no more than a manœuvre to silence the British radicals (cf. Baumgarten *op. cit.*).
[2] Baumgarten *op. cit.*

with the final defeat of the constitutionalists was the appointment, three days after Ferdinand's release, of the priest Saez to the dual dignity of Royal Confessor and Prime Minister of the Realm. A few days later special commissions for the eradication of heresy were established and all clerics who had been adherents of the 'Godless' faction were condemned to incarceration in monasteries of the strictest rule. Political 'purification commissions', at first instituted for officers and civil servants, were later extended to the rank and file of the army, to professors, teachers, students, and even school children. Informers were not only assured of anonymity, but also exempted from any responsibility for their assertions. Not only the actions of an examined person were taken into account, but also his opinions according to hearsay, and even the possibility that his otherwise satisfactory political views might perhaps undergo a future change. In May 1825 a decree was published enabling the police to arrest anyone who had *received* a letter criticising the government. In the summer of the same year all the universities were closed down as hatching-grounds for dangerous ideas (including the University of Cervera, notwithstanding the fact that it had stated in its loyal address to the King that year "Far from us the dangerous novelty of thinking!"). Early in 1825, 112 persons were hanged or shot within eighteen days. During the following October no less than 1,825 officers and men of the former constitutional army were murdered in Catalonia alone, not counting the thousands executed under martial law.[1]

To the mass arrests of the secret police, to the restless activity of the military tribunals and 'purification commissions', to the wholesale banishments and executions and the suppression of every vestige of intellectual freedom,[2] there now was added the organised mob violence of the 'Society of the Exterminating Angel', founded by the Bishop of Osma. "Death to the Blacks" was the cry with which the friars incited the mob to terrorise all persons of property or education. For however undefined the aims of

---

[1] Baumgarten *op. cit.* and H. Butler Clarke, *Modern Spain*, Cambridge, 1906.
[2] On 28 April 1826, when Goya was already in Bordeaux, the members of the Academy of San Fernando in Madrid had to swear: "to defend the mystery of the Immaculate Conception; to be faithful to the King and his laws which govern us; not to belong, or ever to have belonged to any lodge or secret society of whatever nature, nor to accept the absurd principle that the people are free to change the established form of government" (Sánchez Cantón *op. cit.*).

the liberals had been, the class character of the restoration was clear and unconcealed. With the help of the servile masses of starving peasants and beggars in the towns, the Church and the court struck at the entire middle class without reference to the political records of its individual members.

In one of Barcelona's churches there was a black image of the Virgin which had been venerated since time immemorial for its miraculous powers. A rumour was spread that the liberals—the 'Blacks'—had singled out this image for special devotion. It was then that the Black Virgin of Barcelona performed another miracle. Early one morning the priests informed their faithful flock that overnight the holy image had turned as white as snow. Thus did the Mother of God signify to her children her whole-hearted approval of their zeal in rooting out the infamous 'blacks'.[1]

Despite its terrible defeat, the revolution of 1820 had destroyed the foundations of Spanish absolutism. The systematic betrayal by Ferdinand of every rising he himself had instigated against the liberal régime had undermined the confidence of the reactionaries in the legitimate monarch. Increasing numbers of them transferred their allegiance to Ferdinand's equally bigoted, but far less cunning, brother, Don Carlos. The Carlist movement in fact dates from the moment (at dawn 7 July 1822) when Ferdinand, who had stirred up a mutiny of the guards in his favour, turned to the victorious liberal troops and shouted from the balcony of his palace that they should rout the rebels. Consequently in the following period of repression, Ferdinand, the archreactionary, was menaced by armed revolts from the right as well as from the left, and, abandoned by the feudal 'ultras', he was driven into the arms of the conservative bourgeoisie.

Even more important, however, was the fact that the revolution of 1820 had removed the main prop which supported the parasitical system of Spanish absolutism: the exploitation of colonial wealth. The period 1820–23 saw the final emancipation of the major Spanish colonies in America. Deprived of this century-old source of their enrichment, the Spanish ruling classes had to intensify the exploitation of their own people. This they could only do by affording increasing scope to the development of

[1] Inglis, *Spain in 1830*, London, 1837, vol. ii.

capitalism, even though the new capitalist enterprises might largely be controlled by the old feudal orders, especially the Church.

The emergence of capitalism brought in its train not merely the joint exploitation of the Spanish people by their old feudal and new bourgeois masters, but also the birth of a class which alone could provide the democratic masses with the necessary leadership in their struggle for freedom. The industrial working class would be able, in decades of struggle, to liberate the peasants from their spiritual enslavement and to oppose, to the combined forces of their feudal and capitalist exploiters, the unity of all the oppressed.

More than a century of struggle was required to bring about that unity, and when the night of reaction descended on unhappy Spain in 1823, the hope of its achievement as yet lay hidden in the womb of time. All that was clear in 1823 was that for the task of true emancipation the 'respectable' and 'educated' classes were but a broken reed. Freedom, if it were to be won, would have to be won by the oppressed themselves, however benighted, however brutalised, however unconscious or even boastful of their chains they still might be.

GOYA'S LAST YEARS

Goya's personal story during the last nine years of his life need not detain us for long. Little is known of his activities during the Constitutional period. A few portraits date from this time: one of the architect Don Tiburcio Pérez, another of the liberal politician Don Ramón Satué, and, significantly enough, one of Riego's wife.[1] That Goya openly identified himself with the liberal movement is clear, if only from the fact that he now gave the 'Disasters' to his friend Cean Bermúdez to have the captions edited, presumably with a view to publication. Even more significant is the fact that after the restoration Goya went into hiding. He stayed for three months in the house of a learned Aragonese canon, Don José Duaso y Latre (an uncle of Don Ramón Satué), who, though appointed honorary chaplain

---

[1] The portrait of Da. Maria Martinez de Puga was done after the defeat of the Constitutionalists in 1824, before Goya left Madrid, as was also a crayon drawing of his son Xavier.

to the King, editor of the *Gazette*, and general Press censor, used his position to protect a number of intellectuals compromised by their liberalism.[1]

But although Goya escaped persecution, life had become unbearable for him in Madrid. He applied for six months' leave, on the grounds of ill-health, ostensibly to take the waters at Plombières. In June 1824 he arrived in Bordeaux, and after only a few days' rest he continued his journey to Paris (where the Salon of that year contained Ingres' 'Vow of Louis XIII', Delacroix's 'Massacre of Scio', and the pictures of Constable and Bonnington). After a brief stay in which he visited a number of French artists and painted the portraits of his hosts, Don Joaquín Maria Ferrer (a former Cortes member) and his wife (also a small bull-fight composition and a self-portrait drawing), Goya returned to Bordeaux. With the exception of a last journey to Madrid to settle his affairs, he spent the four concluding years of his life in the circle of Spanish exiles in Bordeaux. His last, and in some respects his most magnificent, portraits are of members of this group: his old friend, the poet Moratin (1824), the writer Don Manuel Silvela (*c.* 1825), his adviser in money matters, the banker Santiago Galos (1826), Don Juan Bautista Muguiro (1827), and Don José Pio de Molina (unfinished, 1827), who lived in the house in which Goya died at the age of eighty-two on 16 April 1828.

GOYA'S ARTISTIC TESTAMENT

To understand the final phase in the development of Goya's art we must retrace our steps to the last years before the Revolution of 1820. We have already noted that among the visions of fear and horror which haunted the artist at that period, there emerged one type of image with an opposed significance: the allegorical female figure Truth, Reason, Justice, or Liberty. At the same time Goya's creative fantasy also gave birth to another image, ultimately even more profound in its antithesis to the dominant mood of terror. This we must now examine.

We have noted as a general feature of all Goya's visions in the period 1814–19 their vastness of scale. The unspeakable disaster of brutal reaction after the sacrifices of the war

[1] Mayer wrongly attributes this incident to the reaction of 1814. The facts reported were first published (probably by Vincente Lafuente) as part of a biography of Duaso in the *Boletin del Clero Español* of 1849 (Sánchez Cantón *op. cit.*).

of liberation took shape in Goya's mind in the form of gigantic monsters—whether beasts, such as those in plates 1, 40, and 81 of the 'Disasters', or semi-human and human forms as in the Quinta and the 'Disparates'—whose super-human proportions dwarfed and utterly crushed mankind. But, probably about the time when the ethereal figure of Hope first appeared in Goya's dreams, the irrepressible vitality of the people also began to reassert itself in his imagination in a more elemental form. The very scale of his horror visions brought about this release. For inhuman, monstrous, as were the torments of reaction, the body politic was even vaster. Kings, priests, jailers, torturers must die—the people are eternal. It is this conception which Goya embodied in a series of monumental designs some of which, at least, must date from before 1820.

The main stages in which this new type of image emerged from its satanic opposite can be traced without difficulty. The two paintings in the Quinta with huge figures poised in mid-air above sombre landscapes are transitional in character. The former shows the Fates, aloof, but still predominantly hostile in mood. In the latter, two figures are crouching in the air above what appears to be a battle-field. One is pointing towards a vast, strangely shaped mountain[1] in the distance; the other, apparently a female, is looking backward. The prevailing mood is no longer so ferocious, although it is heavy with mystery and still by no means confident (figs. 108, 109).

Goya's release from the mood of gloom is expressed with triumphant abandon in plate 4 of the 'Disparates'. A youthful giant dances wildly, laughing and shaking his castanets; behind him are the heads of two other shouting giants, facing him the half-crouching figure of a man hiding behind a doll-like, shrouded female figure (possibly, as Young suggests, the wooden statue of a saint) which he is holding up towards the giant. In mood and conception this design is Rabelaisian: Gargantua, embodiment of the people's pristine virility, terrifies the upholders of established super-stition and rises with triumphant laughter above their fears[2] (fig. 110).

---

[1] Mountains play a striking role in Goya's imagery during this period. They occur in a number of designs and paintings, and in two landscape etchings with vast rocks.

[2] I am not, of course, suggesting any direct link between Rabelais and Goya. Un-fortunately there is little documentary evidence regarding the books he read (al-though both Don Quixote and Gulliver appear in his drawings).

From the exuberant joy of release to the confidence of assured conviction was but a small step for Goya. The next stage is a return to the scheme of the two Quinta paintings: the huge form of a giant rising about the clouds in a landscape which again contains a war-like scene below. The giant makes a gesture of defiance; confidence and power are the dominant moods of this picture (Prado) (fig. 112).

But the design most perfect in its simplicity and tranquil force is the famous etching of the 'Giant', of which only a few prints were made before the plate was broken. The immense figure is seated on a gently rising incline before which minute villages appear in the middle distance. Seen from behind, the titan turns his head and looks back towards the sky. The shadow of the earth darkens the greater part of his body, but the first rays of the rising sun fall on his face and shoulders. (Carl Neumann has published two variants of a print after a lost drawing by Brueghel which show a striking formal resemblance to Goya's 'Giant'.[1] Brueghel's giant differs in spirit from Goya's, for he represents the power of wealth before which all mankind abase themselves. Yet it is suggestive that the change in mood from the terror designs of the 'Disparates' to the 'Giant' should be accompanied by a change in affinity —if not in influence—from Bosch to Brueghel, a change, in other words, from the artist who expressed the haunting terrors of the period immediately *before* the revolution to his successor whose art was inspired by the people's cause *in* the revolution) (fig. 113).

In this context a drawing which shows the gigantic head of Gulliver as he lies asleep on the shores of Lilliput also assumes additional significance: the 'grand colossus' need only awaken and stretch his limbs to shake the swarm of petty parasites, who are crawling all over him, into the dust ('Gran coloso dormido'—Berlin, Collection Gerstenberg).

Lastly, we must note a variant of this theme in which the people are no longer represented by a gigantic human form but by a beast. It is plate 21 of the 'Disparates', the 'Disparate de Bestia'. An enormous hump-backed elephant is standing outside a white, semi-elliptical arena and faces

[1] C. Neumann, 'Drei merkwürdige Anregungen bei Runge, Manet und Goya', *Sitzungsberichte der Heidelberger Akademie der Wissenschaften*. Philosophisch-historische Klasse. 1916.

a group of magicians. One of them is holding an open codex of the laws towards the suspicious-looking beast, another a belt of jangling bells, a third seems to be addressing it with honeyed words, while the fourth is turning, as if about to escape. 'Other laws for the People' is the title given to the print, when it was first published in the periodical *L'Art* in 1877. Although probably apocryphal, it expresses its essential meaning, except for the sense of imminent revolt implied both in the posture of the elephant and the expressions of its keepers[1] (fig. 111).

It is unfortunately uncertain at what date Goya returned to a style of documentary realism to express his reassured confidence in the people. But this return to realism is the most striking result of the heroic recovery of his social outlook at the height of the pre-1820 reaction period. There exists a group of three closely related paintings which, with Daumier's paintings and groups of working people, Courbet's 'Roadmakers', a few of the more objective Millets, and some early drawings by van Gogh, belong to the most important pictures of manual workers produced during the nineteenth century. One shows a 'Forge' with three men at work at an anvil (Frick Collection, New York), the other two a 'Knife Grinder' and 'Girl carrying water' respectively (Museum, Budapest). They are wholly documentary paintings of workers at their tasks. The theme which Goya first approached in the 'Fallen Mason' and the 'Muleteers' of 1786–7, and to which he fleetingly returned in the 'Tapestry Workshop' of *c.* 1808–1810, now re-emerges in its most mature form. For in their style also these three groups of works mark three outstanding phases of Goya's artistic development. From the first assertion of realism within the framework of the rococo tradition, through the tense expressionism of doubt and dismay, to the vigorous objectivity of calm conviction—such was the course of a creative struggle which finally enabled Goya to give adequate expression to the theme of the people. On technical grounds the three paintings we are considering are usually dated 1818–19.[2] If this is correct,

---

[1] Among the Bosch paintings taken to Spain in the sixteenth century was his 'Elephant' (Justi *op. cit.*). Although it may have already disappeared by Goya's time, he may well have known Bosch's print of the same subject: a gigantic elephant standing, a tower of strength, amidst the turmoil of a fantastic battle scene.

[2] All three pictures are evidently contemporary; the 'Forge' and the 'Knife Grinder' contain the same model. It is tempting to date them from the Constitutional period. This is impossible, however, in view of the fact that the two Budapest pictures were

Goya had defeated the monsters of reaction in his own mind even before the collapse of political repression. For it is the spirit of freedom, the spirit of the dignity and joy of labour, as both Goya and Shelley understood it, which emanates from these pictures (figs. 114-16).

Goya's sense of confident assurance, his noble triumph over the monsters of despair, was shaken neither by the weaknesses and disappointments of the revolution itself, nor by the renewed horrors of the second restoration. It is to his drawings and last prints that we must turn for his artistic testament. A large number of the drawings[1] date from the artist's last years, although it is not always possible to distinguish those drawn in Bordeaux from the last Madrid designs.

We have already noted a number of drawings which obviously allude to the revolution of 1820. To these must be added a further group of designs of monks and nuns disrobing, an illusion to the secularisation of the religious houses.

Of the later drawings Paul Lafond writes: "Goya, less extreme than in his youth, more contemplative, wiser, more master of himself and of his thoughts, has here in part forsaken the fantastic and the macabre so frequently employed in the Caprichos. . . . This suite of drawings combines something of everything, of philosophy, of morals, of ecstasy, scenes of popular life, and simple incidents found through happy accident."[2]

In this last and most moving cycle of dreams and observations the old master has again traversed the whole range of his creative experience. They are a last version of the Caprichos,[3] but caprichos, imaginative follies, in a calmer, more benevolent, sometimes humorous, but always fundamentally confident mood. It is true that the old monsters still occasionally appear, but more often than not they are now objective studies of idiots ('locos'). And some-

purchased for the Esterhazy Collection from that of Prince Kaunitz on 3 April and 19 October 1820 respectively. Nevertheless they cannot have been painted much before 1819.

[1] Several hundreds of these drawings are preserved in the Prado and in various other collections. A set of 38 is illustrated in Paul Lafond, *Nouveaux Caprices de Goya*, Paris, 1907; many others in *Goya: los Caprichos*, No. 3 of the series *Los Grandes Maestros de la pintura en España*, Madrid, 1909; in F. Zapater, *Goya, Collección de reproduciones . . . etc.*, Madrid, 1924; in Boix and Sánchez Cantón *op. cit.*; in P. d' Acchiardi *op. cit.*; and in Rothe *op. cit.*

[2] Paul Lafond, 'Les Dernières Années de Goya en France', *Gazette des Beaux-Arts*, 1907.

[3] In 1825 Goya's friends in Paris apparently tried to persuade him to issue a new edition of the 'Caprichos', for Goya wrote in December of that year to J. M. Ferrer that he could not do so since he had ceded the plates to the King. He continues: "I would certainly not copy them, since to-day I have got better works, which could be more usefully sold . . ."; cf. Paul Lafond *op. cit.*

times there is a flash of the old ferocity, as in the design in which a man is sawn in two, while bespectacled lawyers watch the ordeal. Again, there is a group of drawings, deeply moving in its mood of pity rather than of ridicule, in which benighted old men or women are counting their beads or praying. One of these might be regarded as a faint echo of the 'man of sorrow' image. And the same is true of another drawing, also in the Prado collection, in which the kneeling figure appears, at first sight, to be an old devil. But Goya's caption quickly dispels the illusion by tracing the old man's horns to a more worldly source: 'He says he was born with them and he has them all his life'—a sardonic allusion to the trials of matrimony. In the serene mood of his final years Goya could make light both of the religious and of the satanic imagery of his troubled past (figs. 92, 93).

But occasional reminiscences such as these scarcely affect the character of the concluding phase of Goya's art. It throbs with the life of the people, their work, troubles, quarrels, and amusements (figs. 117-20).

Roaming through Bordeaux, Goya observed the life of its streets and public places in all its vividness. Many scenes are from circus and fair-ground: the magnificent 'Elephants', the 'living skeleton', the man in the peep-show, the man with the camel, the crocodile, performing animals, and similar marvels. There is also the guillotine performing its gruesome work. But most of the drawings show ordinary folk at their everyday occupations: women at work in their homes, or tending their children; men working or having a drink; children, courting couples, and old people.

Some of these drawings stand out as triumphant manifestations of Goya's faith in the people. Such is the drawing showing a rugged peasant in tattered clothes pulling with all his might at a rope. Such is also the lithograph[1] of the 'Vito'; a girl moving in the measured ecstasy of the dance, surrounded by the uncouth figures of a watching crowd. All the confidence and joy, the unshakable certainty of a better future which inspired the old master, is expressed in this fervent portrayal of Spain, uncouth and barbarous, but triumphant in its irrepressible vitality (figs. 121, 122).

[1] In 1819 Goya took up this new technique; his lithographs are similar in style and spirit to the last drawing. The same applies to the curious miniatures he painted in Bordeaux, when the infirmities of old age rendered work on a large scale difficult for him (though here the fantastic element is rather more in evidence than in the drawings).

In another form this spirit inspired the last of Goya's imaginative paintings, the 'Milkmaid of Bordeaux'. With its brilliant brushwork and exquisite colouring it is technically one of his best productions. A simple peasant girl seated in contemplation. Serene and beautiful, she is Goya's last tribute to those who spend their days in toil.

We have now followed the inspiring course of Goya's creative development to its conclusion. Many important aspects of his art, notably the technical attainments of his supreme craftsmanship in many different media, have been neglected in this study, and whole categories of his work, particularly his portraits, have not been considered. Their exclusion was necessary, since it has been my aim to indicate the underlying rhythm in the development of Goya's outlook and to trace its origin, and the origin of Goya's style, in the social history of his time. In order to pursue this aim and to prevent the main conclusions from being obscured by a multitude of subsidiary details, I had to confine my attention primarily to the theme which links all his productive activity: the people. Yet Goya's work forms a complete and indivisible whole. The portraits, with their majestic progression from his first attempts to get away from the formalised aristocratic portrait of the baroque, through the brilliant works of the 1790's, to the ever more analytical, yet at the same time monumental, portraits of his old age, reveal an integral part of Goya's social and artistic personality. They are a true gallery of the men and women who made the history of his time, both statesmen and intellectuals. In a deeper sense they are documents of that liberation of individual personality which began, though it was not completed, with the bourgeois revolution. In that sense they are the necessary complement of Goya's main theme, the emancipation of the people.

In its formal aspects the development of Goya's art revealed itself as a succession of clearly demarcated phases. It started with the artist's attempt to escape from the baroque tradition and to attain a style of truthful simplicity and naturalness, schooled in the heritage of Spanish realism. The crisis of 1792 led Goya to a more profound formulation of artistic truth. Thenceforth his personality expanded through the creative conflict of its chief elements: reason and fantasy. The cycle completed its course in a sequence of oscillations characterised by the predominance of one or the other of these two creative forces. Tempered by suffering and its mastery, their conflict was at last resolved in the serene but virile harmony of Goya's last works.

And the content of this cycle of creation? I can do no better than return to Shelley who, in describing the theme of his poem 'The Revolt of Islam',[1] has unconsciously epitomised the message of his great comrade-in-arms:

"It is a succession of pictures illustrating the growth and progress of individual mind aspiring after excellence, and devoted to the love of mankind; its influence in refining and making pure the most daring and uncommon impulses of the imagination and the senses; its impatience at 'all the oppressions which are done under the sun'; its tendency to awaken public hope, and to enlighten and improve mankind; the rapid effects of the application of that tendency; the awakening of an immense nation from their slavery and degradation to a true sense of moral dignity and freedom; the bloodless dethronement of their oppressors, and the unveiling of the religious frauds by which they had been deluded into submission; the tranquillity of successful patriotism, and the universal tolerance of benevolence and true philanthropy; the treachery and barbarity of hired soldiers; vice not the object of punishment and hatred, but kindness and pity; the faithlessness of tyrants; the confederacy of the Rulers of the World, and the restoration of the expelled dynasty by foreign arms; the massacre and extermination of the Patriots, and the victory of established power; the consequences of legitimate despotism—civil war, famine, plague, superstition, and an utter extinction of the domestic affections; the judicial murder of the advocates of Liberty; the temporary triumph of oppression, that secure earnest of its final and inevitable fall; the transient nature of ignorance and error, and the eternity of genius and virtue."

[1] Preface to 'The Revolt of Islam', 1817–18.

Appendix

ADDITIONAL NOTES AND DOCUMENTS

I *The German Merchants in the American Trade and the 'Virgen de los Conquistadores'* (*v.* pp. 8-10 and 31)

APART from its significance in the context of the economic revolution of the sixteenth century and its disastrous effects on Spain, the participation of the great German merchant houses in the Spanish-American trade has a special interest for the art-historian. It has been suggested as a tentative explanation of the Teutonic features of several of the portrait heads in Alejo Fernandez' 'Virgen de los Conquistadores' that that picture might have been a donation of the German merchants (Mayer, *Geschichte der spanischen Malerei*, vol. i). This is by no means improbable. Charles had always favoured the participation of his northern subjects in the colonial enterprises of his new realm. In 1517, even before he had come to Spain, he had supported a project of settling Flemish peasants in Yucatan. Five shiploads of them actually sailed for San Lúcar de Barrameda (near Seville), but Diego Columbus was able to uphold the privileges granted to his father, and the Flemish settlers were compelled to return to their own country (*v.* E. Gossart, *Espagnoles et Flamandes: Charles-Quint, roy d'Espagne*, Brussels, 1910). Since the early 1520's both the Fugger and the Welser had made determined efforts to capture a share of the Spanish-American trade. A Fugger agent had bought a cargo which the *Victoria*, the only ship of the Magellan expedition to complete the voyage, had brought back to Spain in 1522. Three years later the Fugger partly financed the expeditions which Garcia de Loaysa and Sebastian Cabot planned to lead to the Moluccas, and in the same year, 1525, the Welser had already established factories at Seville and Santo Domingo. The edict of 1526 in which Charles V granted the right of trade and colonisation to all his subjects thus merely legalised what was already taking place. These developments culminated in two agreements dating from 1528 and 1530 respectively. The former was the contract, mentioned in the text, in which the Welser undertook to colonise Venezuela and to supply the older settlements with negro slaves; they were also granted extensive storage and ship-repairing accommodation in Seville harbour for their exclusive use. The second agreement made the colonisation and commercial exploitation of the entire coastline of what is now the Republic of Chile the monopoly of the Fugger. For some unknown reason, however, the Fugger, unlike the Welser, never made use of their privileges. Nevertheless, both firms were very active in the slave trade with America, until it passed into the hands of the Italians about the middle of the century. For further details *v.* Konrad Häbler, *Geschichte der Fugger'schen Handlung in Spanien* (Weimar, 1897), and the same author's *Die überseeischen Unternehmungen der Welser* (Leipzig, 1903), and C. H. Haring's comprehensive review of the Spanish-American trade (*Trade and Navigation between Spain and the Indies*, Cambridge, Mass., 1918).

The 'Virgen de los Conquistadores' is usually dated from about the 1520's. The picture was painted for the chapel of the Casa de Contratación, the organisation founded by the Catholic Kings in 1503, which served as a ministry controlling all the navigation, trading, and colonial enterprises of Spain. Alejo Fernandez, its painter and the foremost artist of Seville, had designed the decorations of that city for the triumphal entry of the Emperor Charles in 1526, when he legalised the colonial enterprises of his German bankers. The suggestion that Fernandez may have been commissioned by the German merchants to paint the main picture for the Casa de Contratación in celebration of so important a gain is so much the more plausible, since the *Consulado*, the guild of the Spanish merchants concerned in the overseas trade, was not founded until 1543. Alternatively the picture might have been commissioned by the Welser on the occasion of their 1528 agreement. Though much importance cannot be attached to a posthumous engraving (evidently based, however, on a contemporary portrait), the latter assumption derives some support from the fact that the most prominent of the merchants in Fernandez' picture (the richly clothed figure on the extreme left) has the same characteristic profile as a portrait of Bartholomäus Welser by G. C. Eimart (1603–58: a copy in the Print Room of the British Museum, folder of Welser portraits). Bartholomäus Welser (1488–1561) was the head of the main (Augsburg) branch of the Welser firm, in whose name the contracts of 1528 were concluded by his agents or partners, Heinreich and Georg Ehinger and Hieronymus Sailer. Even though this evidence is too slight to establish the Welsers as the *sole* donors of the picture, it is reasonable to conclude that they figured prominently among the donors, who may have included both Spanish and German merchants, in which case 1526 would appear to be the most likely date of the commission.

The chapel of the Casa de Contratación had been endowed by the Catholic Kings as a sanctuary in which special masses were to be read for those who had perished at sea or during the colonial conquests. Hence the 'Virgen de los Conquistadores' was also known as the 'Virgen del Buen Aire': the Virgin of the good winds, patron of sailors. In 1535 Pedro de Mendoza sailed from Seville with a large fleet for the River Plate. There he founded a settlement in 1536 which he called *Nuestra Señora de Buen Ayre*. Thus the Virgin of the sailors' chapel gave its name to the present capital of the Argentine. Although Mendoza's venture was a commercial failure (he himself died on the return journey) and the first Buenos Aires was abandoned within a short period of its foundation, it is curious to note, in the present context, that one of his ships had been equipped by Sebastian Neidhart and Jacob Welser, the head of the Nürnberg branch of the Welser firm.

II. *Bourgoing on the Majos and Majas* (*v.* pp. 15 and 16)

The following passage, in which Bourgoing describes the Madrid majos and majas, may supplement the account given in the text, which was based on Hamilton's analysis of the sainetes:

> The Majos are beaux of the lower class, or rather bullies, whose grave and frigid pomposity is announced by their whole exterior. They have an accent, habit, and gesture peculiar to themselves. Their countenance, half concealed under a brown stuff bonnet, called *Montera*, bears the character of threatening severity, or of wrath, which seems to brave persons the most proper to awe them into respect, and which is not softened even in the presence of their mistress. The officers of justice scarcely dare attack them. The women, intimidated by their terrible aspect, seem to wait with resignation the soft caprice of these petty sultans. If they are provoked by any freedoms, a gesture of impatience, a menacing look, sometimes a long rapier or a poniard concealed under their wide cloak, announce that they cannot permit familiarity with impunity. The Majas, on their parts, rival these caprices as much as their feeble means will permit; they seem to make a study of effrontery. The licentiousness of their manners appears in their attitudes, actions and expressions; and when lewdness in their persons is clothed with every wanton form, all the epithets which admiration can inspire are lavished upon them. This is the disagreeable side of the picture. But if the spectator goes with a disposition, not very scrupulous, to the representations in which the Majas figure; when he becomes familiarised to manners very little conformable to the virtues of the sex, and the means of inspiring ours with favourable sentiments, he sees in each of them the most seducing priestess that ever presided at the altars of Venus. Their impudent affectation is no more than a poignant allurement, which introduces into the senses a delirium that the wisest can scarcely guard against, and which, if it inspires not love, at least promises much pleasure.

III. *Spanish Capitalism on the Eve of the French Revolution*
(*v.* p. 66)

The following details may illustrate the point made in the text that Spanish capitalism had scarcely even begun to emancipate itself from the leading-strings of mercantilism on the Colbert pattern at the time of the French Revolution. Crown enterprises still played a leading role in the economic life of Spain. Townsend gives the following list of state factories in the late 1780's:

2 factories for broadcloth at Guadalajara and Brihuega
1 factory ,, china ware at Buen Retiro near Madrid
2 factories ,, playing cards at Madrid and Malaga
1 factory ,, glass at San Ildefonso
1 ,, ,, paper at Segovia
1 ,, ,, pottery at Talavera
1 ,, ,, saltpetre at Madrid
1 ,, ,, stockings at Valdemoro
1 ,, ,, swords at Toledo
1 ,, ,, tapestries at Madrid
1 ,, ,, tissues at Talavera
1 ,, ,, tobacco and snuff at Seville

The crown also claimed the monopoly for the distribution of brandy, playing cards, gunpowder, lead, quicksilver, sealing wax, salt, sulphur, and tobacco. Among the privately controlled industries the textile and clothing trades appear to have been most flourishing in Barcelona and the silk manufacture in Valencia, where the number of looms had increased from 800 in 1718 to about 5,000 at the time of Townsend's visit. Seville also had regained some of its former importance as a silk manufacturing centre. It is significant, however, that every factory of any importance, mentioned by Townsend, had some kind of privilege from the government—either the monopoly of certain army contracts, or that of certain colonial exports.

While the guilds of the artisans retained their feudal character during the eighteenth century, the great merchant guilds of Madrid underwent a significant transformation during the reform period. The five Major Guilds of Madrid had for a long time enjoyed the monopoly of all wholesale dealings in the capital. During the eighteenth century, however, they formed a joint-stock company which engaged in extensive banking transactions, participated financially in many industrial undertakings, canal constructions, etc., enjoyed lucrative monopolies for army supplies, and engaged in overseas trade. These formidable privileges were to some extent threatened by the Bank of San Carlos, the predecessor of the Bank of Spain, founded in 1781 by the French economist, Count Cabarrús. Apart from issuing State securities, this undertaking sponsored many industrial and trading enterprises. It was the principal shareholder of the Philippine Company founded in 1785. The latter, which operated not only in the Philippines but also in Latin America (for it had absorbed the older Company of Caracas), was the most powerful organisation in the Spanish colonial trade during the reign of Charles IV.

IV. *Pan y Toros* (*v.* pp. 80 *et seq.*)

For a bibliography of *Pan y Toros*, *v.* Julio Somoza de Montsoriu, *Inventario de un Jovellanista*, Madrid, 1901. The pamphlet was certainly not written by Jovellanos; the evidence in favour of Vargas Ponce's authorship is contained in a footnote on p. 266 of vol. ii, *Obras de*

Jovellanos, ed. D. Cándido Nocedal (Biblioteca de Autores Españoles, Madrid, 1859). That *Pan y Toros* remained popular in progressive circles up to the French invasion is shown by the fact that one of the extant manuscript copies bears the date 1804; it was also freely pirated in an article on the treatment of animals which appeared in 1803 in a Seville paper (*v.* M. A. Buchanan, 'Pan y Toros', *Modern Language Notes*, Baltimore, vol. xx, 1905). In a later contribution Buchanan amplifies Somoza's bibliography and discusses the English version of the pamphlet which I have used in the text (*Modern Language Notes*, Baltimore, vol. xl, 1925). It is contained in a rare booklet, of which Buchanan was able to trace only two copies: one in the National Library, Madrid, the other in the British Museum. Its title is:

The
Speech
of
Doctor D. Antonio Joseph Ruiz de Padrón,
Deputy to the Cortes from the Canary Islands,
spoken in the sitting of January 18th, 1813,
relative to the Inquisition.

———

Bread and Bulls
An Apologetic Oration,
on the Flourishing State of Spain in the
Reign of King Charles IV.
delivered
In the Plaza de Toros, Madrid
by Don Gaspar de Jovellanos

———

Mediterranean
Printed on Board His Majesty's Ship Caledonia, off Toulon
1813.

This translation, which is dedicated to Vice-Admiral Sir Edward Pellew, Bart. (later Viscount Exmouth), was made at his request by seven young cadets (including a later Duke of Northumberland), whose education had been entrusted to his care. Even though it may not reflect Pellew's own attitude to the Spanish liberals, it is curious that he should have encouraged his pupils to translate two such notable pieces of liberal propaganda (the speech on the Inquisition is one of the most famous indictments of that institution in the first Cortes) at a time when the British army command was putting its full weight behind the anti-liberal intrigues.

Don José Vargas Ponce is mainly noted as an historian of the Spanish navy. When he was elected President of the Historical Academy in 1805, that institution commissioned Goya to paint his portrait. A letter from Vargas Ponce to Cean Bermúdez, a mutual friend of both painter and sitter, throws an amusing sidelight on Goya's business methods. It also shows that the artist's more intelligent sitters fully appreciated the difference between his 'official' and 'intimate' portraits. For Ponce requests Bermúdez to persuade Goya that he should paint the picture as he himself would like it, *i.e.* not as a fashionable representation piece. He then laments the fact that the Academy cannot afford the price of a standard portrait with head and hands, and suggests, as a compromise, that he should hide one of his hands behind his back and place the other in the lapel of his coat—thus reducing the amount of work required and the fee chargeable. His suggestion seems to have been accepted, for the painting actually shows this pose (*v.* Sánchez Cantón *op. cit.*).

V. *The Decree of 21 July 1814 restoring the Inquisition* (*v.* p. 154)

"The glorious title of Catholic by which the Kings of Spain are distinguished from the other princes of Christendom because they do not tolerate in their realm any person who professes a religion other than the Catholic, Apostolic and Roman, has powerfully moved my heart to employ all means which God has given into my hands, in order to be worthy of it. The grave disturbances and the war which ravaged all the provinces of the kingdom for six years; the presence in it during all that time of foreign troops belonging to many sects, nearly all infected with hatred and abhorrence for the Catholic religion; the disorder which always follows in the wake of such evils, together with the lack of care taken at such times to provide for the needs of religion, gave to the wicked full license to live as they wished and the opportunity to introduce into the kingdom and to instil into many people pernicious opinions by the same means as those employed to propagate them in other countries. In order, therefore, to provide a remedy for so grave an evil and to preserve in my dominions the holy religion of Jesus Christ, which we love and in which my people have their life and live happily, and also in view of the duty which the fundamental laws of the realm impose upon the reigning Prince, and which I have sworn to protect and observe, and because it is the most suitable means of preserving my subjects from internal dissensions and of maintaining them in a state of tranquillity and calmness; I believe that it would be of great benefit in the existing circumstances to restore to the exercise of its jurisdiction the Tribunal of the Holy Office. Wise and virtuous prelates and many important corporations and individuals, both ecclesiastical and secular, have advised me that it was thanks to this tribunal that Spain was not contaminated with the errors which caused such tribulations in other countries during the sixteenth century, while our country flourished in every sphere of letters, in great men, in holiness and virtue; that one of the principal means used by the Oppressor of Europe to sow corruption and discord, so advantageous to him, was the destruction of this tribunal under the pretext that it was no longer compatible with the enlightenment of the age; and that afterwards the so-called Cortes General and Extraordinary used the same pretext and that of

the Constitution to abolish it turbulently and to the grief of the nation.
For which reason they have most earnestly entreated me to re-establish
that tribunal; and I, in acceding to their request and to the wish of
the people, who in the fullness of their love for the religion of their
fathers have already on their own account restored certain lower
tribunals to their functions, I have resolved that henceforth the Council
of the Inquisition and the other Tribunals of the Holy Office shall be
restored and shall continue to function in the exercise of their jurisdiction. . . . At the Palace, 21 July 1814—I THE KING . . ." (*Decretos del
Rey Fernando VII*, Madrid, 1813–34, vol. i, pp. 132-4). The later
sections of the decree provide that the tribunal shall follow the pro-
cedure, both in general matters and in relation to the censorship of
books, in force up to 1808, except for such modifications as may be
recommended "for the good of my subjects" by a commission to be
appointed forthwith. Ferdinand's entire legislation of this period was
guided by the fiction that the momentous period 1808–14 had just
not existed. Note also the reference to the "foreign troops belonging
to many sects" in which Ferdinand pointedly emphasises his hatred
of the heretical British, and not merely of the French.

VI. *Baudelaire on Goya* (*v.* pp. 87, 88-89, 95, 101, and 193)

The following extract reproduces the main section of Baudelaire's
review of the fantastic element in Goya's art, especially the Caprichos. It
is taken from the essay 'Quelques caricaturistes étrangers' (1857). That
essay deals with Hogarth, Cruikshank, Goya, Pinelli, and Brueghel.
After referring the reader to Gautier's article of 1845, as printed in
the *Voyage en Espagne*, Baudelaire continues:

> Je veux seulement ajouter quelques mots sur l'élément très-
> rare que Goya a introduit dans le comique: je veux parler du
> *Fantastique*. Goya n'est précisément rien de spécial, de particulier,
> ni comique absolu, ni comique purement significatif, à la manière
> française. Sans doute il plonge souvent dans le comique féroce et
> s'élève jusqu'au comique absolu; mais l'aspect général sous lequel
> il voit les choses est surtout fantastique. *Los Caprichos* sont une
> œuvre merveilleuse, non-seulement par l'originalité des concep-
> tions, mais encore par exécution. J'imagine devant *Los Caprichos*
> un homme, un curieux, un amateur, n'ayant aucune notion des
> faits historiques auxquels plusieurs de ces planches font allusion,
> un simple esprit d'artiste qui ne sache ce que c'est ni que Godoi,
> ni le roi Charles, ni la reine; il éprouvera toutefois au fond de son
> cerveau une commotion vive, à cause de la manière originale, de
> la plénitude des moyens de l'artiste, et aussi de cette atmosphère
> fantastique qui baigue tous ses sujets. Du reste, il y a dans les
> œuvres issues des profondes individualités quelque chose qui
> ressemble à ces rêves périodiques ou chroniques qui assiègent
> régulièrement notre sommeil. C'est là ce qui marque le véritable
> artiste, toujours durable et vivace même dans ces œuvres fugitives,
> pour ainsi dire suspendues aux événements, qu'on appelle *cari-*

catures; c'est là, dis-je, ce qui distingue les caricaturistes historiques d'avec les caricaturistes artistiques, le comique fugitif d'avec le comique éternel.

Goya est toujours un grand artiste, souvent effrayant. Il unit à la gaieté, à la jovialité, à la satire espagnole du bon temps de Cervantes, un esprit beaucoup plus moderne, ou du moins qui a été beaucoup plus cherché dans les temps modernes, l'amour de l'insaisissable, le sentiment des contrastes violents, des épouvante-ments de la nature et des physionomies humaines étrangement animalisées par les circonstances. C'est chose curieuse à remarquer que cet esprit qui vient après le grand mouvement satirique et démolisseur du XVIIIe siècle, et auquel Voltaire aurait su gré, pour l'idée seulement (car le pauvre grand homme ne s'y con-naissait guère quant au reste), de toutes ces caricatures monacales— moines bâillants, moines goinfrants, têtes carrées d'assassins se préparant à matines, têtes rusées, hypocrites, fines et méchantes comme des profiles d'oiseaux de proie;—il est curieux, dis-je, que ce haïsseur de moines ait tant rêvé sorcières, sabbat, diableries, enfants qu'on fait cuire à la broche, que sais-je? toutes des dé-bauches du rêve, toutes les hyperboles de l'hallucination, et puis toutes ces blanches et sveltes Espagnoles que de vieilles sempiter-nelles lavent et préparent soit pour le sabbat, soit pour la prostitu-tion du soir, sabbat de la civilisation! La lumière et les ténèbres se jouent à travers toutes ces grotesques horreurs. Quelle singulière jovialité! Je me rappelle surtout deux planches extraordinaires.

Then follows the passage quoted on p. 95. The second plate Baudelaire describes as follows:

> L'autre planche représente un être, un malheureux, une monade solitaire et désespérée, qui veut à toute force sortir de son tombeau. Des démons malfaisants, une myriade de vilains gnomes lilliputiens pèsent de tous leurs efforts réunis sur le cou-vercle de la tombe entre-bâillée. Ces gardiens vigilants de la mort se sont coalisés contre l'âme récalcitrante qui se consume dans une lutte impossible. Ce cauchemar s'agite dans l'horreur du vague et de l'infini.

This description is extraordinarily significant for Baudelaire's approach to Goya, for he describes what does not exist in any of the plates of the 'Caprichos'. He evidently combined his own recollection of plate 59—the gaunt man trying to hold up the heavy stone slab— with Gautier's account of the 'Nada' plate in the 'Disasters' (which Baudelaire had not seen himself). Thus he adapted his own mental image to his interpretation of Goya's meaning: a lapse which would be inexcusable to-day in the period of photography and good reproduc-tions, but which reveals how profoundly the younger of these two great artists was stimulated by his predecessor.

After a brief account of the four lithographs, known as the 'Toros de Burdeos', which Goya published during his last years in France, Baudelaire concludes with the paragraph quoted on p. 101.

List of Illustrations

Frontispiece: Fran^co Goya y Lucientes, Pintor. Plate No. 1 of the Caprichos

Illustrations to Chapter I

FIGURE

1 Maja and masked men (La maja y los embozados); tapestry cartoon, 1777, Prado
2 The Sunshade (El quitasol); tapestry cartoon, 1777, Prado
3 The Doctor (El médico); tapestry cartoon, 1779, National Gallery of Scotland, Edinburgh
4 The Pottery Stall (El cacharrero); tapestry cartoon, 1779, Prado
5 The Vintage (La vendimia); tapestry cartoon, 1786, Prado
6 The Wedding Procession (La boda); tapestry cartoon, 1787, Prado
7 A poor family at a well (Los pobres en la fuente); tapestry cartoon, 1787, Prado
8 The injured mason (El albañil herido); tapestry cartoon, 1786, Prado
9 Winter (La nevada); tapestry cartoon, 1786, Prado
10 The Meadow of San Isidro (La Pradera de San Isidro); oil painting, 1787, Prado
11 Domenico Tiepolo: 'Il Mondo Novo' mural from the Villa Zianiga, 1791, now in the Ca' Rezzonico, Venice

Illustrations to Chapter II

12 Birds of a feather (Tal para qual); drawing for Capricho No. 5, Prado
13 It fits well (Bien tirada está), Capricho No. 17
14 On the hunt for teeth (A caza de dientes), Capricho No. 12
15 Sht! (Chitón), Capricho No. 28
16 And then they abducted her (Que se la llevaron!), Capricho No. 8
17 From such dust . . . (Aquellos polbos: short for *De aquellos polbos vienen estos lodos:* from such dust such dirt is made), Capricho No. 23
18 They are overcome by sleep (Las rinde el sueño), Capricho No. 34
19 Don't cry, little fool (No grites, tonta), Capricho No. 74
20 You won't get away (No te escaparás), Capricho No. 72
21 Volaverunt (Volaverunt), Capricho No. 61
22 Dream of Lying and Faithlessness (Sueño de la mentira y de la inconstancia); suppressed plate for the Caprichos
23 Back to his grandfather (Asta su abuelo), Capricho No. 39
24 Of what illness will he die? (De que mal morirá?), Caprico No. 40
25 Drawing for Capricho No. 43 (Prado), with the following two captions: Idioma universal dibujado y grabado p^r Fr^co de Goya, año 1797 (Universal Language drawn and etched by Francisco de Goya in the year

222

List of Illustrations 223

Illustrations to Chapter III

Illustrations to Chapter IV

Acknowledgements: Plates from the Caprichos, Desastres de la Guerra, and Disparates are reproduced by courtesy of Sir John Stirling Maxwell, the Victoria and Albert Museum, London, and The Hispanic Society of America, New York; Goya's paintings by courtesy of the Prado Museum, Madrid, the National Gallery of Scotland, Edinburgh, the Museum of Budapest, and the Frick Collection, New York; Goya's drawings and single prints by courtesy of the Prado Museum, Madrid, the Bibliothèque Nationale, Paris, the Fitzwilliam Museum, Cambridge, and the Metropolitan Museum of Art, New York. Domenico Tiepolo's mural is reproduced from a photograph by Fiorentini, Venice.

THE ILLUSTRATIONS

1. Maja and Majos. *Tapestry Cartoon*, 1777.

2. The Sunshade. *Tapestry Cartoon*, 1777.

3. The Doctor. *Tapestry Cartoon*, 1779.

4. The Pottery Stall. *Tapestry Cartoon*, 1779.

5. The Vintage. *Tapestry Cartoon*, 1786.

6. The Wedding Procession. *Tapestry Cartoon.* 1787.

7. Poor Family at a Well.   8. The Injured Mason.

Tapestry Cartoons, 1786–87.

9. Winter. *Tapestry Cartoon*, 1786.

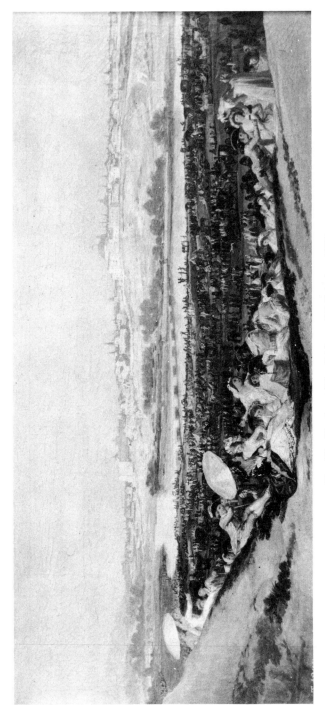

10. The Meadow of San Isidro. *Oil Painting,* 1787.

11. Domenico Tiepolo : Mural *Il Mondo Novo* from the Villa Zianigo, 1791, now in the Ca' Rezzonico, Venice.

12. Birds of a Feather. *Drawing for Capricho*, No. 5.

13. It fits well. *Capricho* No. 17.

15. Sht ! *Capricho No. 28.*

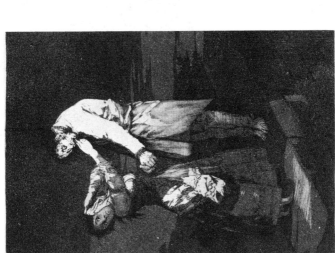

14. On the hunt for teeth. *Capricho No. 12.*

16. And then they abducted her. *Capricho* No. 8.

17. From such dust. . . . *Capricho* No. 23

(A Spanish proverb : *From such dust dust such dirt is made* was Goya's source for the caption of fig. 17.)

18.   They are overcome by sleep.   *Capricho* No. 34

20. You won't get away. *Capricho No. 72.*

19. Don't cry, little fool. *Capricho No. 74.*

21.   Volaverunt.   *Capricho* No. 61.

22. Dream of lies and inconstancy. Suppressed plate for the *Caprichos*.

23.   Back to his grandfather.   *Capricho* No. 39.

24. Of what illness will he die ? *Capricho* No. 40.

25. A universal language. The artist dreaming. His sole intention is to
banish harmful errors and perpetuate with this work of Caprichos the solid
testimony of truth.   *Drawing*, 1797, for *Capricho* No. 43.

26. The Sleep of Reason produces Monsters. *Capricho* No. 43.

27. The Blowers. *Capricho* No. 48.

28. Chinchillas. *Capricho* No. 50.

30. Your Excellency is . . . ahem. as I was saying . . .egad ! Mind you ! Or else . . . *Capricho No. 76*

29. Look, how grave they are ! *Capricho No. 63*

32. Blow! *Capricho No. 69.*

31. Whither, Mamma? *Capricho No. 65.*

33.   Who would have believed it ?   *Capricho* No. 62.

34. Dawn is breaking, we must go. *Capricho* No. 71.

35. What a tailor can do. *Drawing for Capricho No. 52.*

37. It is better to be idle. *Capricho No. 73.*

36. Will no one untie us ? *Capricho No. 75.*

38. Swallow it, dog ! *Capricho* No. 58.

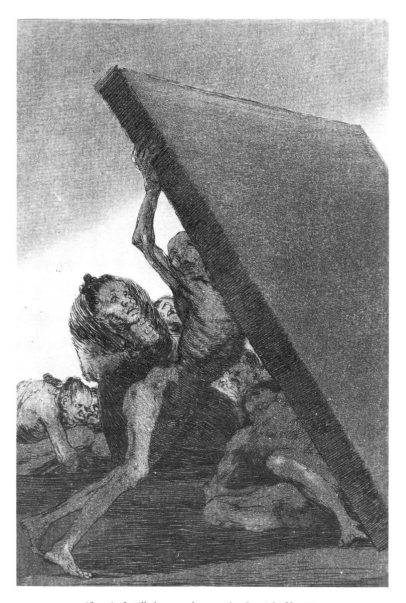

39.   And still they won't move !   *Capricho* No. 59.

41. The hour has come.   *Capricho No. 80.*

40. A golden voice !   *Capricho No. 53.*

Assi suelen acabar los hombres vtiles

42. Thus do the useful end their days. *Drawing.*

43. Street fighting on 2 May, 1808, in Madrid. *Oil Painting*, 1814.

44.   The Firing Squad, 3 May, 1808.   *Oil Painting*, 1814.

45. Guerrilleros making shot. *Sketch in oils,* c. 1814.

46. Guerrilleros making gunpowder. *Sketch in oils.* c. 1814.

47. With reason or without it.

48. And they are like wild beasts. *Los Desastres de la Guerra*, Nos. 2 and 5.

49. Nor for them.

50. For that you were born. *Los Desastres de le Guerra*, Nos. 11 and 12.

51. What valor! *Los Desastres de la Guerra*, No. 7.

52.   And there is no remedy.   *Los Desastres de la Guerra*, No. 15.

53. No time for that now. *Los Desastres de la Guerra*, No. 19.

54. Ravages of War. *Los Desastres de la Guerra,* No. 30.

55.   One cannot bear to see this.

56.   Charity.   *Los Desastres de le Guerra*, Nos. 26 and 27.

57.   That is worse.

58.   I saw it myself.   *Los Desastres de la Guerra*, Nos. 37 and 44.

59.   Unhappy Mother.

60.   Having to beg is worst of all.   *Los Desastres de la Guerra*, Nos. 50 and 55.

61. No one can help them.

62. If they are of different descent. *Los Desastres de la Guerra*, Nos. 60 and 61.

63. Beds of Death. *Los Desastres de la Guerra*, No. 62.

64. Cartloads to the cemetery. *Los Desastres de la Guerra*, No. 64.

65. Rubens : Saturn. *Oil Painting*, 1636.

66. Goya : Saturn. *Oil Painting.*

67.   Bosch : The Cure of Folly.   *Oil Painting.*

68.   Goya : Gran disparate.   *Drawing.*

69. Old Woman and skeleton eating soup. *Oil Painting.*

70. *Disparate* No. 1.

71. *Disparate* No. 3.

72. *Disparate* No. 11.

73. *Disparate No. 2.*

74.   *Disparate* No. 7.

75.   *Disparate* No. 19.

76. *Disparate* No. 10.

77. *Disparate* No. 13.

Some of the Principal Inhabitants of the MOON as they Were Perfectly Discover'd by a Telescope brought to y[e] Greatest Perfection since y[e] last Eclipse Exactly Engraved from the Objects, whereby y[e] Curious may Guess at their Religion Manners, &c.

78. Hogarth: Some of the Principal Inhabitants of the Moon, 1724.

79. The Evacuations. *Anonymous English Caricature,* 1762.

80. Multum in Parvo. *Anonymous English Caricature, 1762.*

81. W. O'Keefe : A Vision. *Caricature, 1796.*

82. That is the worst of it !

83. Farce of Charlatans. *Los Desastres de la Guerra*, Nos. 74 and 75.

84. Nothing—he says so himself.

85. The Carnivorous vulture. *Los Desastres de la Guerra*, Nos. 69 and 76.

86. Torrigiano. *Drawing.*

87. For being a Liberal. *Drawing*.

89.   What cruelty !   Drawing.

88.   For discovering the movement of the earth.   Drawing.

90. May the rope tear. *Drawing for Los Desastres de la Guerra*, No. 77.

91.   Mouk and Boy.   *Drawing.*

93. Old man praying. *Drawing.*

92. He says he has had them since birth, and he passes his life with them. *Drawing.*

94. Sad presentiments of things to come. Frontispiece of *Los Desastres de la Guerra.*

96. The pen is weightier than the sword. *Drawing.*

95. The Communion of St. Joseph of Calasanz. *Oil painting, 1819.*

97. Christ in the Garden. *Oil Painting*, 1819.

98. Divine Freedom. *Drawing*, 1820.

99. Courtaux : La Grande Crucifiée. *Popular Print*, Paris 1871.

101.   Truth beset by evil spirits.   *Drawing.*

100.   He does not know what he is doing.   *Drawing.*

102. Truth has died. *Los Desastres de la Guerra,* No. 79.

103. Will she arise again ? *Los Desastres de la Guerra*, No. 80.

104. Divine Reason, don't spare any of them. *Drawing.*

105.   Lux ex Tenebris.   *Drawing.*

106.   The Light of Justice.   *Drawing.*

107. This is the truth. *Los Desastres de la Guerra*, No. 82.

108. The Fates. *Oil Painting.*

109. Fantastic Vision. *Oil Painting.*

110. *Disparate* No. 4.

111.   *Disparate* No. 21.

112.   The Giant.   *Oil Painting.*

113. The Giant. *Etching*.

114. The Forge. *Oil Painting.*

115. The Knife Grinder. *Oil Painting.*

116.   Girl carrying water.   *Oil Painting.*

117. Peasant Girl and Dog. *Drawing.*

118. Street Performance. *Drawing.*

119. The Telegraph. *Drawing*.

120.   The Meadow of San Isidro.   *Drawing.*

121.   Dancing the Vito.   *Lithograph.*

122.   Peasant.   *Drawing.*

INDEX

INDEX